Reading Essentials and Study Guide
Student Workbook

Mc Graw Hill Glencoe

New York, New York Columbus, Ohio Chicago, Illinois

The McGraw·Hill Companies

Send all inquiries to:
Glencoe/McGraw-Hill
8787 Orion Place
Columbus, Ohio 43240-4027

ISBN 0-07-860533-4

Printed in the United States of America

10 11 WDQ 12 11 10

Table of Contents

Chapter Reading Essentials and Study Guide

To the Student

Glencoe Texas and Texans Reading Essentials and Study Guide provides a condensed version of the important information in each chapter of *Texas and Texans.* These brief summaries of every section contain and define any vocabulary words that may appear in the Student Edition. Each summary ends with a question for you to answer. Accompanying study guides can be used as a quick review of chapter content.

Name ______________________ Date ______________ Class ______________

Reading Essentials and Study Guide

Chapter 1-1

For use with textbook pages 26–30

Understanding Texas Geography

Key Terms

geography The study of the earth's land *(page 26)*

environment Physical surroundings *(page 27)*

location The position of a place on the earth's surface *(page 27)*

absolute location The exact position of a place on the earth's surface *(page 27)*

relative location The position of a place in relation to other places *(page 27)*

place The features and characteristics that give an area its own identity or personality *(page 28)*

region An area that is united by one or more common characteristics *(page 28)*

human-environment interaction The relationships linking people to their surrounding environment *(page 28)*

movement The travel of people, ideas, and goods from one place to another *(page 28)*

cultural diffusion The process of accepting ideas and culture from another place *(page 28)*

diameter The width of a circle *(page 30)*

★DRAWING FROM EXPERIENCE

Have you ever used a map? Do you have a favorite place in Texas? What makes it special? Have you ever planted a garden? Have you moved before? Do you know anyone whose job depends on the land? Do you check the weather before getting dressed each day?

In this section, you will learn the six essential, or basic, elements that geographers study in order to understand our world. You will also discover how geography affects people's lives and how people affect geography.

★ORGANIZING YOUR THOUGHTS

Use the diagram at the top of page 2 to help you take notes as you read the summaries that follow. Think about why you need to know about geography.

(continued)

Name ______________________ Date ______________ Class ______________

Reading Essentials and Study Guide

Chapter 1-1

Six Geographical Elements	
1.	4.
2.	5.
3.	6.

★ **READ TO LEARN** *Write in complete sentences to answer the following questions. Use correct spelling, punctuation, and grammar.*

Six Geographical Questions *(pages 26–27)*

Geography affects almost every detail of your life—what you eat, where you live, and how you dress. **Geography,** the study of the earth's land, explains why people live the way they do in the present. It also explains why certain events occurred in the past. When you study places and events in Texas ask yourself: How do the people who live there interact with the **environment,** the physical surroundings? When you study places and events in Texas, keep in mind the six elements of the National Standards in geography: location, places and regions, human-environment interaction, human systems, physical systems, and uses of geography.

7. How does geography help explain both the present and the past?

The study of earth's land, explains why people people live the way they do in the preasent .It also explain why certain events occurred in the past

Location *(page 27)*

Location answers the question, "Where is it?" There are two types of location: absolute and relative. **Absolute location** is the exact position of a place on the earth. It is identified by latitude and longitude. **Relative location** is the position of a place in relation to other places. It is described using terms like *south of, located next to, between,* and *in the same region.*

(continued)

Name ____________ Date ____________ Class ____________

Reading Essentials and Study Guide

Chapter 1-1

The relative location of Texas has been important to the state's development. To the southeast of Texas is the Gulf of Mexico. It provides jobs in the fishing, oil, tourist, and shipping industries. Texas is next to Mexico. In 2000, Mexican Americans made up about one-third of the population in Texas.

8. How would you describe Texas's relative location?

Texas has been important to the state's development To the southeast of Texas is Gulf Mexico. It provides jobs in the fishing, oil, tourist, and shipping industries

Places and Regions *(page 28)*

Place refers to the characteristics of an area that give it its identity and personality. Places have physical characteristics, such as landforms, climate, plants, and animals. Places also have human characteristics, including language, religion, architecture, music, politics, and way of life.

Geographers group places into regions. **Regions** are areas that are united by one or more common characteristics.

9. What are the two main kinds of characteristics that make up a place?

Religion, and, landform

Human-Environment Interaction *(page 28)*

Human-environment interaction—the relationships linking people to their environment, or physical surroundings—is another element of geography. People cut forests and dam rivers. They do this to build farms and cities. Some of these activities pollute the air and the water. The environment affects human activities as well. The soil and water in a place determine if crops can be grown there. Earthquakes and floods also affect humans.

(continued)

Name ______________ Date ______________ Class ______________

10. How do people sometimes harm the environment?

____

____

____

____

Human Systems *(page 28)*

Geography also includes human systems. People set boundary lines for places. They settle in certain places and not others. They move from place to place. **Movement,** or the travel of people, ideas, and goods, is an important element of geography. People take their ideas and culture to new places. **Cultural diffusion** happens when ideas from another place are accepted in a new location and change its culture.

11. How does human movement cause the culture of a place to change?

____

____

____

____

____

Physical Systems *(page 28)*

Physical systems are another element of geography. They interact and shape the earth. Physical systems include volcanoes, glaciers, and hurricanes. Ecosystems, or communities of plants and animals that depend on each other and the environment for survival, are another example of a physical system.

12. What are ecosystems?

____

____

____

____

(continued)

Name ______________________ Date ______________ Class ______________

Reading Essentials and Study Guide

Chapter 1-1

The Uses of Geography *(page 29)*

There are many tools and technology available to study geography. People use geography and maps every day. Computer software helps people decide how to make the best use of the physical and human environment.

13. What do people use to study geography?

Sizing Up Texas *(pages 29–30)*

Texas is the second largest state in the United States. Its total area is 267,277 square miles. Its boundaries cover 3,822 miles.

Many cities in Texas are very far away from each other. A circle 500 miles in **diameter** with El Paso at its center, for example, includes the capitals of three Mexican and two American states. It does not include Austin, the capital of Texas. The great distance between Texas cities causes problems for many people in the state. People often must travel long distances to get to work and school. Many Texans live so far from other Texans that they have closer business and social ties to people in other states.

14. How do the distances between Texas cities affect Texans' ties with each other?

Name ______________________ Date ______________ Class ______________

Chapter 1-2

For use with textbook pages 31–36

Natural Resources

Key Terms

plain A level, treeless area of land *(page 32)*
barrier island A long thin strip of land covered with sand dunes that protects the mainland shore from ocean waves *(page 32)*
escarpment A long cliff *(page 32)*
fault A weak part of the earth's crust *(page 32)*
plateau A tableland covered with small trees and brush *(page 32)*
aquifer An underground water reservoir *(page 34)*
savanna An area of flat, sometimes rugged land with short grasses, small shrubs, few trees, and rocky soil *(page 36)*
grassland An area of grass with few trees *(page 36)*

★DRAWING FROM EXPERIENCE

What is the land like where you live? Do you live near mountains, rivers, lakes, or plains? Have you ever traveled to other parts of Texas? How was it different from where you live?

In the last section you read about six elements to guide your study of Texas geography. In this section, you will learn about the varying landforms and valuable resources found in Texas.

★ORGANIZING YOUR THOUGHTS

Use the diagram below to help you take notes as you read the summaries that follow. Match Texas's natural resources with economic activities.

Natural Resources	Economic Activities
Water	1. ______________________
Soil	2. ______________________
Forest	3 ______________________
Oil and Gas	4. ______________________

(continued)

Name ______________________ Date ______________ Class ______________

Reading Essentials and Study Guide

Chapter 1-2

★ **READ TO LEARN** *Write in complete sentences to answer the following questions. Use correct spelling, punctuation, and grammar.*

Viewing Texas *(pages 31–33)*

The southern tip of Texas lies on a **plain,** or mostly level land. This land is very near sea level where it meets the Gulf of Mexico. A few miles offshore is Padre Island. This long thin strip of land covered with sand dunes is a **barrier island.** It protects the mainland shore from ocean waves.

As you move north, the land slowly rises and begins to roll. This part of Texas has a dry, hot climate. Tough and prickly plants like mesquite trees and cactus grow here. Grasses and wildflowers such as bluebonnets also grow in South Texas.

The Balcones Escarpment cuts across Texas in an arc. An **escarpment** is a long cliff. The Balcones Escarpment follows a **fault,** or weak part of the earth's crust. The escarpment was formed a long time ago by a giant earthquake. The land to the east and south of the fault sank. The land to the north and west rose very high, forming the escarpment.

A region known as the "Hill Country" begins at the escarpment. This part of Texas is a **plateau,** or tableland covered with small trees and brush. Streams formed the hills on the rim of the plateau. This part of Texas has the most streams and rivers.

To the northwest, the land gets flatter and higher. Only the Caprock Escarpment breaks the plains here. In East Texas, the land starts as a plain and then rises to the west. West of the Balcones Escarpment and "Hill Country," the land is also plains.

West Texas has mountains. No other region in Texas has mountains. Texas has 91 mountains more than one mile high. The highest is Guadalupe Peak.

5. How does the land of Texas change at the Balcones Escarpment?

____

____

____

____

____

(continued)

Name ______________________ Date ______________ Class ______________

Chapter 1-2

Texas's Water Resources *(page 33)*

Water is precious in the hot and rapidly growing region of Texas and the rest of the Southwest United States. The increasing demand for water in this region is a big problem. There are few new water sources for all the additional homes and businesses built here in past decades.

The Gulf of Mexico is a major water resource of Texas. The bays along the Texas coast are also important water resources. The bays are home to many fish and birds. They are also important fishing areas. Rivers empty into the bays. The rivers are often polluted by waste from cities, factories, and fields. This pollution sometimes makes seafood from the bays unsafe to eat.

6. How does the pollution of water resources affect Texans?

____

____

____

____

____

Rivers of Texas *(pages 33–34)*

Texas's river systems vary from region to region. South Texas has few rivers. The Rio Grande forms the southern border of Texas. Most of its water comes from Mexico.

There are two major rivers in the Texas Panhandle. The Red River forms the boundary between Texas and Oklahoma. The Canadian River cuts across the Panhandle from west to east.

There are many rivers in the eastern part of Texas. The Sabine, Neches, Trinity, San Jacinto, Brazos, Colorado, and Pecos Rivers flow across this region.

Texas rivers are sometimes called "wrong-way" rivers because the rivers carry water away from the dry part of the state to the wetter parts in the southeast. The land is higher in the northwest, so almost all the rivers run to the southeast. Dams have been built to control the amount of water that runs from rivers into the Gulf of Mexico. The dams also control floods. The dammed rivers form lakes.

(continued)

7. Why are Texas rivers called "wrong-way" rivers?

Texas Lakes Have Many Uses *(page 34)*

Texas has about 200 major lakes. Only Caddo Lake in East Texas began as a natural lake. The other lakes were formed when rivers were dammed. Even Caddo Lake now holds waters backed up by a dam.

The lakes were first built to control flooding and save water. Today, most Texas lake water is used for irrigation. Texas lakes also supply most of the water needed in cities and for manufacturing.

8. What are two important uses of Texas lakes?

Aquifers Used for Irrigation *(pages 34–35)*

The Balcones Escarpment has many springs. Springs are found where aquifers rise to the surface of the land. An **aquifer** is an underground water reservoir. Many springs get their water from the Edwards Aquifer. The water of this aquifer comes from rainfall in the Hill Country. Lack of rain and heavy use of water in San Antonio and farms to the west can cause the water level of the Edwards Aquifer to drop. Rainfall usually refills this aquifer, making it a good source of water.

The Ogallala Aquifer lies under the Texas High Plains. This aquifer is not easily or quickly refilled by rainfall. As a result, it is losing water. Water from this aquifer is used to irrigate an area larger than New Jersey. Efforts are being made to save this aquifer, but its future is not certain.

(continued)

Name ______________________ Date ______________ Class ______________

9. Where do aquifers get their water?

____

____

____

____

____

Soil Is a Valuable Resource *(page 35)*

Texas's rich soil is one of its most valuable resources. Huge areas of the state can be used for farming. Texas farms produce cotton, watermelons, and spinach. Other crops include wheat, rice, corn, soybeans, vegetables, and peanuts.

Land is also used for ranching. Ranchers raise cattle, sheep, and goats. Ranching, farming, and other businesses connected with them raise about $40 billion in income for Texans each year.

10. What are two uses of Texas land?

____

____

____

____

____

Three Vegetation Regions *(pages 35–36)*

Texas has three types of natural vegetation regions: forests, savannas, and grasslands. The three major forest regions of Texas are located in the eastern third of the state. Forests are an important natural resource in Texas. The timber crop brings a lot of money into the state. Many people have jobs in the lumber, plywood, and paper industries in East Texas.

Texas has several savanna regions. A **savanna** is an area of flat, sometimes rugged land with short grasses, small shrubs, few trees, and rocky soil. The desert savanna of West Texas has limited grazing for animals. Most of the center of Texas has savanna areas.

(continued)

Name ______________________ Date ______________ Class ______________

Reading Essentials and Study Guide

Chapter 1-2

Grasslands are areas of grass with few trees. Early settlers used this land for farming. Even today, grasslands are the most heavily settled regions.

11. What is the main use of grassland regions in Texas?

____

____

____

____

____

Texas Leads in Energy Production *(page 36)*

Petroleum, natural gas, coal, sand, and gravel are Texas's main minerals. Limestone and granite are used for building. Gypsum and salt are other important minerals.

Petroleum and natural gas continue to be the state's most important mineral resources. Oil or gas has been found in most Texas counties. Texas has produced one-fourth of all the energy made throughout the history of the United States.

12. What are Texas's most important mineral resources?

____

____

____

____

____

Name ______________________ Date ______________ Class ______________

Reading Essentials and Study Guide — Chapter 1-3

For use with textbook pages 38–41

The Climate of Texas

Key Terms

middle latitudes The region about halfway between the Equator and the North Pole *(page 38)*

norther A sudden blast of cold air that stretches south from Canada and sweeps across the plains *(page 39)*

★ DRAWING FROM EXPERIENCE

How would you describe winter where you live? What is summer like? Do you live near the Gulf of Mexico? What is the elevation, or height above sea level, where you live?

In this section, you will learn how location and elevation affect the climate of Texas.

★ ORGANIZING YOUR THOUGHTS

Use the diagram below to help you take notes as you read the summaries that follow. Think about how absolute location and relative location affect the climate of Texas.

Absolute Location: Middle Latitudes	Relative Location: Gulf of Mexico
1.	4.
2.	5.
3.	6.

(continued)

Name ______________________ Date ______________ Class ______________

Reading Essentials and Study Guide

★**READ TO LEARN** *Write in complete sentences to answer the following questions. Use correct spelling, punctuation, and grammar.*

Absolute Location Affects Climate *(pages 38–39)*

The absolute location of Texas affects its climate in important ways. The state lies in the **middle latitudes,** the region halfway between the equator and the North Pole. Texas has mild winters because it is not very far north of the equator. The climate of South Texas is much warmer than the climate of North Texas.

Texas does have some periods of cold weather. **Northers,** sudden blasts of cold air from Canada, bring temperatures below freezing. They sweep across the plains. There are no mountains or landforms to block them. Northers usually last only a few days.

Because of its location in the middle latitudes, Texas also has violent storms. Cool air from the north and moist, warm air from the Gulf of Mexico meet in the middle latitudes. The result is thunderstorms and tornadoes.

Texas has an average of 153 tornadoes each year. Most tornadoes strike in April, May, and June.

7. What is one benefit of Texas's location in the middle latitudes?

____

____

____

____

____

Relative Location Also Affects Climate *(pages 40–41)*

Texas's relative location also affects its climate. Texas lies on the Gulf of Mexico. Breezes from the Gulf cool Texas in the summer and warm it in winter. Moisture from the Gulf gives Texas much of its rainfall. More rain falls in East Texas than in West Texas. In the west, winds blow across the deserts and mountains of Mexico before entering Texas. This drier air brings less rainfall to West Texas. Areas of Texas far from the Gulf of Mexico are not greatly affected by it.

The Gulf of Mexico has negative effects on Texas, too. Destructive storms such as hurricanes sometimes sweep in from the Gulf. Terrible hurricanes have struck Galveston, Corpus Christi, and Houston.

(continued)

Name ______________________ Date ______________ Class ______________

8. What is one negative effect of Texas's location by the Gulf of Mexico?

____

____

____

____

____

Elevation and Climate Patterns *(page 41)*

Elevation also affects the Texas climate. The temperature cools by 3 degrees for every 1,000-foot rise in elevation. The temperature rises as elevation decreases.

The warmer temperatures at lower elevations protect some Texans in the winter. By the time a norther reaches Austin, for example, it is much warmer than when it swept across Amarillo. This is because Austin is at a lower elevation than Amarillo.

Elevation also affects rainfall. Warm air holds more moisture than cool air. Mountains in West Texas receive more rain than the surrounding desert. This is because moisture-filled air becomes cooler as it moves up the mountains. Cold air cannot hold a great deal of moisture. As a result, the moisture falls as rain on the mountains.

9. Why do higher elevations receive more rainfall than lower elevations?

____

____

____

____

____

Name ______________________ Date ______________ Class ______________

Reading Essentials and Study Guide

Chapter 2-1

For use with textbook pages 48–54

The Coastal Plains

Key Terms

petrochemical Related to products made from oil or natural gas *(page 51)*

alluvial soils Soils deposited by a river, such as the rich soils of the Rio Grande *(page 54)*

★DRAWING FROM EXPERIENCE

Do you live in a large city or small town? Do you live in the country? What kinds of jobs do people have where you live?

In the last chapter you read about the land, natural resources, and climate of Texas. In this section, you will learn about the Coastal Plains, one of Texas's four natural regions, and how the geography and economic activities are connected.

★ORGANIZING YOUR THOUGHTS

Use the diagram below to help you take notes as you read the summaries that follow. Match the five geographic subsections of the Coastal Plains region with economic activities people do there.

Coastal Plains

Geographic Subsection	Economic Activity
1.	6.
2.	7.
3.	8.
4.	9.
5.	10.

(continued)

Name ______________________ Date ______________ Class ______________

Reading Essentials and Study Guide

Chapter 2-1

★ **READ TO LEARN** *Write in complete sentences to answer the following questions. Use correct spelling, punctuation, and grammar.*

Introduction *(page 48)*

Texas can be divided into four natural regions. The regions are the Coastal Plains, the North Central Plains, the Great Plains, and the Mountains and Basins.

11. What are the four natural regions of Texas?

____

____

____

____

The Most Populated Region *(pages 48–50)*

The Coastal Plains is the largest natural region in the state. This region lies along the coast, the area where the land meets the water. The Gulf of Mexico is the body of water along the southern Texas coast. The elevation of the Coastal Plains is low in general. It varies, however, from being completely flat to having rolling hills.

More Texans live and work in the Coastal Plains than in any other natural region. The Gulf of Mexico gives the region a mild climate. The Coastal Plains are a good place for farming and ranching because they are flat and have plenty of water. The level land makes it easy to build cities. Dallas, Austin, San Antonio, and Houston are a few of the major cities in the region.

The Coastal Plains have many natural resources. The pine forests of East Texas produce lumber and wood products. Other areas provide good soil for growing crops and grasses for raising cattle. Great oil fields are also found in this region. Processing oil and oil products is a major industry. Seaports bring goods to Texas. Many goods come in and go out through ports such as Houston, Galveston, and Corpus Christi. The Gulf Intracoastal Waterway is a protected shipping channel that links Texas to the southeast United States and the world.

Each of the natural regions of Texas is divided into geographic subsections with different types of vegetation. The Coastal Plains region has five subsections: the Piney Woods, the Gulf Coast Plain, the Post Oak Belt, the Blackland Prairie, and the South Texas Plain. Each of these areas has different plants, animals, and natural resources than the others.

(continued)

Name ________________ Date ________________ Class ________________

12. How are the five geographic subsections of the Coastal Plains region alike? How do they differ?

____

____

____

____

The Piney Woods *(page 51)*

Pine trees cover much of the land in the Piney Woods. Four national forests can be found in this part of Texas: the Angelina, Sabine, Sam Houston, and Davy Crockett forests. Big Thicket National Preserve is also here. Besides the trees, there is also a swamp in Big Thicket.

Lumbering and farming are important economic activities in the Piney Woods. A long growing season allows farmers to grow a variety of fruits and vegetables. The area has been settled for hundreds of years. The population increased with the discovery of oil in the 1930s. This area has also developed in the fields of manufacturing, medicine, and education.

13. Why is this part of the Coastal Plain called the Piney Woods?

____

____

____

____

The Gulf Coast Plain *(pages 51–52)*

Cattle raising and farming are important economic activities in the Gulf Coast Plain. Grasses provide feed for cattle, and a long growing season allows various crops to be grown. Rice is an especially important crop.

Some parts of the Gulf Coast Plain are heavily industrialized. The **petrochemical** industry makes products from oil and natural gas. These products include gasoline, plastics, and fertilizer.

Houston is located in the Gulf Coast Plain. Houston is Texas's largest city and the second-busiest seaport in the United States. Ships from around the world use this port. Houston supports a wide variety of businesses

(continued)

Name ______________________ Date ______________ Class ______________

and services. The Johnson Space Center, where astronauts are trained, is located in Houston. It is the center of the state's petrochemical industry. Houston is also important for its financial institutions, medical research, and computer manufacturing.

Corpus Christi is also an important petrochemical center and seaport. It is a center for fishing and shrimping and the home port of the United States Navy. Large numbers of tourists come to Corpus Christi.

14. What are some products of the petrochemical industries in the Gulf Coastal Plain?

____

____

____

____

The Post Oak Belt *(page 52)*

The Post Oak Belt includes many oak trees and other hardwood trees. A band of pine trees runs through an area known as the Lost Pines. Crops grown in the Post Oak Belt include corn, cotton, peanuts, watermelon, and Christmas trees. Livestock is raised here as well.

There are no large cities in the Post Oak Belt. However, the area is an important center for education, medicine, agriculture, and light industry. Tyler, the largest city in the Post Oak Belt, calls itself the "Rose Capital of the World." Texas A&M University is located here.

15. What crops are grown in the Post Oak Belt?

____

____

____

____

The Blackland Prairie *(page 53)*

The Blackland Prairie is home to more of Texas's larger cities and towns than any other geographic subsection. It has excellent transportation systems and many workers. Much of the state's manufacturing takes place here. The area's long growing season and rich soils make farming important.

(continued)

Name ______________________ Date ______________ Class ______________

Reading Essentials and Study Guide

Dallas is the largest city here and the second-largest in the state. It is an important center for insurance, finances, merchandising, technology, and transportation. The Dallas-Fort Worth International Airport is one of the busiest in the United States.

San Antonio is on the edge of the Blackland Prairie and Balcones Escarpment. It is Texas's third-largest city and an important distribution, tourist, and cultural center. San Antonio is the number one tourist distinction in Texas. It attracts visitors to the Alamo, Fiesta Texas, River Walk, and Institute of Texan Cultures.

Austin, the capital of Texas, lies mostly in the Blackland Prairie. This rapidly growing city is a center for state government, computer research, music, and education. Austin is referred to as the live music capital of the world because of the large number of bands and dance halls.

16. What are the major cities of the Blackland Prairie?

____

____

____

The South Texas Plain *(page 54)*

The South Texas Plain is drier than the Gulf Coast Plain. Natural vegetation here includes plants that need little water, such as mesquite and prickly pear cactus. Farming and ranching are important ways of making a living. The Lower Rio Grande Valley is in the southernmost part of this geographic subsection. The Rio Grande has deposited rich **alluvial soils** here over many years. The soils and water from the river make it possible to grow citrus fruits here.

Many people enter Mexico from the city of Laredo. Trucks carrying products developed under the North American Free Trade Agreement (NAFTA) also cross the border here. Brownsville, a farming and tourist center, is also a gateway to Mexico.

17. What helps make farming important in the southernmost part of the South Texas Plain?

____

____

____

____

Name ______________________ Date ______________ Class ______________

Reading Essentials and Study Guide — **Chapter 2-2**

For use with textbook pages 56–59

The North Central Plains

Key Terms

butte A small, flat-topped hill *(page 58)*

agribusiness Large companies that grow, produce, and market agricultural products, supplies, and equipment *(page 59)*

★ DRAWING FROM EXPERIENCE

Have you every traveled to other parts of Texas? What did you see there? Have you ever been on a farm?

In this section, you will read about the geographic subsections of the North Central Plains region of Texas. You will learn about important cities of the region and how people make a living here.

★ ORGANIZING YOUR THOUGHTS

Use the diagram below to help you take notes as you read the summaries that follow. Identify important crops of each geographic subsection of the North Central Plains.

North Central Plains	
Geographic Subsection	**Important Crop**
1.	**4.**
2.	**5.**
3.	**6.**

(continued)

Name ______________________ Date ______________ Class ______________

Reading Essentials and Study Guide

Chapter 2-2

★ **READ TO LEARN** *Write in complete sentences to answer the following questions. Use correct spelling, punctuation, and grammar.*

A Ranching and Farming Region *(pages 56–57)*

The North Central Plains start in Canada, stretch across the middle of the United States, and end in Texas. The Balcones and Caprock escarpments separate the North Central Plains from the rest of Texas. The region is higher in elevation than the Coastal Plains. Rivers have shaped the region into hills and valleys.

The North Central Plains are far from the Gulf of Mexico. As a result, its climate is colder in winter and hotter in summer than the Coastal Plains. The region also gets less rainfall. Grasses and brush cover the land. Ranching and farming are important economic activities. The largest city is Fort Worth.

The North Central Plains are divided into three geographic subsections. They are the Cross Timbers, the Grand Prairie, and the Rolling Plains.

7. How do the North Central Plains differ from the Coastal Plains?

____

____

____

____

____

The Cross Timbers *(page 57)*

The Cross Timbers includes a variety of trees. It is also an agricultural area. The main crops are peanuts, fruit, and vegetables. Dairying and raising livestock are other agricultural activities. Arlington, Denton, and Brownwood are the region's major cities.

8. What agricultural activities are important in the Cross Timbers?

____

____

____

____

(continued)

Name ____________________ Date ____________ Class ____________

Reading Essentials and Study Guide

Chapter 2-2

The Grand Prairie *(page 58)*

The Grand Prairie is covered with grasses and shrubs. Trees grow mostly near streams. Agriculture is the main economic activity. Cattle raising is important. Crops include wheat, peanuts, corn, grain sorghum, and cotton.

Towns are small. Fort Worth and Dallas are the main cities. They are the largest cities in a 20-county area known as the Metroplex. The Metroplex is a major manufacturing and trade area. Dallas is a trade center. Fort Worth is a financial center and is important to aircraft manufacturing. Fort Hood, one of the nation's largest military bases, is also in the Grand Prairie.

9. What is the Metroplex?

____

____

____

____

The Rolling Plains *(pages 58–59)*

The Rolling Plains lie west of the Cross Timbers. This is the largest subsection of the North Central Plains. Most of the land is rolling. In some places there are hills, mesas, and **buttes,** or small flat-topped hills.

Cattle, sheep, and goats are raised in the drier western parts of the Rolling Plains. In the wetter eastern parts, crops such as cotton, wheat, pecans, and peaches are grown.

The Rolling Plains are only lightly settled. Wichita Falls is one of the larger communities. It is home to a large United States Air Force base. Abilene is an oil services and marketing center. San Angelo is a major center for **agribusiness,** or large companies that grow, produce, and market agricultural products, supplies, and equipment. San Angelo is the largest wool producer in the United States.

10. Why do you think the Rolling Plains are only lightly settled?

____

____

____

____

Name ______________________ Date ______________ Class ______________

Reading Essentials and Study Guide

Chapter 2-3

For use with textbook pages 61–65

The Great Plains

Key Terms

drought A long period of less than normal precipitation *(page 62)*

erosion The wearing away of land by the flowing water of a river, for example *(page 63)*

★DRAWING FROM EXPERIENCE

How much rain falls where you live? Do you live on a ranch, or have you visited one? What kinds of wildlife do you see near your home?

In this section, you will read about the geographic subsections of the Great Plains. You will learn about important economic activities and cities in these areas.

★ORGANIZING YOUR THOUGHTS

Use the diagram below to help you take notes as you read the summaries that follow. Locate cities and towns in the geographic subsections of the Great Plains region.

Great Plains	
Geographic Subsection	**Cities and Towns**
1.	4.
2.	5.
3.	6.

(continued)

Name ______________________ Date ______________ Class ______________

Reading Essentials and Study Guide

Chapter 2-3

★ **READ TO LEARN** *Write in complete sentences to answer the following questions. Use correct spelling, punctuation, and grammar.*

The Real "Old West" *(pages 61–62)*

The Great Plains region begins in Canada and runs along the Rocky Mountains through Texas and into Mexico. It has higher elevations than lands to the east. Today cotton and wheat are grown on much of the land.

The region is dry because moist air from the Gulf does not reach it. It often has **droughts,** long periods of less than normal precipitation. Irrigation and new ways of farming make agriculture possible. Summers are often cooler and winters colder here than in other regions because of the Great Plains' high elevation.

The Great Plains has three geographic subsections: the Edwards Plateau, the Llano Basin, and the High Plains.

7. Why is the Great Plains so dry?

____

____

____

____

____

The Edwards Plateau *(pages 62–63)*

The Edwards Plateau ranges between 750 and 2,700 feet above sea level. The land here is level to gently rolling. At its eastern edge is the Balcones Escarpment and the area called the Hill Country.

The thin soil of the Edwards Plateau is not good for growing crops. The most important economic activity is raising cattle, goats, and sheep. Most of the Angora goats in the United States are raised in the Edwards Plateau. Their hair is sold around the world as mohair. The plateau is among the country's most important wool-producing areas.

There are few cities and towns on the Edwards Plateau. The largest city, Del Rio, is located on the Rio Grande. It is a center for business with Mexico and draws many tourists. Kerrville and Fredericksburg are also tourist centers. Kerrville has game ranches, and Fredericksburg is famous for its peaches and German heritage.

(continued)

8. What is the most important activity in the Edwards Plateau?

____

____

____

____

____

The Llano Basin *(page 63)*

The Llano Basin is the smallest geographic subsection in Texas. The elevations here are lower than on the Edwards Plateau. **Erosion,** or the wearing away of land by the flowing waters of rivers, explains why the land is lower. Important rivers in this area include the Llano, San Saba, Pedernales, and Colorado. The land is rolling plains and hills.

Large lakes and reservoirs on the Colorado River take up part of the area. Lake Buchanan is the largest lake. The lakes and hills here have given this area the name Highland Lakes Country.

The Llano Basin has few towns. The main towns are seats of county government. Llano is a tourist, hunting, and livestock center. San Saba is known for pecan growing and processing. The wool and mohair industry is important in Brady.

9. Why is the land of the Llano Basin lower than the land of the Edwards Plateau?

____

____

____

____

____

(continued)

Reading Essentials and Study Guide

Chapter 2-3

The High Plains *(pages 63–65)*

The High Plains make up most of the Texas Panhandle. Elevations reach more than 4,000 feet above sea level. Although mostly very flat, the High Plains also include the rugged land of the Canadian Breaks and the Palo Duro Canyon. This area of the High Plains does not have good soils for farming, so livestock is raised.

Palo Duro Canyon has long been an oasis of life. Buffalo grazed there when ranchers began moving their in 1876. Today, wild turkey, deer, and other wildlife share the Palo Duro Canyon State Park with visitors.

The High Plains are divided into two major parts. The North Plains extends from the Panhandle to around 50 miles north of Lubbock. Wheat, grain sorghum, and cotton are grown there.

The South Plains occupies the southern part of the High Plains. Cotton is the most important crop. More cotton is raised in the South Plains than in any other part of Texas. The crop is irrigated with water from the Ogallala Aquifer.

Amarillo, the largest city of the North Plains, is an important transportation and commercial center. Lubbock, the largest city in the South Plains, produces cotton and serves as a commercial and cultural center. The Permian Basin's Midland and Odessa produce a great deal of petroleum.

10. What helps the farmers of the High Plains grow cotton?

____

____

____

____

____

Name ________________ Date ________________ Class ________________

Chapter 2-4

For use with textbook pages 66–69

The Mountains and Basins

Key Terms

basin A saucer-shaped depression, usually between mountains *(page 67)*

maquiladora A factory in Mexico that assembles parts that are made in the United States and other industrialized nations *(page 69)*

★ DRAWING FROM EXPERIENCE

Can you name some rivers in Texas or the United States? Why are rivers important? Have you ever been to another country? What differences have you noticed in other cultures?

In this section, you will read about the Mountains and Basins region of Texas. You will learn about the region's dry environment and about its largest city, El Paso.

★ ORGANIZING YOUR THOUGHTS

Use the diagram below to help you take notes as you read the summaries that follow. Identify one important mineral, crop, and type of natural vegetation found in the Mountains and Basins region.

Mountains and Basins

1. Mineral	2. Crops	3. Natural Vegetation

(continued)

Name ______________________ Date ______________ Class ______________

Reading Essentials and Study Guide

Chapter 2-4

★ **READ TO LEARN** *Write in complete sentences to answer the following questions. Use correct spelling, punctuation, and grammar.*

The Dry Environment *(pages 66–67)*

The Mountains and Basins region has no subsections. It is part of the Rocky Mountain system that begins in Canada and runs into Mexico. The Mountains and Basins is the most western natural region of Texas. It is also the highest and driest region.

The region is mostly a desert area where little rain falls. Trees grow only along the streams. Desert plants like cactus and yucca grow naturally. Besides mountains and canyons, there are **basins,** or saucer-shaped depressions in the land.

Two-thirds of the people of the Mountains and Basins region live in El Paso. Cotton, pecans, and cantaloupe are the main crops of this region. This area also has close economic and cultural ties to Mexico. Its landforms, climate, and culture are different from the rest of Texas, making it a popular tourist spot.

4. What are the main features of the Mountains and Basins region?

____

____

____

____

____

Mountain Ranges *(pages 67–68)*

All of Texas's mountains are located in this region. The Guadalupe Range is the highest mountain range. The two highest peaks, Guadalupe Peak and El Capitán, stand more than 8,000 feet high.

The Davis Mountains are near the central part of the Mountains and Basins region. South of these mountains is Big Bend Country, named after a sharp bend in the Rio Grande. Important sites in this area include the Chisos Mountains, steep, scenic canyons along the Rio Grande, and Big Bend National Park.

Although much of this region is dry, a few areas are wet enough to support forests and meadowlands. Farming is done mainly along the Rio Grande. The river's water is used for irrigation. Cotton is an important crop. The region also has petroleum and natural gas. Other

(continued)

important minerals include limestone, shale rock, clay, copper, sulphur, salt, and talc. Limestone and other minerals are used to make cement. Talc is used to produce ceramics, paint, and artificial rubber.

5. What are some of the minerals found in this region?

____

____

____

____

____

El Paso *(pages 68–69)*

El Paso is one of Texas's largest cities. It is located where the boundaries of Texas, Mexico, and New Mexico meet. Although far from other Texas cities, it is very close to Mexico and is just across the Rio Grande from Ciudad Juárez. It has commercial ties with both Mexico and neighboring states. It also has a strong Hispanic tradition.

El Paso is an important manufacturing center. Manufacturing has increased as a result of the North American Free Trade Agreement (NAFTA). Many ***maquiladoras,*** or factories that assemble parts, have been built in El Paso and across the border in Mexico. El Paso also has oil refineries and a variety of other factories and businesses. The University of Texas at El Paso is also here.

NAFTA, which took effect in 1994, has greatly affected El Paso and other border cities. Increased trade has helped companies along the United States-Mexico border grow, resulting in many new jobs. Because wages are lower in Mexico, some U.S. and Canadian companies moved their factories there, and hundreds of thousands of U.S. and Canadian workers lost their jobs.

6. What connections does El Paso have with Mexico?

____

____

____

____

____

Name ____________ Date ____________ Class ____________

Chapter 3-1

For use with textbook pages 80–83

The Ancient Texans

Key Terms

archaeologist A scientist who studies artifacts from ancient cultures *(page 81)*

artifact An item belonging to ancient people and studied by archaeologists *(page 81)*

culture The ways a group of people expresses and conducts itself *(page 83)*

anthropologist A scientist who studies cultures *(page 83)*

nomad A person who does not settle in one place but hunts and searches for food *(page 83)*

★ DRAWING FROM EXPERIENCE

Where are your ancestors from? Has your family been in the United States for many generations, or did they come here recently? How long has your family been in Texas? Why did they come here?

In this section, you will learn about the ancient people who came here thousands of years ago and how their cultures changed over time.

★ ORGANIZING YOUR THOUGHTS

Use the diagram to help you take notes as you read the summaries that follow. Try to describe what life was like for ancient people during each period.

Stone Age over 10,000 years ago	Archaic Age 8,000 years ago	A.D. 100 almost 2,000 years ago
1.	2.	3.

(continued)

Name ______________________ Date ______________ Class ______________

Reading Essentials and Study Guide

★ **READ TO LEARN** *Write in complete sentences to answer the following questions. Use correct spelling, punctuation, and grammar.*

The First Texans Arrive *(pages 80–81)*

Before people began writing, they told stories to pass on their knowledge. People lived in Texas thousands of years ago, before Europeans and Africans arrived in North America. They learned about their early history from storytellers.

People began to move to North America 35,000 years ago. They crossed from Asia over a land bridge that connected Siberia and Alaska. Today, there is a body of water covering this land. It is called the Bering Strait. However, during the last Ice Age, water did not always cover this area.

These early people were hunters. They followed herds of animals to Alaska. Over time, people moved farther and farther onto the North American continent. New people continued to cross the Bering Strait. People first reached Texas more than 10,000 years ago.

4. Why did ancient people cross the Bering Strait?

____

____

____

____

Artifacts Are Historical Clues *(pages 81–82)*

Much of what we know about ancient people comes from **archaeologists,** scientists who study artifacts from ancient cultures. **Artifacts** are items belonging to ancient people, including tools, art, bones, pottery, baskets, and shells. Paintings on rocks and in caves in Southwest Texas show how ancient people lived. Changes in pottery or tool styles may suggest new people moved into an area. Human bones like those found near the Texas cities of Midland and Leander show what people looked like and the diseases they had.

5. What do paintings and human bones tell archaeologists about ancient people?

____

____

____

(continued)

Name ________________________ Date ________________ Class ________________

Chapter 3-1

Early People Hunt for Food *(pages 82–83)*

People first arrived in Texas during the late Paleolithic period, or the early Stone Age (more than 10,000 years ago). They hunted large animals, including the mastodon, mammoth, and giant bison. They lived in small groups and did not stay in one place very long. Instead, they followed the herds of animals.

Early people were smaller, weaker, and slower than the animals they hunted. Still, they had several advantages. They used spears, darts, and a notched throwing stick called an *atlatl.* Another advantage they had was strategy. One strategy was called "surround," in which hunters surrounded a herd of animals and then killed them as they tried to escape.

During the Archaic Age 8,000 years ago, life in early Texas changed. People hunted smaller animals. They also began gathering berries, nuts, seeds, and roots. They made new tools to prepare the food. Tools were made of bone or stone and included axes, picks, drills, choppers, scrapers, and grinders. They stayed in one place longer than earlier hunters.

6. What two advantages did early people have over the large animals that they hunted?

____

____

____

____

____

Hunters Become Farmers *(page 83)*

While people in Texas were hunting and gathering food, people in Mexico were growing food. In A.D. 100, groups of people in Texas began growing crops. They grew peanuts, corn, tomatoes, beans, pumpkins, squash, and cotton.

Farming changed the way people lived. It meant they had a steady source of food. It also meant they could not leave their farms. People no longer roamed searching for food. Instead, they stayed in one place for a number of years. They built villages which led to more complex societies. Their societies included craft workers, warriors, and political and religious leaders.

(continued)

7. How did farming change the way ancient people lived?

____

____

____

____

____

Different Cultures Emerge *(page 83)*

The early people of Texas developed into cultures. **Culture** is all the ways a group of people express and conduct itself. It includes language, customs, clothing, shelter, ways of working and playing, and beliefs.

When the first Europeans arrived in what they called the Americas, there were many groups of Native Americans in Texas. They belonged to one of four cultures. **Anthropologists,** scientists who study cultures, have named these the Southeastern, Pueblo, Gulf, and Plains cultures.

Each culture developed differently. Each had to live a certain way because of its environment, or physical surroundings. The Native Americans who lived in the fertile and wet land of East Texas farmed. They had permanent settlements. The land of the Gulf people could not be farmed. These people were nomads. **Nomads** hunt and search for food. They do not settle in one place.

The Native American cultures influenced European settlers. The Europeans learned to travel over new land, prepare new foods, grow new plants, and hunt new animals. Europeans began to use Native American words for places, foods, and animals.

8. How was the East Texas culture different from the Gulf culture?

____

____

____

____

____

Name ____________________ Date ______________ Class ______________

Chapter 3-2

For use with textbook pages 85–89

Southeastern and Gulf Cultures

Key Terms

confederacy A large group made up of smaller groups *(page 87)*

matrilineal Tracing descent through the mother *(page 87)*

shaman A person believed to have the power to cure the sick *(page 88)*

★ DRAWING FROM EXPERIENCE

Where does most of the food you eat come from? Have you ever gone fishing and eaten the fish you caught? Have you ever eaten food that you grew yourself?

The last section discussed the movement of ancient people to present-day Texas and changes in their way of life. In this section, you will learn about ways of life among Native American groups of the Southeastern and Gulf cultures.

★ ORGANIZING YOUR THOUGHTS

Use the diagram to help you take notes as you read the summaries that follow. Think about the similarities and differences among the groups of Native Americans who first lived in Texas.

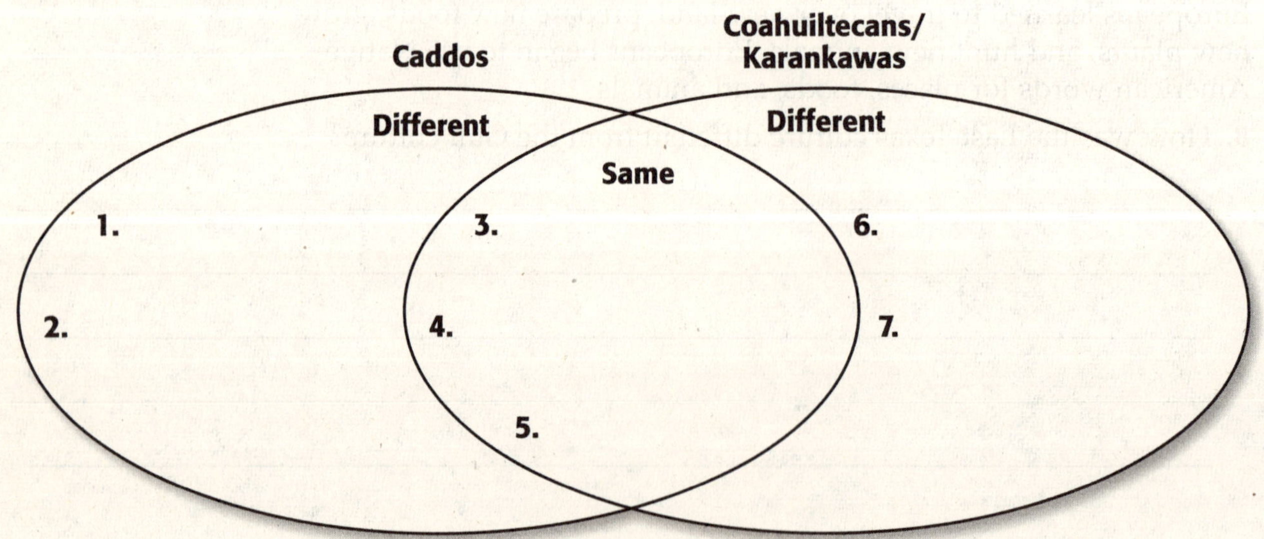

(continued)

Name ______________________ Date ______________ Class ______________

Reading Essentials and Study Guide

★ **READ TO LEARN** *Write in complete sentences to answer the following questions. Use correct spelling, punctuation, and grammar.*

Early People *(pages 85–86)*

The groups of Native Americans who lived in Texas before Europeans arrived were similar in many ways. They lived in small groups and had leaders. They believed spirits caused rain, fire, and the change of seasons.

These groups were also different from each other in some ways. They did not speak the same language. Some were peaceful. Others liked to go to war. Some lived in communities. Others moved frequently.

8. How did early Native American groups in Texas differ?

____

____

____

____

____

Southeastern Farmers and Gatherers *(page 86)*

The people of the Southeastern and Gulf cultures included the Caddos, Karankawas, and Coahuiltecans. These groups differed in many ways. Some farmed, others fished, and many gathered foods. During the 1600s, as new groups joined them, they turned to raising crops. They built settlements and began to trade.

9. What three Native American groups lived in southeastern Texas?

____

____

____

____

____

(continued)

Name ______________________ Date ______________ Class ______________

Reading Essentials and Study Guide

Chapter 3-2

The Caddos *(page 87)*

Many groups made up the Caddo people. These groups were part of larger groups called **confederacies.** Two of the confederacies lived in the area now called Texas. They were **matrilineal.** This means they traced descent through their mothers.

Each group had its own government. The government had two leaders. One leader handled war and peace. The other leader handled religion. The leaders had many helpers. Both men and women could hold positions of power. The Caddos were the largest and most advanced of all native Texan groups.

The Caddos lived in the East Texas timberlands. They grew squash, beans, pumpkins, melons, sunflowers, plums, and corn. Men cleared the fields. Women planted and took care of the crops. The Caddos also gathered fruit and berries and hunted and fished. They hung trotlines across streams. A trotline is a long, heavy fishing line with many baited hooks. People still fish this way today.

Most Caddos lived in permanent villages. Their houses were dome-shaped. They used mud, poles, and straw to build their houses.

The Caddos often went to war. They fought with other Native Americans and European settlers. They were friendly with the French. The French traded with them. The Caddos sided with France when there was trouble between the French and Spanish.

In time, disease reduced their numbers. In 1859, the Caddos were forced to move to present-day Oklahoma. Their descendants still live there today.

10. What are three ways, besides farming, that the Caddos met their need for food?

____

____

____

____

The Search for Food *(page 87)*

The Coahuiltecans, the Karankawas, and other Native American people lived along the Gulf of Mexico. They were nomads. They could not farm like the Caddos. The land along the coast was too muddy for farming. The Gulf people ate small animals, nuts, and plants.

(continued)

Name ____________________ Date ____________ Class ____________

11. Why were the Coahuiltecans and the Karankawas unable to farm?

____

____

____

____

____

The Coahuiltecans *(pages 87–88)*

The Coahuiltecans lived on the South Texas plain. They used bows and arrows to hunt javelina, deer, and bison. The javelina is a small animal that looks like a wild boar. The Coahuiltecans also gathered plants. They used plants to make flour. Sometimes they ate worms and lizards. They moved to a new place every few weeks.

All members of Coahuiltecan society were equal. They shared food and water. Women took care of the camp. Men hunted. Everyone worked. **Shamans** were important to the Coahuiltecans, as they were to other Native Americans. Shamans were people believed to have the power to cure the sick. They led religious ceremonies, made medicine, and cared for the sick.

Most of the Coahuiltecans disappeared by the time Texas became a state. Many had died in battle. Some moved to Mexico or other places. Others died from diseases brought by the Europeans.

12. Where did the Coahuiltecans get their food?

____

____

____

____

____

The Karankawas *(page 88)*

The Karankawas lived along the Gulf Coast and on the small islands between Galveston and Corpus Christi Bays. They traveled in search of food. During the spring and summer, they lived near forests. There they gathered nuts and berries and hunted. In the fall and winter, they

(continued)

Name ______________________ Date ______________ Class ______________

lived near the sea. The Karankawas used canoes to catch fish and gather sea plants for food.

The Karankawas made tools, pottery, and baskets. They used tar to make the baskets waterproof. In the 1820s, North American settlers moved to the Coastal Plain. All Karankawas were driven out of Texas or killed by the mid-1800s.

13. In what two places did the Karankawas live during the year?

____

____

____

____

____

Other Southeastern Cultures *(page 88)*

During the early 1500s, new Native American groups moved to the region just west of the Caddos. Many came from north of Texas. Some were escaping from war. Others were looking for an easier life. Many began to trade with other Native Americans and Europeans.

14. Why did new Native American groups move to Texas in the 1500s?

____

____

____

____

____

The Wichitas *(pages 88–89)*

The Wichitas lived on the prairies and oak timberlands that extend to the Red River. During the 1600s, they moved from present-day Kansas to the land near the Trinity, Red, and Brazos Rivers.

The Wichitas built villages, farmed, and hunted. Women were leaders and shared work with the men.

(continued)

Name ______________________ Date ______________ Class ______________

The Wichitas were often at war with others. This was because other people wanted their land. They traded with the French. They fought with Spanish settlers until the Spaniards began to trade with them. Anglo American settlers forced the Wichitas to give up their land. Today, descendants of the Wichitas live in Oklahoma.

15. What was the role of women in Wichita society?

____

____

____

____

____

More Native American Groups Arrive *(page 89)*

The Atakapans lived along the coast between Galveston Bay and the Sabine River. They are considered part of the Southeastern culture, although they followed the practices of other cultures.

About 1820, the Cherokees moved from the eastern United States to Texas. They settled in woodlands north of Nacogdoches. In 1839, Anglo American settlers forced the Cherokees to move to present-day Oklahoma.

Between 1780 and 1816, the Alabama and Coushatta nations settled near the Trinity River in Texas. They left during the Texas war for independence. In 1854, they accepted a reservation near present-day Livingston.

16. What are three Native American groups who moved to Texas?

____

____

____

____

____

Name ______________________ Date ______________ Class ______________

Chapter 3-3

For use with textbook pages 90–95

Pueblo and Plains Cultures

Key Terms

middlemen Dealers or agents acting as go-betweens for the producers of goods and the retailers or consumers *(page 90)*

adobe Sun-dried earth and straw *(page 91)*

tepee A shelter made of tanned hides fastened to a framework of poles *(page 95)*

★DRAWING FROM EXPERIENCE

Do you know what a pueblo or a tepee looks like? Have you ever seen a Native American ceremony or artwork painted on a buffalo skin?

The last section looked at the ways of life of the people of the Southeastern and Gulf cultures. In this section, you will learn about the Pueblo and Plains cultures. You will discover what kinds of houses they built, what they ate, and why the buffalo and horse were important to them.

★ORGANIZING YOUR THOUGHTS

Use the diagram to help you take notes as you read the summaries that follow. Think about what the different peoples of the Pueblo and Plains cultures did to protect their way of life.

Protecting Ways of Life

1. Jumanos

2. Tiguas

3. Tonkawas

4. Apaches

5. Comanches

6. Kiowas

(continued)

Name ______________________ Date ______________ Class ______________

Reading Essentials and Study Guide

Chapter 3-3

★ **READ TO LEARN** *Write in complete sentences to answer the following questions. Use correct spelling, punctuation, and grammar.*

The Jumanos and the Tiguas *(pages 90–91)*

The Jumanos were a Pueblo group who hunted bison and traded. They roamed in Texas, New Mexico, and northern Mexico. They were **middlemen,** or go-betweens, for eastern farming tribes, such as the Caddos, and the western Pueblo people. The Jumanos traded crops for animal skins and meat. They also traded items like paint, turquoise, and feathers. Many eastern Indians wanted to trade for the Jumanos' bows and arrows.

The Jumanos had striped tattoos on their faces that marked them as peaceful traders. Men had short hair with one long lock decorated with feathers. Women wore braids.

Some Jumanos settled along the Rio Grande. They were farmers who used irrigation to grow corn, squash, beans, other vegetables, and possibly cotton. When there was no rain and crops failed, the Jumanos gathered and ate cactus plants and other foods. They also hunted small animals, deer, and buffalo.

Jumano farmhouses were large. They were made of **adobe.** Adobe is made of sun-dried earth and straw. Adobe houses stay cool in summer and warm in winter. These houses lasted a long time in the dry climate.

Another group of Native Americans, the Apaches, moved south onto the Plains. The Jumanos fought to keep their land and trade ties, but the Apaches were stronger. Some Jumanos moved into Mexico. Some joined other Native American groups.

The Tiguas were also Pueblo people. They moved from New Mexico to Ysleta, near present-day El Paso. Their descendants are still there today. Texas has recognized the Tigua people and set up a reservation. The Tiguas still hold religious ceremonies and celebrate feasts like their ancestors did.

7. What items did the Jumanos trade with other groups?

____

____

____

____

____

(continued)

Name ______________________ Date ______________ Class ______________

Reading Essentials and Study Guide

Chapter 3-3

The Plains Cultures *(page 92)*

The Plains culture changed with the arrival of horses. Horses crossed from Asia to North America many thousands of years ago. However, they died off before the end of the Ice Age. The Spanish brought horses back to the Americas around 1500. The horses were swift and strong and could eat any kind of grass. The horses helped the people of the Plains culture become great hunters and warriors.

Buffalo had roamed the Plains for hundreds of years. They lived almost everywhere in Texas except the Piney Woods. By the end of the 1800s, white hunters had killed millions of these animals. The Plains people needed the buffalo for food. The loss of the buffalo meant the end of the Plains people's way of life.

8. What happened to the buffalo?

____

____

____

____

____

The Tonkawas *(page 92)*

The Tonkawas came to Texas in the 1600s. They lived along the Edwards Plateau, near present-day Austin.

Although they needed buffalo for food and shelter, there were not many buffalo on their hunting grounds. There were a lot of buffalo on the plains to the west. However, the Apaches and Comanches would not allow the Tonkawas to hunt there. The Tonkawas had to hunt deer, rabbits, turtles, and snakes instead.

The Tonkawas lost many members fighting with other Native Americans and European settlers. Yet they managed to survive.

9. Why did the Tonkawas hunt small animals?

____

____

____

____

(continued)

Name ______________________ Date ______________ Class ______________

Reading Essentials and Study Guide

Chapter 3-3

The Apaches *(page 93)*

Anthropologists believe that the ancestors of the Apaches came from very far north. This is because their language is similar to the language of Native Americans in Canada and Alaska. By 1700, several groups of Apaches had entered Texas. The Mescaleros lived in the mountains of West Texas. The Lipans lived in the Hill Country of Central Texas.

The Lipans were often at war. The Spanish threatened them from the south, and the Comanches threatened them from the north. The Lipans left Central Texas and moved to the mountains of West Texas. Today, most Apaches live on reservations in New Mexico.

10. What are the names of two Apache groups?

____

____

____

____

____

The Comanches *(pages 93–94)*

The Comanches lived in western Texas. Their huge territory covered parts of Mexico, Texas, Kansas, Oklahoma, Colorado, and New Mexico. Their language was similar to languages of Native Americans in the northern Rockies and of the Aztecs of Mexico.

The Comanches were divided into many groups. Each group had its own leader and council of older men to make decisions. No leader or council of one group could make a decision for another group. No person or group council could speak for all the Comanche people.

Comanche life centered on hunting and war. The Comanches hunted bear, elk, antelope, and buffalo. A buffalo hunt involved most of the group. The hunters rode horses and surrounded the buffalo herd. They forced the herd to move in a circle. The hunters then used bows and arrows and spears to kill the buffalo as they passed.

The Apaches, Wichitas, Tonkawas, and white settlers threatened the Comanches. They had to fight to keep control of their land. They also fought to take horses from their enemies. The Comanches fought hard to keep their way of life. By 1875, however, the destruction of the buffalo and the loss of their horses forced them to move to a reservation in present-day Oklahoma.

(continued)

Name ____________________ Date ____________________ Class ____________________

Chapter 3-3

11. Who made important decisions for a group of Comanches?

____

____

____

____

____

The Kiowas *(page 95)*

The Kiowas lived on the same plains as the Comanches. They were nomadic people. They moved quickly and often. They lived in **tepees,** shelters made of tanned hides fastened around poles. The hides were decorated with paintings. The tepee entrance usually faced east. This was so the sun would warm the tepee in the morning. The Kiowas built a fire in the center of the tepee. Beds made of branches and animal skins lined the sides.

Like other Plains Indians, the horse and buffalo were extremely important to the Kiowas. The horse was used for freedom of movement and speed for hunting. The buffalo provided food, hides for robes and tepees, and horns for spoons and needles.

Tradition and ceremony were very important to the Kiowas. They kept written records of their travels. They painted pictures of important events on buffalo hides. They had ceremonies for every season. The most important was the sun dance in June. They believed that honoring the sun would bring happiness, buffalo, and victory.

All men were warriors. The Kiowas also fought to keep their way of life. In the end, though, they too were forced to live on reservations.

12. How were Kiowa homes different from Jumano shelters?

____

____

____

____

____

Name ______________________ Date ______________ Class ______________

Chapter 4-1

For use with textbook pages 102–105

First Steps in a New Land

Key Terms

conquistador A Spanish soldier who sought riches and power for himself and wealth and glory for Spain *(page 103)*

friar A member of a Catholic religious order *(page 103)*

mission A religious settlement built by friars in the Americas *(page 103)*

★ DRAWING FROM EXPERIENCE

Would you like to explore outer space? Would you volunteer to travel to a space station or another planet? What qualities do you think explorers have?

In the last chapter, you read about Native American groups that lived in Texas before European explorers arrived. In this section, you will learn about the first European explorers to reach the Americas and what their goals were.

★ ORGANIZING YOUR THOUGHTS

Use the diagram below to help you take notes as you read the summaries that follow. Think about why each explorer came to the Americas and what he did there.

Explorer	Achievements
1. Christopher Columbus →	
2. Hernán Cortés →	
3. Alonso Álvarez de Pineda →	
4. Alvar Núñez Cabeza de Vaca →	

(continued)

Name ____________________ Date ____________ Class ____________

Reading Essentials and Study Guide

Chapter 4-1

★ **READ TO LEARN** *Write in complete sentences to answer the following questions. Use correct spelling, punctuation, and grammar.*

Columbus Sights a New World *(pages 102–103)*

Christopher Columbus sailed west across the Atlantic Ocean in 1492. He was looking for a new route to Asia for the Spanish. On his journey Columbus reached new lands unknown to Europe. The Europeans called these new lands the Americas. Columbus made three more trips to the Americas and set up a colony on an island there. From there, the Spanish explored the American mainland.

5. What did Columbus find while searching for a route to Asia?

____

____

____

____

New Spain *(page 103)*

Spanish soldiers called **conquistadores** explored the Americas after Columbus. They were looking for riches and power for themselves. They also wanted to make Spain wealthy and powerful. The conquistadores defeated Native Americans as they made their way through the Americas. They made it possible for others to follow them and build towns, roads, mines, farms, and ranches.

Friars, members of Catholic religious groups, also helped Spain in the Americas. Most of the people in Spain were Catholics. Spanish rulers wanted Native Americans to become Catholic too. Friars set up religious settlements called **missions** to teach Native Americans about the Catholic religion. A mission was often the first Spanish settlement in an area.

6. How did the friars' goals in the Americas differ from those of the conquistadores?

____

____

____

____

(continued)

Reading Essentials and Study Guide

Cortés Lands in Mexico *(pages 103–104)*

In 1519, the Spanish explorer Hernán Cortés landed on the eastern coast of Mexico. He marched with an army of 500 soldiers to Tenochtitlán, the capital city of the Aztec people. The Aztecs had a large empire. On his way to Tenochtitlán, Cortés persuaded thousands of Native Americans who suffered under the Aztecs to join his forces.

The Aztecs welcomed Cortés to Tenochtitlán because they thought he was one of their gods. They destroyed Tenochtitlán and stole its treasures. They built a new city in the same location. They named it Mexico City. Mexico City became the capital of New Spain.

Cortés's success inspired other Spaniards to come to the Americas. They had many reasons for coming. Some were searching for treasure. Some were just curious and wanted adventure. Others wanted to settle there. Still others wanted to help spread the Catholic faith.

7. How did Cortés treat the Aztecs?

____

____

____

____

____

Álvarez de Pineda Explores Texas *(pages 104–105)*

Alonso Álvarez de Pineda was the first European to explore the Texas coast. He arrived the same year Cortés landed in Mexico. Pineda made maps of the lands he saw as he sailed from Florida to Mexico.

8. How did Pineda help the Spanish in the Americas?

____

____

____

____

____

(continued)

Reading Essentials and Study Guide

Shipwrecked in Texas *(page 105)*

Alvar Núñez Cabeza de Vaca came to the Americas in 1527 with a group sent to conquer the area between Florida and Mexico. They did not achieve this goal. The ships that were supposed to pick them up never arrived. They built boats and sailed along the coast toward Mexico. A storm tossed the boats and forced them to an island near Galveston. Cabeza de Vaca called the island *Malhado,* the isle of misfortune.

Cabeza de Vaca and his men were the first Europeans to enter what became Texas. The Karankawas helped them by building fires and giving them food. Most of the men in the group died because of disease or exposure. Disease also spread to the Karankawas.

Cabeza de Vaca and his remaining men survived by following the ways of the Native Americans. A man from Morocco named Estevanico joined them. Estevanico was the first black man to enter Texas. Estevanico and Cabeza de Vaca became shamans. Cabeza de Vaca also became a trader. On his travels, he learned a lot about the land and people of what is now Texas.

After almost six years in South Texas, Cabeza de Vaca and his group traveled west toward Mexico. They probably passed through South and West Texas on their way.

9. What were Cabeza de Vaca and his group supposed to do in the Americas?

____

____

____

____

____

Name ______________________ Date ______________ Class ______________

Reading Essentials and Study Guide **Chapter 4-2**

For use with textbook pages 107–111

The Spanish Explore Texas

Key Terms

viceroy An official who represents the monarch *(page 108)*

pueblo A series of connected flat-roofed buildings *(page 108)*

★DRAWING FROM EXPERIENCE

Have you ever traveled to an unfamiliar place? Why did you go? What did you see and do there? What did you bring home to remember your trip?

In the last section, you learned that the Spanish were the first Europeans to reach Texas. In this section, you will discover why other Spanish explorers came to Texas and what they found there.

★ORGANIZING YOUR THOUGHTS

Use the diagram below to help you take notes as you read the summaries that follow. Compare and contrast what the Spanish hoped to find in Texas and what they actually found there.

1. What They Hoped to Find	Spanish Explorers in Texas	2. What They Found

(continued)

Name ______________________ Date ______________ Class ______________

Chapter 4-2

★ **READ TO LEARN** *Write in complete sentences to answer the following questions. Use correct spelling, punctuation, and grammar.*

The Quest for Texas Gold *(pages 107–108)*

Cabeza de Vaca wrote a report about what he had seen in Texas. He said that Texas was very large and beautiful. He also said its land would be good for growing food. He was the first European to report seeing buffalo. He described them as huge "cows" with small horns.

Cabeza de Vaca said he had not seen gold, but passed on stories he heard of rich cities in Texas filled with valuable items such as gold and jewels. He suggested that the Spanish send a group to look for these treasures in the north of what is now Texas. Many who wanted to be conquistadores were eager to go.

Antonio de Mendoza read Cabeza de Vaca's report. Mendoza was a **viceroy,** or official who represents the monarch. Mendoza had heard about seven cities with treasures in the north of Texas. He decided to find out if the stories were true. Mendoza had to find others to lead the search because Cabeza de Vaca had returned to Spain.

3. Why did Mendoza think the Spanish should explore the north of Texas?

____

____

____

____

____

Fray Marcos Leads a New Expedition *(pages 108–109)*

Viceroy Mendoza sent a small group of men to check on the stories of riches in the lands to the north. A priest named Fray Marcos de Niza led the group. Estevanico went along as a guide because he knew the land and some of the Native Americans.

After riding ahead, Estevanico reported that a land named Cíbola was 30 days away. He said that Cíbola had seven cities and was filled with gold, silver, and gems. Beyond Cíbola were richer lands. When Estevanico was killed by Native Americans, Fray Marcos continued north. He saw Cíbola from a distance. When he returned to Mexico, he described Cíbola as a golden city with great riches. Fray Marco

(continued)

Name ______________________ Date ______________ Class ______________

may have seen the city at sunset. Cíbola was really only a pueblo. A **pueblo** is a group of connected buildings with flat roofs.

4. What did Estevanico tell Fray Marcos that encouraged him to travel north?

____

____

____

____

____

Coronado Is Disappointed *(pages 109–110)*

Viceroy Mendoza sent a a huge group of soldiers and Native Americans to find Cíbola. The group was led by Francisco Vázquez de Coronado. In 1540, Coronado found Cíbola. It did not contain any riches. It was made of only mud and stone. Coronado was very disappointed.

Even so, Coronado believed there must be riches somewhere in the area. He stayed to explore. He sent one group west across New Mexico and Arizona. They reached the Grand Canyon. Coronado and another group headed east. They met a Native American named the Turk. The Turk told them of a rich place named Quivira farther east. Coronado decided to go there. The Turk led the way. The trip was very long. They traveled across the plains of Texas to Kansas. They reached a Native American settlement but found no treasure. Coronado killed the Turk and claimed the land for Spain. Coronado's group headed back to New Spain.

Coronado reported to the king of Spain about Texas. He said it was a beautiful land that had good soils for farming. He noted that it did not contain any gold or other riches, only little villages.

5. What did Coronado find instead of Quivira?

____

____

____

____

(continued)

Name ______________________ Date ______________ Class ______________

Reading Essentials and Study Guide

Chapter 4-2

Moscoso Explores East Texas *(pages 110–111)*

Hernán de Soto was marching west from Florida with an army around the same time Coronado was traveling across the Great Plains. In 1541, de Soto reached the Mississippi River. This was the first time Europeans had reached the Mississippi River. De Soto died there.

Luis de Moscoso became the leader of the group. He led the soldiers into East Texas as far as the lower Brazos River. The group met many Native Americans. They did not find any riches. Moscoso led the soldiers back to the Mississippi River. They sailed down the river and then along the coast of Mexico.

6. What area did Moscoso and his army explore?

____

____

____

____

____

New Mexico Is Founded *(page 111)*

By 1543 Spaniards had seen much of the land that is now Texas. They found no riches like those in Mexico City. Because of this, Spain lost interest in Texas. They did not build settlements there. They decided it would be better to build towns in other areas.

In 1609, Spaniards set up a colony along the Rio Grande. They named this colony New Mexico. The capital city was named Santa Fe. The Spanish explored the surrounding area. They traded with the Jumanos. Then they left and did not return for many years.

7. Why did Spain decide not to settle Texas?

____

____

____

____

____

Name ______________________ Date ______________ Class ______________

Chapter 4-3

For use with textbook pages 112–115

La Salle Awakens Spanish Interest

Key Terms

stockade A fort designed to protect those who live in it *(page 114)*

sandbar A shallow sandy spot in a body of water such as a river or ocean *(page 114)*

★DRAWING FROM EXPERIENCE

Have you ever been so busy with some activities that you have forgotten to pay attention to others? What happened as a result?

In the last section, you read that Spain decided not to build settlements in Texas. In this section, you will learn how France challenged Spain's claims to Texas.

★ORGANIZING YOUR THOUGHTS

Use the diagram below to help you take notes as you read the summaries that follow. Think about the events that led up to and followed the building of Fort St. Louis in Texas.

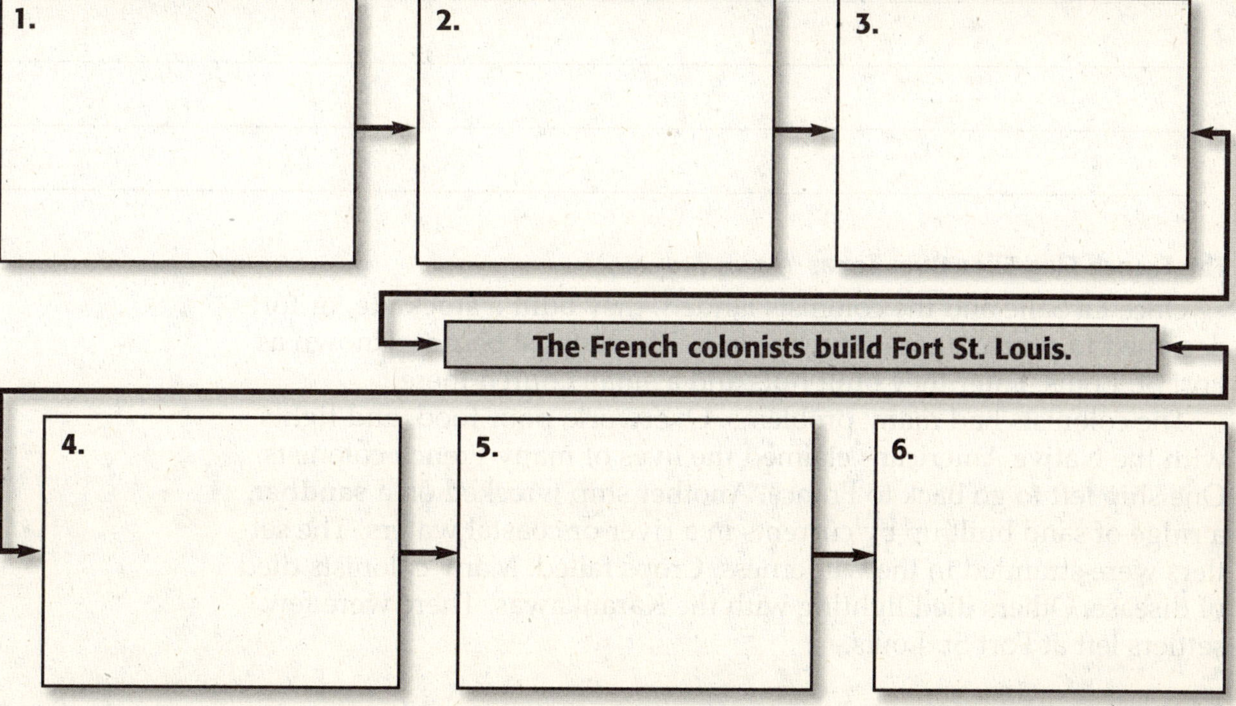

(continued)

Name ____________________ Date ____________ Class ____________

Reading Essentials and Study Guide

Chapter 4-3

★ **READ TO LEARN** *Write in complete sentences to answer the following questions. Use correct spelling, punctuation, and grammar.*

France Challenges Spanish Claims *(pages 112–113)*

In the early 1600s, countries other than Spain began claiming land in the Americas. England started colonies in North America. France started a colony in Canada. Some years later, France challenged Spain's claim to Texas.

The French explorer René Robert Cavelier, Sieur de La Salle, led a group to set up an empire in Texas. In 1682 La Salle traveled down the Mississippi River to the Gulf of Mexico. He was the first European to make this trip. La Salle claimed all the land around the Mississippi River for France. He named the land Louisiana.

La Salle wanted to start a French colony at the mouth of the Mississippi. In 1684 he sailed with 300 colonists to settle there. They ran into many problems, including missing the Mississippi River. They sailed to the west, along the coast of Texas. After searching unsuccessfully for the mouth of that river, La Salle finally decided to go ashore. He chose a spot on Matagorda Bay.

7. Why did La Salle and his group sail along the coast of Texas?

____

____

____

____

____

The French Flag Flies Over Texas *(pages 114–115)*

Once La Salle and the colonists landed, they built a **stockade,** or fort designed to protect those who live in it. The outpost became known as Fort St. Louis. Later they built huts and a small church there.

The colonists had many problems. Overwork, poor food, and fights with the Native Americans claimed the lives of many French colonists. One ship left to go back to France. Another ship wrecked on a **sandbar,** a ridge of sand built up by currents in a river or coastal waters. The settlers were stranded in the wilderness. Crops failed. Many colonists died of disease. Others died fighting with the Karankawas. There were few settlers left at Fort St. Louis.

(continued)

La Salle decided to head east to try to find the Mississippi River. On a second trip he and his group wandered into East Texas. Members of the group refused to continue looking for the Mississippi. In the end they murdered La Salle.

Now the French colony had no leader. Some in La Salle's expedition traveled to Quebec, a French settlement in Canada. Other colonists were attacked by the Karankawas. Most of the colonists were killed or taken into Karankawa camps. No one was left at Fort St. Louis.

Even though Fort St. Louis failed as a settlement, it had other results. It established trade with the Native Americans of the Mississippi Valley.

La Salle's journey in Texas gave the United States a reason to claim Texas as part of the Louisiana Purchase. Some Americans argued that France regarded Texas as part of the Louisiana Purchase.

France now had a claim to Texas. The Spanish had been busy settling areas of New Spain and New Mexico. The Spanish feared France might take Texas away from them. Spain decided it was time to settle Texas. The Spanish began exploration of the northern Gulf shore.

8. Why did the Spanish decide to settle Texas?

____

____

____

____

____

Name ______________________ Date ______________ Class ______________

Reading Essentials and Study Guide

Chapter 5-1

For use with textbook pages 120–123

First Missions Are Built

Key Terms

presidio A Spanish military post *(page 121)*

council A group of advisers *(page 123)*

★DRAWING FROM EXPERIENCE

Have you ever visited a mission? What Spanish influence do you see in your neighborhood? Do any streets in your community have Spanish names?

In this section, you will learn about the early missions the Spanish built in Texas. You will also learn about relations between the Spanish and French.

★ORGANIZING YOUR THOUGHTS

Use the diagram below to help you take notes as you read the summaries that follow. Think about the activities of the Spanish and French in Texas and whether they were successful.

Event (Cause)	What Happened as a Result (Effect)
The French began to settle Texas around 1685.	1.
The Spanish met the *Tejas* in East Texas.	2.
Drought and disease caused problems for the mission in East Texas.	3.
Father Hidalgo asked the French for help in building a mission in East Texas.	4.
The Spanish did not believe the French had no plans to settle East Texas.	5.

(continued)

Name ______________________ Date ______________ Class ______________

Reading Essentials and Study Guide

Chapter 5-1

★**READ TO LEARN** *Write in complete sentences to answer the following questions. Use correct spelling, punctuation, and grammar.*

Spain Looks to Texas *(pages 120–121)*

The Spanish considered Texas part of what they called New Spain. Catholic friars started the first permanent settlement of Europeans in Texas in 1682 near El Paso. This settlement was the mission of Corpus Christi de la Ysleta. Most Spanish settlements were in the eastern part of Texas near Louisiana. When the French began to settle in Texas after 1684, the Spanish made a stronger effort to establish colonies. Spain built missions, military outposts called **presidios,** and towns on Native American lands.

6. What led the Spanish to build presidios?

____

____

____

____

____

A Tejas Mission *(page 121)*

De León led his troops northeast. Near the Colorado River they met a group of Hasinai people, whom they called the *Tejas*, a word meaning "friend."

When the expedition returned to Mexico, Massanet asked the viceroy for permission to found a mission among the Tejas. In 1690, the Spanish built the first Spanish mission in East Texas. The mission was named San Francisco de los Tejas.

7. Why do you think the Spanish called the Native Americans they met *Tejas*?

____

____

____

____

____

(continued)

Name ______________________ Date ______________ Class ______________

Reading Essentials and Study Guide

A Mission Abandoned *(page 122)*

The mission had many problems. Drought ruined the Tejas's crops. Disease killed many of the Native Americans and one of the friars. The Tejas people rejected the Catholic religion and resented the Spaniards' attempts to change the way they lived.

The Spanish decided to leave the mission in East Texas. There was no threat from the French there, and the mission was far from Spanish settlements. Even though the mission failed, its presence made Spanish land claims in Texas stronger.

Spanish settlements continued to grow along the Rio Grande. The mission San Juan Bautista was built in 1699. It eventually grew into a complex of three missions, a presidio, and a town. The mission was called the "Mother of Texas Missions." Father Francisco Hidalgo was one of the friars at the mission.

8. Why do you think the Tejas people rejected the Catholic religion?

____

____

____

____

France Threatens Again *(pages 122–123)*

In 1699 the French set up a colony on the Gulf Coast at Biloxi in present-day Mississippi. The French were interested only in trade. Friends of the Native Americans, French traders also wanted to trade with the Spanish. Spanish law did not allow trading with foreigners in the colonies of New Spain.

Father Hidalgo asked for French help in building a mission among the Tejas. He wanted to be the friar there. The French wanted the trade. A Frenchman, Louis de St. Denis, was sent to talk to the Spanish. St. Denis said the French did not plan to settle in East Texas. The Spanish viceroy and his **council,** or advisers, did not believe St. Denis. The Spanish ordered new missions to be built in East Texas.

9. Why do you suppose Father Hidalgo asked for French help?

____

____

____

Name ________________ Date ________________ Class ________________

Reading Essentials and Study Guide — Chapter 5-2

For use with textbook pages 124–128

Spanish Settlements

Key Terms

province A district of land with a governor as leader *(page 126)*

★ DRAWING FROM EXPERIENCE

Have you ever been to the Alamo in San Antonio? If you have, what did you find most interesting about it? If you have not, what do you know about the Alamo? Why do you think the missions and presidios were built in different areas of a settlement?

In the last section, you learned about early Spanish missions in Texas. In this section you will learn about new Spanish settlements in Texas and the problems the Spanish faced in setting them up.

★ ORGANIZING YOUR THOUGHTS

Use the diagram below to help you take notes as you read the summaries that follow. Identify important events in the Spanish settlement of Texas.

Date	Event
1716	1.
1718	2.
1719	3.
1727	4.
1757	5.

(continued)

Name ______________________ Date ______________ Class ______________

Reading Essentials and Study Guide

Chapter 5-2

★ **READ TO LEARN** *Write in complete sentences to answer the following questions. Use correct spelling, punctuation, and grammar.*

Missions Are Established in East Texas *(pages 124–125)*

St. Denis guided the Spanish to the location of the first mission in East Texas, San Francisco de los Tejas. This time, Spanish families came to live there. Within a year, the Spanish built six more missions and a small fort.

6. Where did Spanish families first settle in East Texas?

____

____

____

____

____

San Antonio Is Founded *(pages 125–126)*

The Spanish saw that a settlement at a location between New Spain and the new missions was needed. The 500-mile journey from the Rio Grande to East Texas was dangerous. In 1718, the Spanish built a fort-town called Presidio San Antonio de Béxar on one side of the San Antonio River. Many soldiers brought their families to the presidio and settled permanently. The men dug irrigation canals for farming. The women worked the land, cooked, and took care of the children. The settlement became the city of San Antonio. On the other side, they built a mission called San Antonio de Valero. The mission chapel later became the Alamo.

7. What made the settlement along the San Antonio River permanent?

____

____

____

____

____

(continued)

Name ______________________ Date ______________ Class ______________

Reading Essentials and Study Guide

Aguayo Defends the Missions *(page 126)*

The settlement of East Texas stopped when a war broke out between Spain and France in 1719. The French seized East Texas. The viceroy of New Spain sent the Marqués de San Miguel de Aguayo and an army to retake East Texas from the French. Aguayo was the governor of Coahuila, a **province,** or district, of New Spain that included Texas. Aguayo set up the missions there again and moved the presidio to the banks of the Angelina River.

8. Why did the viceroy of New Spain choose Aguayo to retake East Texas?

____

____

____

____

____

Aguayo Founds Two Cities *(page 126)*

Near the French post of Natchitoches, Aguayo built a large presidio called Nuestra Señora del Pilar de los Adaes. A force of 100 soldiers and their families built a village nearby. Soon after Los Adaes was established, it became the capital of Texas. It was the capital for almost 50 years. From Los Adaes, Aguayo traveled southwest and built a mission and presidio near La Salle's ruined fort. Both were later moved to the San Antonio River near present-day Goliad. The Spanish called the new settlement La Bahía.

Since 1691, the Spanish had treated Texas as a province with a governor. Spanish officials had governed the province from northern Mexico. Because of French threats, the Spanish now felt they needed to keep a closer watch on Texas.

9. Why did the Spanish feel they had to establish a capital in Texas?

____

____

____

____

(continued)

Name ____________________ Date ____________ Class ____________

An Uneasy Peace *(pages 126–127)*

When Aguayo returned to Coahuila, there were nine missions, four presidios, and two villages in Texas. By 1727, the Spanish felt it was too expensive to keep the settlements. They closed the presidio, cut back on the number of soldiers at Los Adaes, and moved several missions to San Antonio.

The French continued to be active in East Texas. They traded with Native Americans but did not claim land west of a certain boundary. Although the Spanish did not like the French trading in East Texas, relations between the two countries were peaceful most of the time.

10. Why did the Spanish and French have peaceful relations?

____

____

____

____

____

Plains People Resent Missions *(pages 127–128)*

The Native Americans in East Texas got along with the Spanish. The people were not interested in Catholicism. They also didn't threaten the lives of the friars or settlers.

The Native Americans of the Plains, however, did not want the Spanish to enter their hunting grounds. The Apaches and Comanches fought the Spanish. Spanish friars still wanted to spread the Catholic religion and Spanish culture. Three more missions were founded between 1748 and 1751 to serve the Tonkawa and other peoples. The missionaries suffered bad luck. The Apaches attacked the settlements, disease struck the settlers, drought (lack of rain) ruined the crops, and the Tonkawas left. The friars left one mission and moved the other two to San Antonio.

(continued)

11. Which two Native American groups of the Plains fought the Spanish? Why?

____

____

____

____

____

San Sabá Mission Fails *(page 128)*

In 1757, the Spanish built Mission Santa Cruz de San Sabá. A presidio was set up a few miles away. The location of the settlement was dangerous. The nearest Spanish settlement was 100 miles away, and Apaches and Comanches roamed the plains nearby.

The Spanish missionaries built this mission because they wanted the Apaches to become Christians. The Apaches wanted the mission as protection against their Comanche enemies. The Apaches came to the mission for food and gifts but never stayed long. The Apaches and Comanches did not want to give up their life as nomads.

12. Why did the Apaches come to the mission of San Sabá?

____

____

____

____

____

Name ______________________ Date ______________ Class ______________

Reading Essentials and Study Guide

Chapter 5-3

For use with textbook pages 130–133

Building Communities

Key Terms

ayuntamiento A city council elected by landowners in Spanish Texas *(page 132)*

alcalde A chief official elected by landowners in Texas *(page 132)*

mestizo A person of mixed Spanish and Native American heritage *(page 132)*

Tejano A person of Mexican heritage who considers Texas home *(page 133)*

★ DRAWING FROM EXPERIENCE

What kinds of jobs do men and women do today? Do you know any women who are farmers or ranchers? Do you think the life of a soldier is much different today than it was in the past? Have you or someone in your family traced your heritage, or family history?

You have read about how the Spanish started missions in Texas. In this section you will learn about life at the missions, presidios, and settlements.

★ ORGANIZING YOUR THOUGHTS

Use the diagram below to help you take notes as you read the summaries that follow. Think about what life was like for various groups in Spanish Texas.

Group	Description of Life in Texas
1. Native Americans	
2. Soldiers	
3. African Americans	
4. Women	

(continued)

Reading Essentials and Study Guide

★ **READ TO LEARN** *Write in complete sentences to answer the following questions. Use correct spelling, punctuation, and grammar.*

Life in the Missions *(pages 130–131)*

Spanish missions were busy centers of activity. The friars tried to get the Native Americans to live close to the missions. They wanted to teach the Native Americans the Spanish way of life. The Spaniards sometimes used gifts to get the Native Americans to move close to the missions. Sometimes they used force.

Native Americans who accepted mission life were kept busy. The day usually started with prayer. The children would go to school, the women wove cloth, molded pottery, and cooked. The men would work in the fields or learn to be carpenters and blacksmiths. At the end of the day the friars held religion classes for adults, followed by prayers.

Although some Native Americans adapted to mission life, most would not stay at the missions. They were not used to the strict lifestyle. They did not want to be farmers, carpenters, or blacksmiths. They found it difficult to leave behind a way of life they had practiced for centuries.

5. Why did the Spanish want the Native Americans to settle near the missions?

____

____

____

____

____

Soldiers Face Hardships *(page 132)*

The life of a Spanish soldier was difficult and dangerous. Soldiers had to protect the mission and nearby settlements, control the Native Americans in the missions, and scout the countryside. Most soldiers were also settlers who brought their families to the new towns. They even farmed as well as being soldiers.

The soldier-settlers sometimes traded with the Native Americans. The friars felt that sometimes the soldiers took advantage of the Native Americans because they did not know Spanish ways. The soldiers sometimes said the friars took away the Native Americans' freedoms.

(continued)

6. Why were the soldiers important to the new settlements?

Important Settlements in Spanish Texas *(page 132)*

By 1772, San Antonio was the largest settlement and served as the capital of Texas. The people there had some say in their government. Landowners elected a city council called an ***ayuntamiento*** and a chief official called an ***alcalde.*** Goliad, Los Adaes, and Nacogdoches were other important settlements.

To increase the population of San Antonio, 15 families came to Texas in 1731 from the Canary Islands. The Canary Islands are off the coast of Africa. Many families of San Antonio can trace their ancestors back to these people from the Canary Islands. Some of these newcomers became very wealthy, including many women. María Betancour owned a cattle ranch, and María Josefa Granados owned a general store. María Pérez Cassiano ran the government when her husband was out of town.

7. How did the Spanish try to increase the population of San Antonio?

Living in Spanish Texas *(pages 132–133)*

The people of Texas made their living in several ways. Some were farmers and ranchers. Others worked as shopkeepers, fishers, barbers, and blacksmiths, among other jobs. A variety of people lived in Texas. There were Americans, Spaniards, and **mestizos.** A mestizo is a person of mixed Spanish and Native American heritage. There were also

(continued)

African Americans living in Texas. Some were free, and others were slaves.

Most men and women were married. Widows, women whose husbands had died, and widowers, whose wives had died, made up 10 percent of the population. Some women became storekeepers, ranchers, and farm managers. Many became wealthy from inheriting land.

8. What is the term for a person of Spanish and Native American heritage?

____

____

____

____

____

A Tejano Heritage Takes Shape *(page 133)*

A Tejano character developed in Texas. The term ***Tejano*** describes a person of Mexican heritage who considers Texas home. The Tejano heritage is reflected in the population, religion, language, institutions, and customs of today.

The settlers wanted to improve community life. They hired teachers to educate their children. They guarded public health by forbidding practices such as dumping trash and washing clothes in the drinking water supply. Although life was hard, communities often held dances, horse races, and fairs for recreation.

9. Why do you think the early people of Texas thought of themselves as Tejano instead of Mexican or Spanish?

____

____

____

____

____

Name ______________________ Date ______________ Class ______________

Chapter 6-1

For use with textbook pages 138–142

Spanish Texas 1763–1819

Key Terms

alliance An agreement between two or more groups to work together *(page 139)*

filibuster An individual who carries out rebellious activities in a foreign country *(page 142)*

★DRAWING FROM EXPERIENCE

What is another name for the Fourth of July? Why do we celebrate this holiday? What states were part of the United States when it won its independence? How far west did the United States stretch?

In this section, you will learn that many areas of North America passed from one country's control to another's as the result of war. You will also learn how agreements among several countries affected the boundaries and settlement of Texas.

★ORGANIZING YOUR THOUGHTS

Use the diagram below to help you take notes as you read the summaries that follow. Match countries with events in 1763–1819.

Event	Country
1. Bought Louisiana from France	
2. Provided supplies to the Americans during the American Revolution	
3. Lost land and power in North America following the French and Indian War	
4. Fought to gain independence from Great Britain	
5. Closed most of its missions in Texas because they were too spread out and costly	
6. Had a dispute with the United States over the boundary between Louisiana and Spanish Texas	
7. As a result of the French and Indian War, gained control over most of the land east of the Mississippi	
8. Shares a border with Canada	

(continued)

Name ______________________ Date ______________ Class ______________

Reading Essentials and Study Guide

Chapter 6-1

★**READ TO LEARN** *Write in complete sentences to answer the following questions. Use correct spelling, punctuation, and grammar.*

Spain Acquires Louisiana *(pages 138–139)*

From 1756 to 1763, Great Britain and France were involved in the French and Indian War (the Seven Years' War). Great Britain won the war. As a result, Great Britain gained control of Canada and all French land east of the Mississippi River, except New Orleans. Spain gained control of New Orleans and all French land west of the Mississippi River. France no longer had power in North America. Spain questioned whether the missions and presidios in East Texas were still needed.

9. Why did Spain question whether the settlements in East Texas were needed after the French and Indian War?

____

____

____

____

____

Spain Closes East Texas Missions *(page 139)*

The Spanish decided to close all their missions in Texas except those at San Antonio and Goliad. Then they could focus on forming an **alliance,** or working agreement, with the Comanches to fight together against the Apaches.

The Spanish governor of Texas ordered the East Texas settlers to move closer to San Antonio for safety. Many did not want to move. San Antonio was hot and dry. They would need irrigation for their crops. The best land had already been taken.

10. How did the East Texas settlers feel about moving closer to San Antonio? Why?

____

____

____

____

(continued)

Name ____________________ Date ____________ Class ____________

Reading Essentials and Study Guide

Chapter 6-1

Nacogdoches Founded *(pages 139–140)*

The leader of the East Texans asked that the settlers be allowed to go back to their East Texas homes. The governor would not allow this. However, he did allow some of them to settle along the Trinity River. For the first four years, this new colony did well. Then the settlers had many problems. Their crops did not grow and many settlers became ill. They also had to fight the Comanches. Because of these problems, the settlers moved back to where they used to live. They built a town named Nacogdoches.

11. What kinds of problems did the settlers along the Trinity River face?

____

____

____

____

____

Settlers Face Many Dangers *(page 140)*

Conflict with the Apaches and Comanches stopped the Spanish from colonizing Texas during the late 1700s. There were not enough Spanish soldiers to protect the settlers. Spain began to lose control of Texas. In the 1790s, Spain insisted that the churches support themselves.

12. What caused Spain to begin to lose control of Texas?

____

____

____

____

____

Spain Helps the American Colonists *(pages 140–141)*

While Spain was having problems in Texas, Americans east of the Mississippi River were fighting for independence from Great Britain. This war was known as the American Revolution. Both France and Spain were on the side of the Americans. The Spanish governor of

(continued)

New Orleans opened the port to American ships. He also provided weapons, clothing, money, and medical supplies to American troops.

When Spain entered the war in 1779, the governor of New Orleans gathered an army of soldiers from Spain, Mexico, and Cuba. He also invited African and Native Americans to fight. These efforts helped keep the British from taking New Orleans and the lower Mississippi Valley.

13. Why was New Orleans important to the Americans during the American Revolution?

____

____

____

____

____

The United States Buys Louisiana *(page 141)*

In 1800, Spain was forced to give Louisiana back to France. In 1803, the United States purchased the Louisiana Territory from France. The United States became twice as large after buying Louisiana. After the purchase of Louisiana, Anglos began pushing across the Mississippi River to Spanish Texas.

14. How did the purchase of Louisiana change the size of the United States?

____

____

____

____

____

Disputes About Boundaries *(pages 141–142)*

The United States and Spain disagreed about the boundary between Spanish Texas and Louisiana. Some of the land near the boundary was

(continued)

claimed by both countries. The two countries argued about the boundary for several years. Finally, they came to an agreement. They decided that neither of them would claim the land near the boundary. The land became known as the Neutral Ground.

In 1819, the United States and Spain signed the Adams–Onís Treaty. The treaty settled the disagreement about the boundary. Spain gave Florida to the United States. The United States agreed that Texas belonged to Spain. The eastern boundary of Texas was the Sabine River. The Neutral Ground became part of the United States.

15. What was the Neutral Ground?

____

____

____

____

____

Americans Migrate to Texas *(page 142)*

Many Americans moved to Spanish Texas. These people were mainly farmers and traders. Some were **filibusters,** adventurers who were trying to help the United States take control of Texas from Spain. One of these men was Philip Nolan. He and a group of men came to Texas to catch wild horses, which they then sold. In 1801, Nolan and his group were attacked by a group of Spanish soldiers. These soldiers believed Nolan's group was trying to take Texas from Spain. Most of Nolan's group were killed or later died in a Mexican prison.

16. Besides filibusters, what Americans moved to Texas?

____

____

____

____

____

Name ________________________ Date ________________ Class ________________

Reading Essentials and Study Guide

Chapter 6-2

For use with textbook pages 144–148

Unrest Grows in Texas

Key Terms

liberation The freeing of an individual, group, or nation *(page 145)*

republic A government in which voters choose people to represent them *(page 145)*

★DRAWING FROM EXPERIENCE

What does the term *freedom* mean to you? Why do you think people are willing to fight for freedom? What would you be willing to do to keep the freedoms you enjoy?

In the last section, you read about the Americans' fight for freedom from Great Britain. The Mexicans and Texans saw the United States gain its independence from Great Britain. In this section, you will find out what happened when the Mexicans and Texans began to ask for freedom from Spain.

★ORGANIZING YOUR THOUGHTS

Use the diagram below to help you take notes as you read the summaries that follow. Think about the goals of different individuals and groups.

Group	Goals
Hidalgo and followers	1.
Republican Army of the North	2.
Laffite	3.
James Long	4.

(continued)

Name ______________________ Date ______________ Class ______________

Chapter 6-2

★ **READ TO LEARN** *Write in complete sentences to answer the following questions. Use correct spelling, punctuation, and grammar.*

Hidalgo Calls for Independence *(pages 144–145)*

Many Mexicans did not like being ruled by Spain. The best jobs in Mexico were given to men sent from Spain. Spain taxed Mexicans to help pay for wars in Europe. In 1810, a priest named Father Miguel Hidalgo y Costilla called for Mexico's freedom from Spain. Hidalgo's followers fought with the Spanish. At first, Hidalgo's soldiers did well, but they could not capture Mexico City. In 1811, Hidalgo was captured and killed. One of his followers, Juan Bautista de las Casas, took over San Antonio and other towns, but the Spanish regained control of Texas.

5. Why were many Mexicans unhappy with Spanish rule?

____

____

____

Gutiérrez-Magee Expedition *(pages 145–146)*

The fight for freedom continued. Another member of Hidalgo's group, Bernardo Gutiérrez de Lara, planned to invade Texas. He formed an army to fight for the **liberation,** or freeing, of Texas. Gutiérrez de Lara and an American soldier named Augustus Magee wanted to set up a **republic,** a government in which people would vote to determine who would represent them. The forces were known as the Republican Army of the North. The army included Tejanos, Native Americans, and Anglo Americans. It quickly grew in size.

The Republican Army captured Goliad. The Spanish surrounded the town for three months. Magee died there in 1813. Samuel Kemper replaced him as commander of the troops. When the Spanish retreated, Kemper and his troops followed them to San Antonio. The Republican Army defeated the Spanish there. Then the leaders of the Republican Army issued a declaration of independence for the State of Texas.

6. Why was the Republican Army of the North created?

____

____

____

(continued)

Name ______________________ Date ______________________ Class ______________________

Reading Essentials and Study Guide

Disagreements and Defeats *(page 146)*

Soon there were disagreements within the Republican Army. The Americans thought the leaders of Texas's new government should be elected by voters, as they were in the United States. The Mexicans thought government leaders should be appointed, as they were in New Spain. Gutiérrez de Lara thought Texas should remain part of Mexico. The Americans thought Texas should be independent or become part of the United States.

In 1813, Spanish soldiers defeated the Republican Army. Most of the Republican soldiers were killed. The Spanish soldiers killed settlers in San Antonio and East Texas whom they believed had helped the Republican Army. Other settlers were forced to leave Texas.

7. What were the Mexicans' and Americans' disagreements about the new government of Texas?

____

____

____

____

____

Revolutionaries and Pirates *(pages 146–147)*

The Republican Army's fight to free Texas from Spain had failed. However, some of the remaining soldiers continued to look for ways to fight against Spain. These soldiers found a safe place to live on Galveston Island. It was easy to attack Spanish ships that were sailing in the Gulf of Mexico from the island.

A French pirate named Louis Michel Aury captured Spanish ships along the coast of Texas. Another pirate named Jean Laffite said he was fighting to free Mexico from Spanish rule. However, Laffite was really more interested in stealing riches from Spanish ships. When Laffite began attacking American ships, the United States Navy stopped him. Laffite left Galveston Island.

8. Why did pirates stay on Galveston Island?

____

____

____

(continued)

Name ______________________ Date ______________ Class ______________

Reading Essentials and Study Guide

Chapter 6-2

Spain Exiles French Colonists *(pages 147–148)*

At this same time, a group of French colonists tried to settle along the Trinity River in East Texas. They built two forts. The Spanish governor in Texas sent soldiers to remove the colonists. The colony was abandoned in 1818.

9. Why do you think the Spanish governor forced the French colonists to leave their settlement?

____

____

____

____

____

James Long Invades Texas *(page 148)*

James Long was a filibuster who tried to free Texas from Spain. He did not think the United States should give up its claim to Texas.

In 1819, Long's men captured the town of Nacogdoches in East Texas. By this time, very few people were living in Nacogdoches. Long declared that Texas was free and independent from Spain. He was elected president of Texas.

Long traveled to Galveston Island to meet with Laffite. While he was away, Spanish troops defeated his soldiers. Long went to New Orleans to get more soldiers and returned to invade Texas by sea. Long's soldiers sailed along the coast of Texas and went inland. They captured Goliad, but Spanish troops attacked them, and Long surrendered.

10. Why did James Long invade Texas?

____

____

____

____

____

Name ______________________ Date ______________ Class ______________

Reading Essentials and Study Guide

Chapter 6-3

For use with textbook pages 150–153

Spanish Rule Ends in Texas

Key Terms

lariat A long, light rope used with a running noose to catch livestock *(page 153)*

vaquero A Spanish cowhand who took care of large herds of cattle on the long cattle drives *(page 153)*

★DRAWING FROM EXPERIENCE

Why do you think the United States is sometimes called a multicultural nation? What foods do you eat that can be traced to other cultures? Which buildings in your community show the influence of other cultures? What other signs of different cultures do you see around you every day?

In the last section, you read about how people in Mexico and Texas called for freedom from Spain. In this section, you will discover how Spanish rule ended in Texas. You will also learn how Spanish culture continues to influence Texas.

★ORGANIZING YOUR THOUGHTS

Use the diagram below to help you take notes as you read the summaries that follow. Think about some of the effects of Spanish rule in Texas.

Effects of Spanish Rule

1.

2.

3.

4.

5.

(continued)

Name ______________ Date ______________ Class ______________

Chapter 6-3

★ **READ TO LEARN** *Write in complete sentences to answer the following questions. Use correct spelling, punctuation, and grammar.*

Texas at the End of Spain's Rule *(pages 150–151)*

Mexico became free from Spain in 1821. The province of Texas was a part of the new country of Mexico. Although Texas had been under Spanish rule for 300 years, there were few Spanish settlements there. San Antonio, Goliad, and Nacogdoches were the only settlements inland in Texas. As time went on, fewer and fewer people lived in these settlements.

Settlements on Texas's borders, such as Laredo, were not considered part of the province of Texas. Some settlers lived near El Paso. They were controlled by the Spanish authorities in New Mexico. Large areas of northern and western Texas had very few settlers. Native Americans roamed these areas as nomads. The Native Americans did not recognize Spanish government.

6. Why do you suppose there were so few settlers in northern and western Texas?

____

____

____

____

____

Spanish Neglect *(pages 151–152)*

There were several reasons why Spain could not attract Spanish settlers to Texas. First, there was no gold or silver in Texas to attract people there. Also, Texas was remote and unsophisticated compared to Mexico City. Mexico City had universities, artists, physicians, and the many comforts of a civilized society.

Mexico offered plenty of fertile, open land for farming and ranching. In addition, the Native Americans in Mexico were peaceful and willing to work. Those in Texas were mostly unfriendly and uninterested in Spanish culture and religion.

During the time Texas was ruled by Spain, the Spanish paid very little attention to the province. Near the end of Spanish rule, conditions were very bad in many parts of Texas, including San Antonio.

(continued)

Name ____________________ Date ____________ Class ____________

7. Why couldn't Spain attract settlers to Texas?

Spanish Legacy *(page 153)*

Even though Spain did little to settle Texas, Spanish rule had a great influence on the area. Spaniards mapped and explored the land. They gave many Texas rivers and cities Spanish names. Spaniards also built the first roads. Spanish settlers brought horses, cattle, sheep, and pigs into Texas. Texans used the Spanish ranching system with its special terms, such as **lariat,** a long rope, and chaps. Spanish cowhands, called ***vaqueros,*** took care of the large herds of cattle on the long cattle drives. The settlers adapted, or changed, Spanish customs to meet the conditions they found in Texas.

After Mexico became independent, many Spanish settlers stayed in Texas. As time went on, more settlers came to Texas from Mexico. Today, many Texans have Spanish names. In addition, many Texans speak, read, and write Spanish.

8. Why did settlers in Texas change some of their customs?

Name ______________________ Date ______________ Class ______________

For use with textbook pages 164–170

Austin Establishes a Colony

Key Terms

depression A time in which money loses value and people lose jobs *(page 165)*

survey To measure land to determine size and boundaries *(page 167)*

empresario The Spanish word for a land agent whose job is to bring in new settlers to an area *(page 168)*

militia A temporary army unit *(page 169)*

★DRAWING FROM EXPERIENCE

Have you ever been to Austin, the capital of our state? Do you know why it is called Austin?

In this section, you will learn about Moses Austin and his son, Stephen F. Austin, who were responsible for bringing American settlers to Texas.

★ORGANIZING YOUR THOUGHTS

Use the diagram below and on the next page to help you take notes as you read the summaries that follow. Think about the part each person played in the colonization of Texas.

Setting Up a Colony in Texas	
Moses Austin	**Baron de Bastrop**
1.	2.

(continued)

Reading Essentials and Study Guide

Setting Up a Colony in Texas, continued	
Antonio Martínez	**Stephen F. Austin**
3.	**4.**

★ **READ TO LEARN** *Write in complete sentences to answer the following questions. Use correct spelling, punctuation, and grammar.*

Moses Austin Paves the Way *(pages 164–165)*

Moses Austin moved from Connecticut in 1798 to what is now Missouri. At that time, Missouri still belonged to Spain.

At first, Moses Austin was very successful. However, in 1819, a depression in the United States ruined his business. A **depression** is a time in which money loses value and people lose jobs. He wanted to regain his fortune, and decided to talk to the Spanish governor about colonizing Texas.

In 1820 Austin and an enslaved African American named Richmond left for Texas. With the help of Baron de Bastrop, Austin convinced Governor Antonio Martínez to allow 300 American families to settle in Texas. Before Austin could carry out his plans, he became ill with pneumonia and died. He wanted his son to carry out his plans.

5. Why did Moses Austin want to colonize Texas?

(continued)

Name ______________________ Date ______________ Class ______________

Reading Essentials and Study Guide

Chapter 7-1

Stephen F. Austin Continues His Father's Work *(pages 165–166)*

Stephen F. Austin was on his way to help his father set up the colony in June of 1821 when Moses Austin died. Stephen had been studying law and working for a newspaper in New Orleans.

Stephen F. Austin was determined to carry out his father's plan. He went to see Governor Martínez. Governor Martínez welcomed him and discussed plans for settlement.

6. What did Stephen F. Austin do before he went to colonize Texas?

____

____

____

____

Austin Sets Colony Boundaries *(page 166)*

Austin decided that the region between the Colorado and the Brazos Rivers was a good place for a colony. It had good soil, plenty of water, natural resources, a mild climate, and no other settlements.

Austin wrote a full report to Governor Martínez outlining the boundaries he wanted for his colony. He also requested more land along the coast. He knew he would need a port where settlers could land and get supplies.

7. Why did Stephen F. Austin choose the area between the Colorado and Brazos Rivers for the colony?

____

____

____

____

____

Advertising for Colonists *(page 167)*

Austin advertised for settlers to come to his colony. Every man would receive 640 acres for himself, 320 acres for his wife, 160 acres for each child, and 80 acres for each slave.

Austin **surveyed,** or measured, the land himself to decide on grant sizes and boundaries. Settlers would pay him 12.5 cents per acre.

(continued)

Austin would use the money to do the surveys. He also used the money to advertise for new settlers, prepare the titles, and register the grants. Austin gave the settlers credit, giving them time to pay.

Settlers coming to Texas had to become citizens of Mexico. They also had to become Catholic and have good morals.

8. What was required of the new settlers when they moved to the colony?

____

____

____

____

____

Good Land and Low Prices Attract Settlers *(page 167)*

Many people wanted to settle in Texas because it had good farmland at low prices. In late 1821, Austin outfitted a ship called the *Lively* to take people and supplies from New Orleans to the new colony.

Austin began to have problems. In the spring of 1822, the *Lively* wrecked on Galveston Island. Many colonists and badly needed supplies were lost. In March 1822, Austin learned that Mexico had won its independence from Spain. The new government did not recognize Austin's right to colonize Texas. Governor Martínez told Austin to travel to Mexico City. He would need to get approval from the new government.

9. Why did Austin have to travel to Mexico City?

____

____

____

____

____

Austin Impresses Mexican Leaders *(page 168)*

After spending more than a year in Mexico City, Austin was given a contract for colonization of Texas. Under this new contract in 1823, the amount of land each settler received was more than that granted by Governor Martínez. Families who raised livestock and farmed could

(continued)

receive 4,605 acres. Austin would get 100,000 acres of land for his services as **empresario,** or land agent. He would still be able to settle 300 families.

10. What are two ways that the new contract for colonization was better than the first one?

____

____

____

____

____

Problems Develop in the Colony *(pages 168–169)*

Many problems developed in the colony. Some colonists left Texas because of drought. Others needed their land to be surveyed. People disagreed over land ownership. Austin and Baron de Bastrop, the land commissioner, settled claims to the land.

Native Americans did not like the colonists on their territory. The Karankawas and Tonkawas raided settlements and stole livestock. Austin had to command a militia for protection. A **militia** is a temporary army unit. Soon, relations between the settlers and the Native Americans became quiet.

11. What were the problems Austin faced when he returned from Mexico?

____

____

____

____

____

Men and Women of the Old Three Hundred *(pages 169–170)*

By 1825, Austin had given land to nearly 300 families. The settlers in the colony became known as the Old Three Hundred. Most had come from Alabama, Arkansas, Louisiana, Missouri, and Tennessee. They chose the best land for their homes and farms.

(continued)

Name ______________________ Date ______________ Class ______________

Several members of the Old Three Hundred had been in Texas before Austin. Jane Long held a land title on the lower Brazos River. R. M. Williamsom, a lawyer, became a leader in the Texas independence movement.

Some women received land of their own. Rebekah Cummings came to Texas with her children. Nancy Spencer and Elizabeth Tumlinson stayed in Texas and became members of the Old Three Hundred after Native Americans killed their husbands.

12. Where did most of the settlers come from?

____

____

____

____

____

The Colony Gets a Capital *(page 170)*

The colony was growing and needed a capital. Austin thought the west bank of the Brazos River would be a good place. The town was named San Felipe de Austin in honor of both Austin and the patron saint of Texas Governor Luciano Garcia. By 1828, about 200 people lived in San Felipe.

13. Why was the new capital named San Felipe de Austin?

____

____

____

____

____

Name ______________________ Date ______________ Class ______________

Reading Essentials and Study Guide

For use with textbook pages 172–179

The Colonies Grow

Key Terms

Federalist A person who believes in sharing power between the states and the national government *(page 172)*

Centralist A person who thinks power should rest in the national, or central, government *(page 173)*

dowry The valuable goods (money, land, and furnishings) a bride brings to a marriage *(page 176)*

department A major administrative unit, similar to a territory *(page 177)*

★DRAWING FROM EXPERIENCE

Are you of Mexican descent? Do you know people of Mexican, Irish, German, or African American descent? Who are some important women in your community, state, or country?

In this section, you will learn about the growth of the colonies under the Mexican government.

★ORGANIZING YOUR THOUGHTS

Use the diagram below and on the next page to help you take notes as you read the summaries that follow. Identify the three major empresarios during this period, the large settlements they set up, and the important towns they established.

Empresario	Location of Settlement	Central Town
1.	2.	3.

(continued)

Name ______________________ Date ______________ Class ______________

Reading Essentials and Study Guide

Chapter 7-2

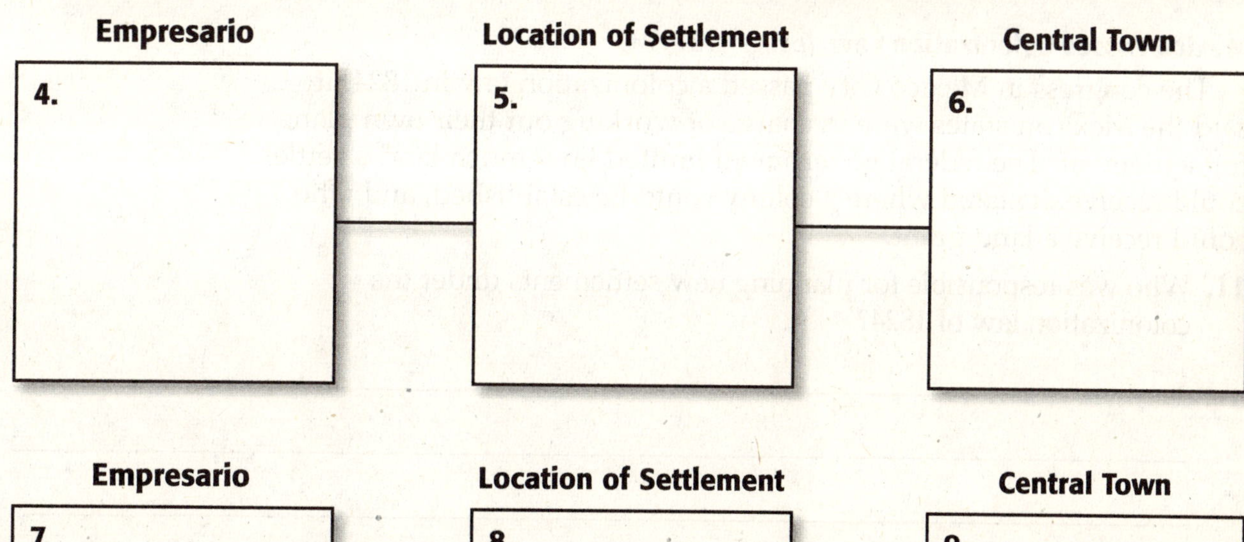

Empresario	Location of Settlement	Central Town
7.	8.	9.

★ **READ TO LEARN** *Write in complete sentences to answer the following questions. Use correct spelling, punctuation, and grammar.*

The Constitution of 1824 *(pages 172–173)*

In March 1823, the emperor of Mexico was overthrown. **Federalists** formed the new government. Federalists believed in sharing power between states and the national government. Their rivals, the **Centralists,** believed that power should be in the central government of Mexico City. The Federalists wrote a constitution for Mexico in 1824.

10. What is the difference between a Federalist and a Centralist?

____

____

____

____

____

(continued)

Name ______________________ Date ______________ Class ______________

Reading Essentials and Study Guide

Chapter 7-2

Mexico Passes Colonization Law *(pages 173–174)*

The congress in Mexico City passed a colonization law in 1824. It said the Mexican states were in charge of working out their own plans for settlement. The federal government limited how much land a settler could receive. It stated where a colony could be established, and who could receive a land grant.

11. Who was responsible for planning new settlements under the colonization law of 1824?

____

____

____

____

____

How State Colonization Laws Worked *(pages 174–175)*

In 1825, lawmakers at Saltillo passed their own law for colonization. Under this law, foreigners were invited to move to Texas. These settlers could receive land as individuals or through an empresario.

Families paid $30.00 for 4,428 acres of land, one league. Single men received less land. If a man married a Mexican woman, he received a bonus of additional land.

Although individual families were able to settle on their own, most settlers came as part of an empresario contract. This was because most settlers could not speak Spanish and needed the help of an empresario. Also, most of the best lands were held by empresarios.

Empresario contracts lasted for six years. The empresarios needed at least 100 families to settle on the land in six years, or their contract was cancelled.

12. What are two reasons settlers came to Texas with an empresario?

____

____

____

____

(continued)

Name ______________________ Date ______________ Class ______________

Reading Essentials and Study Guide

The Most Successful Empresario *(page 175)*

Stephen F. Austin was the most successful empresario. He received four new contracts. The first one allowed the settlement of 500 more families within his first colony. The second contract allowed the settlement of 100 families. They would live east of the Colorado River and north of the San Antonio Road, providing protection for travelers going to San Antonio. The town of Bastrop became "Little Colony," the name given to the land covered by the new contract.

In 1828, Austin received permission for the settlement of 300 families along the coast. In 1831, Austin received his last contract. Austin and his partner, Samuel M. Williams, could settle 800 families in the area to the north and northwest of the first colony.

13. How did Austin's second contract help travelers?

____

____

____

____

____

Why Austin's Colonies Succeeded *(pages 175–176)*

Austin was successful for many reasons. He dealt well with Mexican authorities. His colonists had an easy time getting titles to their land. Native Americans became less of a threat. Austin also had some of the most fertile soil in Texas. Settlers were looking for fresh land to grow cotton. Texas had what they needed. The land was well watered. There were enough trees for homes and fuel. There were roads and rivers that provided a means of transportation.

14. Why were Austin's colonies successful?

____

____

____

____

____

(continued)

Name ______________________ Date ______________ Class ______________

Reading Essentials and Study Guide

Chapter 7-2

Green DeWitt's Success *(page 176)*

Green DeWitt was another successful empresario. In 1825, he brought 400 families to Texas. His colony was west of Austin's first colony and south of San Antonio Road. The town of Gonzales was headquarters for the colony.

15. Who was Green DeWitt?

____

____

____

____

Martín de León, Empresario *(page 176)*

Martín de León was another successful empresario. In 1805, he established a ranch on the Aransas River. He received permission to bring Mexican settlers to Texas. He settled between 100 and 200 families along the Guadalupe River. His wife Patricia helped found the town of Victoria in 1824. Bringing valuable goods, or a **dowry** to her marriage, Patricia gave money, land, and furnishings to help build the first church in Victoria. She sided with the Texans during their war for independence from Mexico.

Native American raids troubled the colony. However, the colonists prospered by farming and ranching. By the 1830s thousands of cattle grazed on the rich grasses. Victoria became an important center for trade between Texas and Mexico.

16. What were two ways that Patricia de León supported Texas?

____

____

____

____

____

Other Contracts *(pages 176–177)*

James Power and James Hewetson settled Irish immigrants along the Gulf Coast. Their central town was Refugio. John McMullen and James McGloin established a colony of Irish settlers at San Patricio.

(continued)

Reading Essentials and Study Guide

Many other empresarios had contracts to bring settlers to Texas. Two of them, David Burnet and Lorenzo de Zavala, became active in the independence movement.

17. Where were Irish settlements located?

____

____

____

____

____

Various Nationalities Settle in Texas *(page 177)*

The people in Texas during the 1820s were of different nationalities. More than 3,000 people were Mexican. Most Mexicans lived in the Department of Béxar. A **department** is a major administrative unit, similar to a territory. More than 2,000 African American slaves also lived in Texas.

Not all African Americans in early Texas were slaves. Greenbury Logan, Lewis B. Jones, William Goyens, and Hendrick Arnold were free African Americans. By the time of the Texas Declaration of Independence, 150 free African Americans lived in Texas.

18. How many African Americans in Texas were slaves, and how many were free?

____

____

____

____

____

Women Play Important Roles *(page 178)*

Mary Austin Holley, Austin's cousin, came to Texas in 1831. She wrote about everyday life in Austin's colony.

(continued)

Life was hard for early female settlers. They worked alongside the men building houses and raising livestock. They also defended their land. However, they had few rights. They could buy and sell land. They could sue for survivor benefits. But they could not vote, hold public office, or serve on a jury.

In spite of the problems, women made important contributions. Holley's books about Texas helped attract settlers. María Calvillo was the daughter and wife of ranchers. She became the sole owner of her father's ranch, and improved and expanded her holdings. Jane McManus brought German colonists to Texas. Tamar Morgan, a slave, purchased her freedom and became a successful landowner.

19. Why was life difficult for women in the colonies?

____

____

____

____

____

Education in the Colonies *(page 179)*

The Mexican government did not have money for public education. Therefore, the colonists educated their own children. Wealthy colonists hired private teachers. Others sent their children to schools in the United States. Most settlers joined together to establish private schools in new communities. By the 1830s almost every town in the new settlements had one teacher.

20. How did children in the new settlements receive an education?

____

____

____

____

____

Name ______________________ Date ______________ Class ______________

Reading Essentials and Study Guide

Chapter 8-1

For use with textbook pages 186–189

The Difficulties Begin

Key Terms

decree An order given by someone of authority *(page 188)*

exempt To excuse or release from something required *(page 188)*

customs duty A tax on goods made in foreign nations *(page 189)*

★DRAWING FROM EXPERIENCE

What rules do you have at home? What rules do you follow at school? How do you feel when you have to follow a rule you think is unfair?

In this section, you will learn about the problems and solutions between the settlers of Texas and the Mexican government.

★ORGANIZING YOUR THOUGHTS

Use the diagram below to help you take notes as you read the summaries that follow. Think about the problems that arose both for settlers in Texas and for the Mexican government.

Settlers' Problems	Mexicans' Problems
1.	4.
2.	5.
3.	6.

(continued)

Name ______________________ Date ______________ Class ______________

Reading Essentials and Study Guide

★ **READ TO LEARN** *Write in complete sentences to answer the following questions. Use correct spelling, punctuation, and grammar.*

Differences Create Tension *(pages 186–187)*

Texas changed as a result of settlement in the early 1820s. Trade expanded. The population grew. Farms and plantations produced corn, cotton, and sugarcane. Tensions developed between Mexican officials and Anglo American settlers.

When the Federalists were in power in Mexico, the Anglo American settlers were left alone. The settlers started their own schools and newspapers. Some used slaves, even though the Mexican government was against it.

When the Centralist Party came into power in Mexico, more control was placed over the Anglo Americans. The settlers thought the changes were unfair. A series of clashes eventually led to a revolution.

7. How did the Federalist and the Centralist parties differ in their treatment of settlers?

____

____

____

____

Trouble Begins in East Texas *(page 187)*

One of the first clashes between colonists and Mexican authorities took place in 1826. A large land grant in the Nacogdoches area had been given to Haden Edwards. He brought in 800 families to settle there. Some people already living in the area had proof of owning the land. Edwards told the people who had no proof that they would have to leave or buy the title to the land. Many of these people had ancestors who had lived on the land for decades. They did not want to buy the land that they already owned.

8. What did Haden Edwards do when he got the land grant?

____

____

____

____

(continued)

The Republic of Fredonia *(pages 187–188)*

Haden Edwards' brother Benjamin thought the only solution was to revolt and declare their colony independent from Mexico. With the help of a Cherokee chief named Richard Fields, Benjamin and a group of settlers took over the Old Stone Fort in Nacogdoches. On December 16, 1826, they raised a red and white flag with the words "Independence, Liberty, and Justice" over the fort. They announced the creation of the Republic of Fredonia.

The Edwards brothers were not successful. Mexican troops were sent from San Antonio to put down the revolt. The brothers tried to get help from Austin's colony and from the United States, but no help came. Some of the Fredonians were captured, and some fled to the United States.

9. What happened to the Edwards brothers' revolt?

____

____

____

____

____

Mier y Terán Investigates *(page 188)*

The Fredonian revolt was a minor event, but it worried Mexican officials. They thought the United States wanted to take over Texas. When the U.S. ambassador to Mexico, Anthony Butler, asked Mexican officials to sell Texas to the United States, the Mexicans became even more worried.

The Mexican government decided to send General Manuel de Mier y Terán to East Texas to observe the settlers. Anglo Americans outnumbered the Mexican settlers there. In his report, Mier y Terán told the Mexican officials that Anglo American influence was strong. He said something should be done or Texas would be lost.

The Anglo American settlers were worried about Mexican rule. The colonists wanted to keep their slaves, but the Mexican government wanted to abolish, or get rid of, slavery. In 1829, the president

(continued)

of Mexico issued a **decree,** or order, abolishing slavery. Texans tried to persuade Mexican officials to **exempt,** or excuse, Texas from the decree. Although not put into effect in Texas, it worried settlers who had slaves.

10. Why do you think the president of Mexico decided to exempt Texas from the decree abolishing slavery?

____

____

____

____

____

The Law of April 6, 1830 *(page 189)*

On April 6, 1830, the Centralist government in Mexico issued a law stopping immigration from the United States. The government encouraged immigration from Mexico and Europe. The law also set up new forts. Soldiers in the fort would prevent smuggling, the introduction of slaves, and illegal land speculation. The Mexican government discouraged trade between foreign countries and Texas. The government placed a tax, called a **customs duty,** on goods made in foreign countries. The Law of April 6, 1830 alarmed the colonists. Many had strong ties with the United States. The decree marked a turning point in relations between the colonists and the Mexican government. Each side began to distrust the other. Stephen F. Austin tried to talk to the Mexican leaders, but the damage had already occurred in the relationship.

11. Why were Anglo American settlers in Texas concerned about the Law of April 6, 1830?

____

____

____

____

____

Name ______________________ Date ______________ Class ______________

Reading Essentials and Study Guide

Chapter 8-2

For use with textbook pages 190–193

Rebellions, 1831–1832

Key Terms

commerce The exchange of goods *(page 190)*
import To bring goods into a country, usually for sale *(page 191)*
skirmish A fight, usually on a small scale *(page 191)*
resolution A statement expressing a formal opinion *(page 191)*

★DRAWING FROM EXPERIENCE

Have you ever made resolutions at the beginning of a new year? Have you ever promised that you would do something and then not do it? Would you like to be part of a group that made the rules?

In this section, you will learn about the continuing conflict between settlers in Texas and the Mexican government. You will learn about the changes settlers in Texas wanted.

★ORGANIZING YOUR THOUGHTS

Use the diagram below and on the next page to help you take notes as you read the summaries that follow. Match events (causes) in the period 1831–1832 with their results (effects).

Events (Causes)		Results (Effects)
Bradburn strictly enforces laws and puts two men in prison	→	1.
Mexican president Bustamante ignores constitution	→	2.

(continued)

Name ______________________ Date ______________ Class ______________

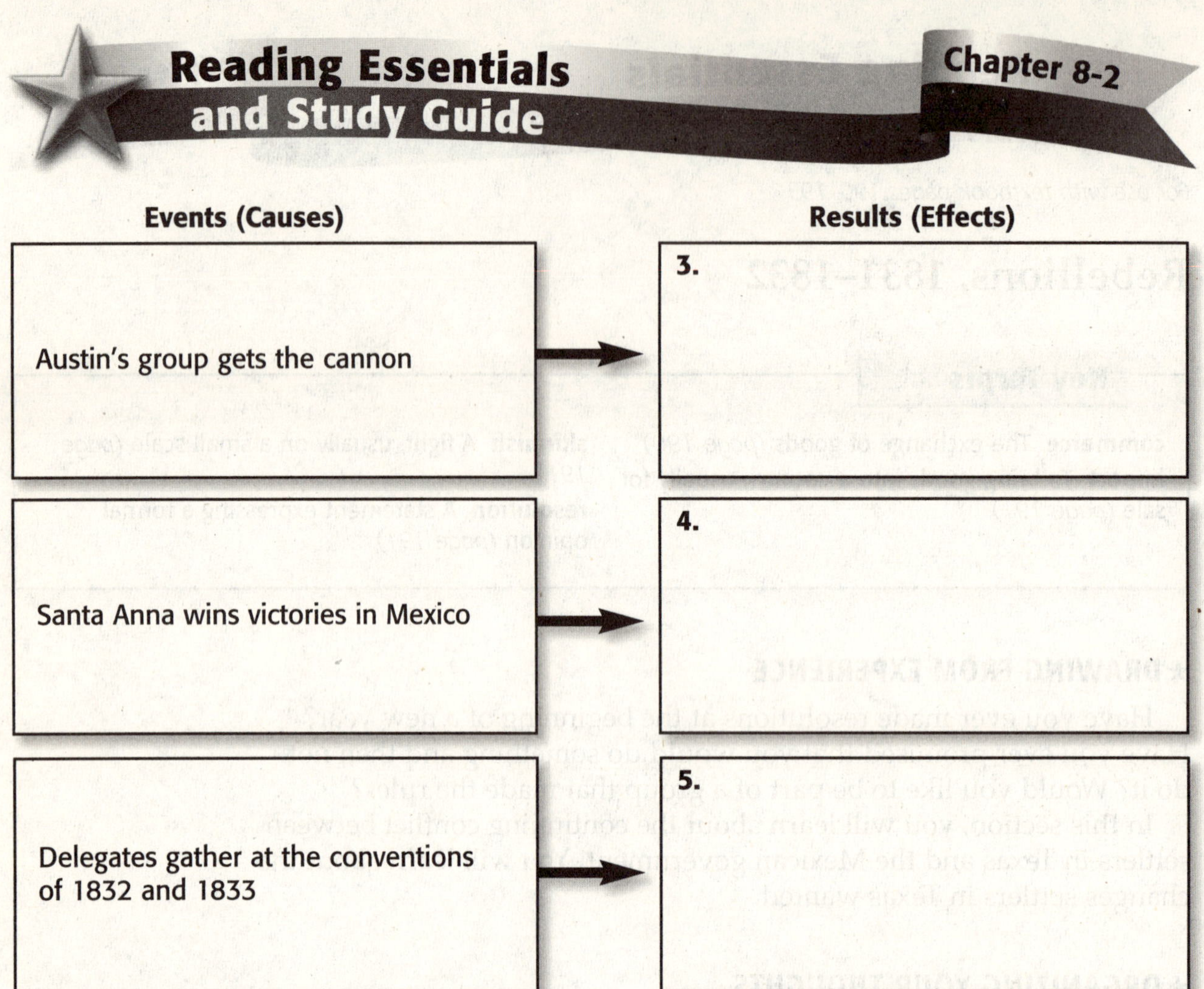

★ **READ TO LEARN** *Write in complete sentences to answer the following questions. Use correct spelling, punctuation, and grammar.*

Settlers Protest at Anahuac *(pages 190–191)*

The first serious conflict between Mexican authorities and colonists happened at the port town of Anahuac. Mexican soldiers at the port controlled **commerce,** or the exchange of goods, into Mexico.

John Davis Bradburn was in command at Anahuac. The colonists accused him of taking supplies. He believed in strict enforcement of the Mexican laws. Taxes were collected on goods **imported,** or brought, into Mexico. The merchants became angry. The final blow came when Bradburn arrested two lawyers in 1832. Bradburn put the two men in prison for interfering with law enforcement.

About 160 settlers marched to Anahuac to demand the release of the two prisoners, William B. Travis and Patrick C. Jack. A small **skirmish,** or fight, broke out between the colonists and Bradburn. Bradburn had agreed to let the prisoners go, but didn't. After another skirmish,

(continued)

Name ______________________ Date ______________ Class ______________

Reading Essentials and Study Guide **Chapter 8-2**

the colonists made camp at Turtle Bayou and sent John Austin to get a cannon.

6. Why were Travis and Jack put in prison?

____

____

____

____

____

Colonists Adopt the Turtle Bayou Resolutions *(pages 191–192)*

While waiting for John Austin to return, the colonists made **resolutions,** or statements of formal opinions. They declared their loyalty to Mexico. The colonists said they supported Antonio López de Santa Anna, who was fighting against the Centralist president, Anastasio Bustamante. Bustamante was ignoring the Mexican Constitution of 1824. The colonists and Santa Anna wanted to follow the constitution. Bradburn was finally replaced, and the prisoners were released. The soldiers at Anahuac declared support for Santa Anna.

7. To what country did the colonists declare their loyalty?

____

____

____

____

____

Clash at Velasco *(page 192)*

John Austin's group got the cannon and loaded it on a ship. The Mexican authorities considered them rebels. The Mexican commander at Velasco, Colonel Domingo de Ugartechea, would not let the group pass when they reached Velasco. Fighting broke out between the Texans and Mexican troops. The Battle of Velasco was bitter. There was loss of life on both sides. Ugartechea surrendered.

Meanwhile, those supporting Santa Anna were winning battles. By 1832, President Bustamante had resigned, and in 1833 Santa Anna

(continued)

began serving as president. The colonists were pleased because they thought he was a Federalist.

8. Why did the Mexican commander stop Austin and his group?

____

____

____

____

____

Conventions of 1832 and 1833 *(pages 192–193)*

A convention was called in San Felipe in 1832 to discuss changes needed in Texas. Stephen F. Austin was elected president of the convention, and 58 delegates participated. The delegates wanted

A. Texas to be made a separate Mexican state

B. immigration from the United States to be permitted again

C. Texas to be exempt from some import taxes

D. better education in Texas

E. better protection from Native Americans

F. land titles for settlers in East Texas

These resolutions were never presented to officials in Mexico.

Another convention met in San Felipe in 1833. These delegates wanted similar things. These delegates, among whom was Sam Houston, wrote a constitution for the proposed Mexican state of Texas. Austin made the trip to Mexico City to present the resolutions.

9. What was the main difference between the conventions of 1832 and 1833?

____

____

____

____

____

Name ____________________ Date ____________ Class ____________

Reading Essentials and Study Guide

Chapter 8-3

For use with textbook pages 194–198

Increased Tensions, 1833–1835

Key Terms

cholera A disease caused by deadly bacteria *(page 194)*

repeal To do away with, such as getting rid of a law *(page 195)*

malaria A disease carried by mosquitoes *(page 196)*

dictator A ruler with strong power *(page 198)*

★ DRAWING FROM EXPERIENCE

Have you ever known anyone who was willing to fight for his or her beliefs? What do you feel strongly about? Can you name a country that has a dictator? Do you know what life is like in countries with dictators?

In this section, you will learn about the struggles of Stephen F. Austin and the reforms he and others worked to get. You will also learn about the changes President Santa Anna made.

★ ORGANIZING YOUR THOUGHTS

Use the diagram below and on the next page to help you take notes as you read the summaries that follow.

Event	Person or Group
Agrees to some of Austin's reforms but does not allow Texas to become a separate state	**1.**
Writes a letter about difficulties in Mexico City; is arrested and imprisoned	**2.**
Die from cholera	**3.**
Believe relations with national government are improving	**4.**

(continued)

Name ______________________ Date ______________ Class ______________

Reading Essentials and Study Guide

Chapter 8-3

Event	Person or Group
Orders people disloyal to Santa Anna arrested	**5.**
Approves of the Consultation; is concerned that Santa Anna is becoming a dictator	**6.**

★ **READ TO LEARN** *Write in complete sentences to answer the following questions. Use correct spelling, punctuation, and grammar.*

Austin's Mission Is Stalled *(pages 194–195)*

It took three months for Stephen F. Austin to get to Mexico City in 1833. When he arrived, Santa Anna was not there. Santa Anna's government was not well organized. Large numbers of people in the city had **cholera,** a disease caused by deadly bacteria. Austin was discouraged and wrote a letter to the authorities in Texas telling of the problems he faced.

7. What did Austin find when he got to Mexico City?

____

____

____

____

____

Austin Is Imprisoned and Released *(pages 195–196)*

In November 1833, Santa Anna finally returned to Mexico City. He agreed to some of the reforms, or changes, Austin wanted. He did not agree to let Texas become a separate state. Santa Anna did **repeal,** or do away with, the law restricting immigration from the United States.

On his way back to Texas, Austin was arrested because of the letter he had written. Austin was taken back to Mexico City and spent a year in prison. He wrote letters to family and friends. Local officials worked for his release. On Christmas Day 1834, Austin was released on bail. His case was finally decided, and he went back to Texas. By the time he returned to Texas, he had been away for over two years.

(continued)

Name ______________________ Date ______________ Class ______________

Reading Essentials and Study Guide

8. Which law did Santa Anna repeal?

____

____

____

____

____

Reforms Begin in Texas *(page 196)*

While Austin was away, many changes took place in Texas. The cholera epidemic struck hard. Over 80 people died, including eight members of the Austin family. Heavy rains in 1833 and **malaria,** a disease carried by mosquitoes, added to the suffering.

Things had improved by 1834. Some of the reforms promised by Santa Anna began. English was used as the official language for business, allowing immigration from the United States. The court system was improved, and Texans had more representatives in the state legislature of Coahuila. There was even religious tolerance. Although people were still concerned about Austin's imprisonment by the Mexican government, they felt relations with the national government were improving.

9. Why were people concerned about Austin's imprisonment?

____

____

____

____

Trouble Erupts Again *(page 197)*

In early 1835, there was trouble again in Anahuac. The commander of the troops in Anahuac was Antonio Tenorio. Residents of the port city were angry with Tenorio because customs duties were collected in Anahuac, but not in other ports. One merchant refused to pay and was arrested. A group of colonists led by William B. Travis forced Tenorio to leave Texas. Some Texans were not happy with the action Travis took. They wrote a letter of apology to General Cós, Santa Anna's brother-in-law and commander of the Mexican forces in Coahuila.

(continued)

10. What caused the conflict between Tenorio and colonists in Anahuac?

____

____

____

General Cós Rejects the Apology *(page 197)*

General Cós did not accept the apology. He was angered by the disturbances and wanted all those disloyal to Santa Anna to be arrested. General Cós was acting on orders from Santa Anna. Santa Anna was no longer a Federalist, but a Centralist. Cós ordered the arrest of Lorenzo de Zavala, a Mexican politician who had helped write the Mexican Constitution of 1824. Cós took soldiers to Texas to arrest people who were disloyal.

11. What happened to people who were disloyal to Santa Anna?

____

____

____

Texans Call for a Consultation *(pages 197–198)*

Texans were very concerned about these arrests. On August 15, 1835, leaders in the town of Columbia called for a convention to discuss the situation. The convention was to be known as the Consultation. The colonists in the Peace Party wanted to stay friendly with Mexico and were afraid the Consultation would cause problems. Members of the War Party wanted the Consultation and hoped for independence from Mexico. They would even go to war if necessary. Austin gave his approval for the Consultation. He was concerned that Santa Anna was becoming a **dictator,** or a ruler with strong power. He was also concerned that troops were being sent to Texas.

12. What worried Austin?

____

____

____

____

Name ______________________ Date ______________ Class ______________

Reading Essentials and Study Guide **Chapter 9-1**

For use with textbook pages 204–208

The Revolution Begins

Key Terms

committee of correspondence A local group sharing political and military information with other groups *(page 205)*

siege A military blockade of a city or fortress *(page 206)*

provisional government A temporary government *(page 208)*

municipality A locally governed area *(page 208)*

regular army An army of full-time, paid soldiers *(page 208)*

★DRAWING FROM EXPERIENCE

Have you ever played a game in which you or your team was leading at the beginning? Did your early lead make you feel you could easily win the game? In this section, you will read about the Texans' early victories over the Mexicans during the Texas Revolution, and the steps taken to govern themselves.

★ORGANIZING YOUR THOUGHTS

Use the diagram below and on the next page to help you take notes as you read the summaries that follow. Recall details about the steps delegates to the Consultation took to set up a government for Texas.

Vote on Independence

1.

↓

Declaration of the People

2.

↓

Provisional Government

3.

↓

(continued)

Reading Essentials and Study Guide

Regular Army

4.

Commissioners to United States

5.

★ **READ TO LEARN** *Write in complete sentences to answer the following questions. Use correct spelling, punctuation, and grammar.*

A Mexican Army Arrives in Texas *(pages 204–205)*

Mexican officials were concerned about whether they could keep Texas under their control. More Mexican soldiers were needed in Texas. When more soldiers were sent to San Antonio, the colonists became concerned for their safety. To make certain they were safe from the soldiers, the colonists formed committees of safety. These committees watched the roads. They warned the colonists when Mexican soldiers were coming. The settlers heard many rumors. One rumor was that the Mexicans planned to arrest all the Texan leaders. Local groups were formed to share political and military information among the settlers. These groups were called **committees of correspondence.**

6. What was the purpose of the committees of safety?

____

____

____

Gonzales—The Lexington of Texas *(pages 205–206)*

The first fighting between the colonists and the Mexican troops was in Gonzales in October 1835. The first battle of the American Revolution took place in Lexington, Massachusetts. In both Gonzales and Lexington, the government tried to take away the colonists' weapons. Because these two battles were similar, Gonzales is called the "Lexington of Texas."

Colonel Ugartechea ordered the people to surrender their cannon. They buried it and waited for more reinforcements. The Texan forces dug it up and mounted it on a wagon. They decorated the cannon with a white flag that said "Come and Take It."

(continued)

Reading Essentials and Study Guide

The fighting began at Gonzales early in the morning and was soon over. The Mexican leaders told their soldiers to return to San Antonio. Only one person, a Mexican soldier, was killed in the battle.

News of the fight spread quickly through Texas. Many colonists were excited that Texas had won this battle. Mexico saw the Battle of Gonzales as the beginning of a war.

7. Why was Gonzales called the "Lexington of Texas"?

____

____

____

On to San Antonio *(page 206)*

One week after the fighting in Gonzales, a group of Texans attacked the garrison at Goliad. The Mexicans quickly surrendered. There was only one large group of Mexican soldiers left in Texas. That group was at San Antonio. Texans began gathering for the march against Cós. The cry was "On to San Antonio!"

Stephen F. Austin was chosen to lead a group of several hundred Texan soldiers to San Antonio. As they marched along, more soldiers joined the group. The soldiers did not believe they could defeat the Mexican soldiers in a battle. So, they decided to camp and lay **siege** (set up a military blockade) around San Antonio. The Texans hoped the Mexicans would run out of supplies and be forced to surrender.

8. What did the Texans hope would happen when they laid siege to San Antonio?

____

____

____

Peace Party Prevails at the Consultation *(page 207)*

At this same time, other Texans were meeting at San Felipe for a Consultation. The delegates came from 14 different towns and districts. Members of the War Party wanted to declare immediately that Texas was free from Mexico. Members of the Peace Party opposed Santa Anna but did not want to declare independence from Mexico. They

(continued)

wanted the Consultation to declare that Texas was fighting for the Constitution of 1824, which Santa Anna had overthrown.

The Consultation took a vote on whether to declare independence from Mexico immediately. The majority of delegates voted not to do so. The next day, the group made a statement that Texans were loyal citizens of Mexico, supported the Constitution of 1824, and would take up arms only to defend themselves and to oppose Santa Anna. This statement is referred to as the Declaration of the People of Texas.

9. How did the delegates differ about declaring independence from Mexico?

____

____

____

____

A Provisional Government Begins *(page 208)*

Next, the Consultation created a **provisional government,** or temporary government, for Texas. The provisional government had a governor and a lieutenant (assistant) governor. It also had a council with one representative from each **municipality,** or locally governed area.

The consultation chose two members of the War Party as governor and lieutenant governor. Both supported independence for Texas. Most of the members chosen for the council were members of the Peace Party. The two parties continued to argue.

The Consultation created a **regular army** of full-time, paid soldiers. Sam Houston was named its commander.

The Consultation chose Stephen F. Austin and two other people as commissioners representing Texas in the United States. They were told to ask the United States for soldiers, supplies, and money to fight against Santa Anna.

10. Why did the Consultation send representatives to the United States?

____

____

____

____

Name ____________________ Date ____________ Class ____________

Reading Essentials and Study Guide

Chapter 9-2

For use with textbook pages 210–213

The Capture of San Antonio

Key Terms

veto To reject *(page 213)*

override To overrule *(page 213)*

★DRAWING FROM EXPERIENCE

Have you ever worked together with others in your school or community to carry out a project or achieve a goal? When have U.S. citizens come together to do something or to support our country? In this section, you will learn how people of many backgrounds worked together to make Texas strong and fight for its independence. You will also discover some of the problems they had along the way.

★ORGANIZING YOUR THOUGHTS

Use the diagram below and on the next page to help you take notes as you read the summaries that follow. Think about what different individuals and groups did to help in the fight for Texas independence.

Texas Fight for Independence
1. Ben Milam and Frank W. Johnson
2. African Americans

(continued)

Name ______________________ Date ______________ Class ______________

Reading Essentials and Study Guide

Chapter 9-2

Texas Fight for Independence, continued
3. Tejanos
4. Provisional Government

★ **READ TO LEARN** *Write in complete sentences to answer the following questions. Use correct spelling, punctuation, and grammar.*

The Grass Fight *(pages 210–211)*

The Texans laying siege to San Antonio heard that a group of Mexicans were headed there with mules carrying bags of silver. The Texans believed this silver was going to be used to pay the Mexican soldiers. A group of Texan soldiers met the Mexican mule train and attacked it. They were disappointed to find that the mules were carrying grass, not silver. This skirmish became known as the "Grass Fight."

Except for the Grass Fight, very little was happening at San Antonio. The Texan volunteer soldiers were tired of waiting for the Mexicans to surrender. They were hungry and winter was coming. Many of the soldiers left. The siege was called off in December.

5. Why did the Texans attack the group of Mexicans traveling to San Antonio?

___

___

___

___

___

(continued)

Name ______________________ Date ______________ Class ______________

Reading Essentials and Study Guide

The Assault on San Antonio *(pages 211–212)*

As the Texans got ready to leave, they heard that the Mexican army at San Antonio was weak and could not win a major fight. By this time hundreds of volunteer soldiers had begun to arrive in Texas from the United States.

A group of about 300 volunteers led by Ben Milam and Frank W. Johnson decided to attack San Antonio. The Texans forced the Mexican soldiers into the center of town. The Mexicans took refuge in an old mission known as the Alamo. After only four days, Cós, the Mexican commander, admitted that he had lost the battle. He promised he would never again fight against the colonists or the Constitution of 1824. He and his soldiers were allowed to return to Mexico.

The capture of San Antonio was a great victory for the Texans. The Mexicans had more than twice as many soldiers as the Texans, but the colonists won anyway. Now there were no Mexican soldiers on Texas land. The Texas volunteers then began to go home.

6. What did the Mexican commander promise after he lost the battle at the Alamo?

____

____

____

____

____

Tejanos and African Americans Join the Fight *(page 212)*

Many Tejanos (Texans whose ancestors were Mexicans) could not decide whether to be on the side of Texas or the side of Mexico. Most did not take either side. Some Tejanos, however, joined Cós to fight for Mexico. Others joined the Texas army commanded by Captain Juan N. Seguín. Seguín supported the Texas movement for independence.

There were also a number of free African Americans who fought in the Texas army. One of them was Hendrick Arnold, who led part of the Texas army into battle.

(continued)

7. Why do you think it was hard for the Tejanos to choose between the Texans and the Mexicans?

____

____

____

____

The Provisional Government *(page 213)*

The provisional government continued its work as the fighting went on. A post office was created. Plans were made to set up an army and a navy. The government also asked the United States to loan it money.

There were many arguments between the governor and members of the Council. The Council voted to hold a convention. However, the governor **vetoed,** or rejected, this idea. The Council then **overrode** (overruled) the governor's veto. The convention would be held, even though the governor was against it.

Because of the disagreements between the governor and the Council, the government could not work properly. Neither side would cooperate with the other side. The Texans should have been preparing to fight the Mexican leader Santa Anna. Instead, they were spending time arguing with each other.

8. What did the governor do when the Council voted to hold a convention? How did the Council react? What finally happened?

____

____

____

____

____

Name ______________ Date ______________ Class ______________

Reading Essentials and Study Guide

Chapter 9-3

For use with textbook pages 214–219

The Convention of 1836

Key Terms

petition To request something from an individual or body such as a government *(page 215)*

executive Having to do with the chief officer of a government *(page 216)*

legislative Having to do with the lawmaking body of a government *(page 216)*

judicial Having to do with the courts *(page 216)*

civil rights Freedoms guaranteed to all citizens *(page 216)*

ad interim Temporary government *(page 217)*

★ DRAWING FROM EXPERIENCE

Do you belong to a club or organization? Does the club have officers, or leaders? What kinds of rules does the club have? How did members of the club decide on rules? In this section, you will learn more about the new Texas government. You will discover how Texans chose leaders and rules.

★ ORGANIZING YOUR THOUGHTS

Use the diagram below to help you take notes as you read the summaries that follow. Think about the work the Convention of 1836 did to set up a government for Texas.

Branches of Government	Civil Rights	Other Decisions
1.	4.	7.
2.	5.	8.
3.	6.	

(continued)

Name ______________________ Date ______________ Class ______________

Chapter 9-3

★ **READ TO LEARN** *Write in complete sentences to answer the following questions. Use correct spelling, punctuation, and grammar.*

Santa Anna Crosses into Texas *(pages 214–215)*

The council called for a new convention to be held in March 1836. Texans hoped that the Mexican army would not come to Texas until after the convention. However, the Texans found out that Santa Anna was already on his way with a large army. The Mexican soldiers arrived at San Antonio in February. For safety, those Texans who were still in San Antonio moved into the Alamo mission.

9. What did the Texans in San Antonio do when Santa Anna's army arrived?

____

____

____

____

The Convention Declares Independence *(page 215)*

At the end of February, delegates started arriving in the small town of Washington-on-the-Brazos for the new convention. The Convention of 1836 began on March 1, 1836, with 59 delegates. Only two of the delegates attending had been born in Texas. Most of the other delegates were from different parts of the United States.

The Convention decided to choose a committee to write a document stating that Texas was free of Mexico. The Texas Declaration of Independence was similar to the U.S. Declaration of Independence. It stated that the Mexican government led by Santa Anna had not treated the Texans fairly, and had not given them many freedoms. Texans were denied the freedom of religion, freedom to carry weapons, and the right to **petition,** or request something from the government. In addition, the Mexican government did not provide schools for Texan children. The Texas Declaration of Independence stated that the people of Texas were declaring that they were free from Mexico.

On March 2, 1836, all of the delegates voted to adopt the Declaration of Independence. March 2 is known as Texas Independence Day.

(continued)

10. What are two reasons the Texans believed the Mexican government was treating them unfairly?

The Delegates Write a Constitution *(pages 216–217)*

The Convention then began writing a constitution for the Republic of Texas. The delegates worked as quickly as possible because Santa Anna was in Texas. The constitution was completed and approved only two weeks after the Declaration of Independence was signed.

The Texas constitution was similar to the Constitution of the United States. It set up three branches, or parts, of government. At the head of the **executive** branch was the chief governing officer. The **legislative** branch made the laws. The courts made up the **judicial** branch. The Texas constitution also contained a Bill of Rights that promised certain **civil rights** to the citizens of Texas. These rights included freedom of speech, freedom of the press, and freedom of religion.

The Texas constitution made it legal to own slaves. Free African Americans were not allowed to live in Texas without special permission. Those African Americans who had fought to free Texas could not live freely in the republic.

11. What are some of the civil rights protected by the Texas constitution?

The Ad Interim Government Takes Control *(page 217)*

The constitution stated that elections should be held so that Texans could elect their representatives. Elections could not be held while there were Mexican soldiers in Texas. To get around this problem, the Convention chose people to be part of a temporary, or **ad interim** government. These people would govern only until there could be regular elections.

(continued)

12. Why did Texans set up an ad interim government?

____

____

____

____

A Convention Diary *(pages 217–218)*

Colonel William F. Gray was a visitor at the Convention. He kept a diary, or written record, of what happened. He described many of the interesting people who came to the Convention. He spoke about how much people there liked Sam Houston. He also wrote about how the Convention regularly received news of the fighting at the Alamo in San Antonio.

13. How did the delegates at the Convention feel about Sam Houston?

____

____

____

____

Santa Anna Advances *(pages 218–219)*

On March 15, the Convention learned that the Texans had lost their fight at the Alamo. Santa Anna had won. Santa Anna's army was now heading toward Washington-on-the-Brazos, where the Convention was being held. The Convention ended on March 17. The delegates left town very quickly. Santa Anna continued his march through Texas. The new government of Texas had to move to different places as Santa Anna approached. The war had begun. The future of the new Republic of Texas did not look good.

14. Why did the Convention end quickly?

____

____

____

Name ______________________ Date ______________ Class ______________

Chapter 10-1

For use with textbook pages 224–228

A Clash of Armies

Key Terms

recruit To enlist in the army *(page 226)*

★DRAWING FROM EXPERIENCE

Do you know anyone who is in the army? Do you know anyone who has ever fought in a war? Why did that person join?

In this section, you will learn about the many people who joined the Texan army to fight for independence. You will learn why they joined and the strengths and weaknesses of both the Texan and the Mexican troops.

★ORGANIZING YOUR THOUGHTS

Use the diagram below to help you take notes as you read the summaries that follow. Identify the commanders of Texas troops at these scattered places.

Texas Commanders by Location

San Patricio	Goliad	San Antonio
1.	3.	4.
2.		5.
		6.

(continued)

Name ______________________ Date ______________ Class ______________

Reading Essentials and Study Guide

Chapter 10-1

★ **READ TO LEARN** *Write in complete sentences to answer the following questions. Use correct spelling, punctuation, and grammar.*

A Missed Opportunity *(pages 224–225)*

General Cós surrendered San Antonio to the Texans in December 1835. Santa Anna was furious. Santa Anna wanted to punish the Anglo rebels in Texas and the Tejanos who had gone against him. Mexico City was very far from Texas. It would take Santa Anna a long time to get to Texas. However, the Texans did not use the time well. During the first two months of 1836, Texas had no leadership. The Texans did not organize. Instead, the volunteer soldiers who captured San Antonio returned home. The Texas army became very small.

Most of those who stayed in the army were new arrivals from the United States. Some had come for land. Some had come because they believed in liberty. Some had come for the adventure.

Some volunteers were well-known figures. David (Davy) Crockett of Tennessee had been a U.S. congressman. Others were unknown farmers, hunters, and clerks. They represented various nations, including England, Wales, Ireland, Scotland, and Germany.

7. What are three reasons people came from the United States to join the war?

____

____

____

Texas Forces Are Divided *(page 225)*

The Texan forces were divided at the end of 1835. General Sam Houston was commander of the regular Texas army. He could not bring together the military units. The volunteers did not recognize his authority. Some volunteers were used to electing their own leaders. In addition, Texas Governor Smith gave the same assignment to several commanders. For example, he assigned three leaders to attack the Mexican city of Matamoros.

Texan forces remained scattered. About 100 men were still in San Antonio. Their commander was Colonel James C. Neill. Colonel Frank W. Johnson and Dr. James Grant each had about 50 men in San Patricio. Colonel James W. Fannin had about 450 men at Goliad. Another force was formed at Gonzales. These different units had little communication and did not work together in any way.

(continued)

8. What was the major problem for the Texan forces?

____

____

____

____

____

Santa Anna Moves North *(page 226)*

Santa Anna moved 6,000 soldiers northward. Many members of the army had been **recruited,** or enlisted quickly. They were untrained and undisciplined. They were poorly clothed and fed. They had poor equipment. Many were forced to fight.

Texans thought Santa Anna would wait until the spring to move north. However, Santa Anna began marching in the winter. He hoped to surprise the Texans. He divided his army into two main columns. He led the larger column across the Rio Grande at Paso de Francia and headed toward San Antonio. General José Urrea led the other column. They crossed the Rio Grande at Matamoros and moved toward Goliad.

9. What were four weaknesses of the Mexican troops?

____

____

____

____

____

Texans Occupy the Alamo *(pages 226–227)*

Texan troops in San Antonio stayed in an abandoned mission. It once housed a Spanish colonial company from Alamo de Parras. For this reason, the building was called the Alamo.

Colonel Neill had 104 soldiers in the Alamo. In January, he asked for more guns and troops. Houston ordered Colonel James Bowie and about 25 Texans in Goliad to go to the Alamo. Bowie was a well-known person. He was famous for a large knife he carried.

(continued)

Name ______________________ Date ______________ Class ______________

10. Why was the building that the Texan troops stayed in called the Alamo?

____

____

____

____

Travis Arrives at the Alamo *(pages 227–228)*

In February, Colonel William B. Travis and about 30 soldiers from San Felipe came to the Alamo. David Crockett and 12 more volunteers also came. Crockett was a frontier legend. He was a sharpshooter, hunter, and storyteller. He had been a colonel in the Tennessee militia. He had also been in the Tennessee legislature and the U.S. Congress. He was nearly 50 years old when he came to Texas. Travis offered him a command, but he wanted to remain a private.

Tejanos were active, first in the uprisings against Spain and then against Mexico. They risked not only their lives but also their land, homes, and families. They had more to lose than the Anglo Americans who were seeking land, liberty, and adventure. The Tejanos saw Santa Anna as a dictator. He did not follow the Constitution of 1824 that guaranteed a democratic government in Mexico. At least nine Tejanos helped defend the Alamo.

In February, Colonel Neill left the Alamo because of an illness in the family. Bowie was made commander of the volunteers. Travis became commander of the regular army soldiers. At the end of February, Bowie became sick and passed his command to Travis.

Travis and the troops did not think that Santa Anna would enter Texas until the spring. A party of scouts reported that Santa Anna's army had crossed the Rio Grande in early February. However, Travis still believed that he would have more time.

11. How did the Tejanos' reasons for fighting differ from the Anglo Americans' reasons?

____

____

____

____

Name ______________________ Date ______________ Class ______________

Reading Essentials and Study Guide

Chapter 10-2

For use with textbook pages 230–235

Texans Defend the Alamo

Key Terms

fortify Strengthen *(page 231)*

bombard Attack *(page 233)*

★ DRAWING FROM EXPERIENCE

Have you ever heard the saying "Remember the Alamo"? What does the saying mean to you? Have you ever visited the Alamo? What were your impressions of the site? Today, it is a popular tourist attraction, but in 1836 it was the site of one of the most violent and bloody battles between Texas and Mexico.

The last section discussed the problems facing Texan troops as Santa Anna and Mexican forces advanced. In this section, you will learn about the Alamo and the courageous men who lost their lives fighting to defend it. You will also learn how the battle helped Texas's struggle for independence.

★ ORGANIZING YOUR THOUGHTS

Use the diagram below and on the next page to help you take notes as you read the summaries that follow. Explain some of the factors that contributed to the Texans' defeat at the Alamo.

1. The Alamo Structure

(continued)

Reading Essentials and Study Guide

2. The Troops

3. The Timing

★ **READ TO LEARN** *Write in complete sentences to answer the following questions. Use correct spelling, punctuation, and grammar.*

In Defense of the Alamo *(pages 230–231)*

When Bowie got to the Alamo, he knew there were not enough soldiers to defend it. He and Travis believed that holding the Alamo was very important to the future of Texas. They strengthened its defenses.

On February 23, Travis was surprised when part of Santa Anna's army arrived at San Antonio. The Texans barely made it inside the Alamo before Santa Anna's cavalry arrived.

The Texans had some protection. The walls of the Alamo were 2 to 3 feet thick and 12 feet high. Twenty-one cannons **fortified,** or strengthened, the mission. They had one powerful 18-pound cannon. The Texans had a lot of beef, corn, and water.

(continued)

Name ______________________ Date ______________ Class ______________

The Alamo had weaknesses as well. The wall surrounding the main plaza had a gap between the south wall and the old chapel. The Texans closed it with only a fence of sticks and dirt. Also, the mission was very large, and Travis had fewer than 200 men.

4. What were the strengths of the Alamo?

____

____

____

____

____

Travis Declares "Victory or Death" *(pages 231–232)*

Travis was determined to hold the Alamo. He wrote to the people of Texas and the United States. He asked for help. His letters received little response. The Texas forces were poorly organized and scattered. Travis hoped that Fannin would come with his army from Goliad. However, Fannin did not have enough wagons to move his supplies. Only 32 volunteers came from Gonzales. Albert Martin and George C. Kimball led them into the Alamo on March 1.

Santa Anna's headquarters were at the San Fernando Church. It faced the Alamo. Santa Anna raised the red flag of "no quarter." This meant he would not take any prisoners in the battle.

On March 3, Travis wrote to the president of the Convention of 1836. He described the fighting that had already happened. He asked again for help. He concluded by saying that he and his troops intended to hold the Alamo.

5. How did Travis try to get help to strengthen the Alamo?

____

____

____

____

____

(continued)

Name ______________________ Date ______________ Class ______________

Reading Essentials and Study Guide

Chapter 10-2

Facing Certain Death *(page 233)*

Mexican troops surrounded the Alamo. It became clear that Travis and his troops had no chance for victory. Travis told his army that staying in the Alamo meant certain death. According to legend, Travis drew a line on the ground with his sword. All those who wished to stay and fight were asked to cross over the line. All but one of the men crossed over the line. Almost 200 men, mostly volunteers, decided to stay and fight for a cause in which they believed.

The Texans held the Alamo against the odds. The Mexican cannons had **bombarded** (attacked) the Alamo daily. However, there was little damage. The Texans were able to shoot Mexican troops from a great distance with their rifles.

6. Why was it so courageous for the men to stay at the Alamo?

____

____

____

____

____

Texan Troops Give Ground *(pages 233–234)*

Santa Anna ordered the attack on the Alamo to begin at dawn on March 6. As many as 1,800 Mexican troops helped with the attack. They moved in five columns to attack the Alamo at three different points. Mexican buglers played "El Degüello." This is an ancient chant that meant they would show no mercy.

The Texans were ready for the attack. The first and second groups of Mexican attackers were riddled by cannon and rifle fire. The Texans, however, were forced to give ground as the third wave attacked. The Mexican forces stormed over the walls of the Alamo. They fought in the yard of the mission with knives and clubs. Mexican forces continued to attack until the Alamo was overpowered. By 8 A.M., the battle was over.

After the fighting ended, the bodies of the dead were burned. Because of this, it is not known how many people died. Santa Anna claimed that 600 Texans died. Historians first believed that at least 189 Texans died. New research estimates that 250 defenders died. Bowie, Travis, and Crockett were killed. A Mexican officer, Colonel José Enrique de la Peña, wrote that Crockett survived the battle but was executed immediately afterward.

(continued)

It is uncertain how many Mexicans died. Santa Anna claimed that he lost 70 men. Many Texans believe that 1,000 Mexicans were killed or wounded. Historians believe it was 600.

7. Why is Santa Anna's claim that 600 Texans died probably not true?

____

____

____

____

____

A Battle Cry for Victory *(pages 234–235)*

Although Santa Anna ordered that all defenders of the Alamo be put to death, several survived. Santa Anna released the women and children who had been inside the Alamo during the battle. They went to Gonzales to tell the other Texans about the disaster.

Historians believe that losing the Alamo helped Texas win its independence. Santa Anna lost many good soldiers in the battle and was delayed for two weeks.

After the battle, Texans wanted to win their independence even more. People of the United States began to help Texas in their struggle for freedom. Texans were inspired by the heroism of those in the battle. "Remember the Alamo" became the battle cry of Houston's army.

8. What are two reasons that the defeat at the Alamo was a good thing for Texas?

____

____

____

____

____

Name ______________________ Date ______________ Class ______________

Chapter 10-3

For use with textbook pages 237–241

Defeat in South Texas

Key Terms

dispatch To send off or away with speed on official business *(page 238)*

★DRAWING FROM EXPERIENCE

Have you ever heard the saying "Remember Goliad"? Have you ever been to Goliad? Why do you think Goliad is important?

The last section discussed the defeat of Travis and his troops at the Alamo by Santa Anna and his men. In this section, you will learn about the defeat of Colonel Fannin by José Urrea at Goliad.

★ORGANIZING YOUR THOUGHTS

Use the diagram below to help you take notes as you read the summaries that follow. List examples of how Mexicans showed the defeated Texans mercy.

Mexicans Show Mercy for Texans

José Urrea	Mexican Soldiers	Francita Alavez
1.	2.	3.

(continued)

Name ______________________ Date ______________ Class ______________

Reading Essentials and Study Guide

Chapter 10-3

★ **READ TO LEARN** *Write in complete sentences to answer the following questions. Use correct spelling, punctuation, and grammar.*

Urrea Sweeps Northward to Refugio *(pages 237–238)*

While troops fought at the Alamo, José Urrea was leading Mexican troops through South Texas. He defeated Frank W. Johnson's command at San Patricio and Dr. James Grant's men at Agua Dulce.

The people at Refugio asked Colonel Fannin to send help. He **dispatched,** sent off, Captain Amon B. King and about 30 soldiers to help them. They were surrounded by Urrea's army. They asked Fannin to send more troops.

Colonel William B. Ward and more men were sent to help King. Most of his men were captured or killed. The loss of lives was a major setback for the Texan cause.

4. Who was leading the Mexican troops through South Texas?

____

____

____

Fannin Delays His Departure *(page 238)*

Fannin was the commander of the Texan troops at Goliad. He had trouble making a decision and sticking to it. Fannin had tried to help Travis at the Alamo. However, he did not have enough wagons and had to return to Goliad. On March 14, General Houston ordered Fannin to retreat toward Victoria. Houston did not think the Texans were ready to meet the Mexican army. Fannin waited several days. He wanted to know what happened to King and Ward. Fannin then lost a skirmish, or fight, with the Mexican troops. He finally began his withdrawal on March 19.

Fannin had a heavy cannon that had to be pulled by oxen. This slowed his withdrawal. On March 19, his men stopped to rest and eat. They were near Coleto Creek in an open prairie. They were surrounded by Urrea's troops. Fannin had about 300 men, and Urrea had 300 to 500 men. During the attack, seven Texans were killed and 60 were wounded, including Fannin.

Overnight, both sides prepared for battle. The Mexicans had a better position in the woods. The Texans had no cover and no water. Their spirits remained high. They thought they would receive reinforcements

(continued)

from Victoria. However, it was Urrea who received reinforcements. In the morning, Mexican cannons opened fire on the Texans. Fannin agreed to surrender.

5. Why did Fannin delay his departure from Goliad until March 19?

____

____

____

Texans Surrender *(page 239)*

The Texans under Fannin believed that they were surrendering as prisoners of war. They thought they would be treated fairly by the Mexicans. However, the surrender agreement actually states that the Texans surrendered completely. They placed themselves at the mercy of the Mexican commander.

Urrea assured Fannin that the Texans would be treated fairly. According to survivors, Mexican officers said that the Texans would be released. Fannin and his troops were marched back to Goliad. They were imprisoned in the old presidio.

6. What were the Texans expecting once they surrendered to Urrea?

____

____

____

Santa Anna's "Cruel Necessity" *(pages 239–240)*

General Urrea asked Santa Anna to spare the prisoners' lives. However, Santa Anna ordered their execution. He feared that the Texans would join others in rebellion. He also was following the Mexican law that required the execution of those who took up arms against the government.

On March 27, the prisoners were marched out onto the prairie. They believed they were to do work there or possibly go home. They were shot by Mexican soldiers. Wounded prisoners were killed later that morning. A few managed to escape. Colonel Fannin was the last to be shot. About 350 Texans were executed. General Urrea felt sorry about Santa Anna's decision.

(continued)

Several prisoners, including two physicians and some workers, were not killed. The Mexicans needed them for their skills. Many of the Mexicans living in Goliad did not want to execute the soldiers. Some Mexican soldiers shot over the heads of the Texans and allowed them to escape. Señora Francita Alavez was the wife of a Mexican officer. She cared for the Texans during their imprisonment. She also helped some avoid being killed. The survivors called her the "Angel of Goliad."

7. Why did Santa Anna order the execution of the prisoners?

____

____

____

The Lessons of the Alamo and Goliad *(pages 240–241)*

After the Alamo and Goliad, Santa Anna thought it would be easy to drive the rest of the rebels out of Texas. Texans may never have won their independence without the Battle of the Alamo. The battle cost Santa Anna many lives. U.S. citizens sent people and money into Texas to aid their freedom. Santa Anna thought Texans would give up after the fall of the Alamo. It had the opposite effect.

One historian wrote that Americans never fought more bravely than in Texas and never managed affairs more poorly. The fighting in South Texas showed the lack of teamwork among the Texans. The defeats in South Texas convinced General Houston that he must not let his forces split into small groups. The defeats also taught the Texans that it was not wise to fight the Mexican army on the open plains of South Texas. The plains gave the Mexican cavalry a huge advantage.

News of the defeats at the Alamo and Goliad spread rapidly. The defeats angered Texans. "Remember Goliad" joined "Remember the Alamo" as a motto of the Texan soldiers.

8. What did Sam Houston and the Texan troops learn from the defeats in South Texas?

____

____

____

Name ______________________ Date ______________ Class ______________

Chapter 11-1

For use with textbook pages 246–250

The Road to San Jacinto

Key Terms

massacre Violent and cruel killing off of people, especially those who are unarmed *(page 248)*

★DRAWING FROM EXPERIENCE

Have you ever wanted something that you thought you would never be able to get? Have you ever taken a risk and done something really different from what you usually do? What things would you do to protect your family or where you live?

In this section, you will learn about the determination of Sam Houston and how he worked to make Texas independent from Mexico. You will also learn about Houston and his conflict with Santa Anna.

★ORGANIZING YOUR THOUGHTS

Use the diagram below and on the next page to help you take notes as you read the summaries that follow. List the activities and movements of Sam Houston and his troops in the proper order before they met Santa Anna in battle.

Sam Houston builds an army.

↓

1.

↓

2.

↓

(continued)

Name ______________________ Date ______________ Class ______________

Reading Essentials and Study Guide

3.

4.

5.

Houston's army waits at Buffalo Bayou.

★**READ TO LEARN** *Write in complete sentences to answer the following questions. Use correct spelling, punctuation, and grammar.*

Santa Anna Remains in Texas *(pages 246–247)*

The Texas cause seemed hopeless in March 1836. The fall of the Alamo and the losses in South Texas opened the way for the Mexican army to move farther into Texas. Santa Anna ordered his troops to burn every town in their path.

Santa Anna wanted to return to Mexico to take care of other matters. He thought the Texas rebellion was crushed except in central and East Texas. Santa Anna felt General Vicente Filisola could arrest David Burnet and the temporary government. Filisola, however, was not sure the fight was over. He believed the Texans would fight more to protect their homes and land. Filisola convinced Santa Anna to delay his return to Mexico.

(continued)

6. Why did the Texas cause seem hopeless?

____

____

____

____

____

Houston Builds the Texas Army *(page 247)*

Sam Houston also knew the campaign was not over. He was named commander in chief of the army at the Convention of 1836. He went to join the army at Gonzales after the convention. When he arrived at Gonzales, he found 370 volunteers. They were all anxious to fight Santa Anna.

At Gonzales, Houston learned that the Alamo had fallen. He had to decide whether to fight or flee. The army at Gonzales was small and untrained. Houston decided to retreat eastward toward the Colorado River. He hoped to pick up more soldiers along the way. Houston also ordered Fannin to bring his troops from Goliad to Gonzales.

7. Who was named commander in chief of the army at the Convention of 1836?

____

____

____

____

____

Houston's Army Retreats *(pages 247–248)*

Houston's army began to retreat from Gonzales on March 13, 1836. The army crossed the Colorado River at Burnham's Crossing and waited for others to join them. The troops drilled and trained. The number of soldiers grew to almost 1,400 as volunteers came in from the United States.

(continued)

Reading Essentials and Study Guide

Houston was concerned about Fannin and his troops. They never arrived because Santa Anna's army captured them. Santa Anna's army was moving toward the Colorado River. Some of Houston's men wanted to stay and fight. Houston didn't believe his army was strong enough to win, so he moved them to the Brazos River. He hoped that Santa Anna's army would have trouble getting supplies as they followed the Texans east. Houston also hoped he would get more help from the United States.

8. Why did Houston retreat from Gonzales?

____

____

____

____

____

Panic Causes Runaway Scrape *(page 248)*

Families living between the Colorado and Brazos Rivers were panicked. They heard about the disaster at the Alamo. Soon after that they learned of the **massacre,** or killing off, of Fannin's unit. They were scared when they found out about Houston's retreat. Hundreds of families packed all their belongings and moved east toward the Sabine River. The trip was miserable, and many got sick. Their journey is known as the Runaway Scrape.

9. Why did the families pack their belongings and move east?

____

____

____

____

____

Houston Trains His Army *(pages 249–250)*

On March 29, 1836, Houston and his Texas army reached the Brazos River. While some of the troops guarded the river, other soldiers went to Groce's Plantation. There Houston trained the soldiers in the basics

(continued)

Name ______________________ Date ______________ Class ______________

Reading Essentials and Study Guide

of warfare. Many of Houston's men did not like the drilling and marching. Some left the army. Others talked about choosing a new general.

Texas President David G. Burnet sent a letter to Houston urging him to attack Santa Anna. Houston did not want to move his troops until they were ready. As the troops trained, Hendrick Arnold, an African American scout, kept Houston informed of Santa Anna's movements.

10. Why didn't Houston fight when his troops reached the Brazos River?

____

____

____

____

____

The Mexican Army Moves East *(page 250)*

On April 5, 1836, Santa Anna crossed the Colorado River to overtake the Texans. Santa Anna divided his army to attack different places. His soldiers failed to take Houston's troops at the Brazos River. Santa Anna traveled downriver to find President Burnet and the Texas government. The Texan officials, however, kept moving and stayed ahead of Santa Anna.

General Houston moved his army southeast toward the San Jacinto River. At Groce's Landing he received two six-pound cannons. They were named "The Twin Sisters." Santa Anna was also moving toward the San Jacinto River. When Houston and his troops reached Buffalo Bayou, they waited there to meet the Mexicans.

11. Why do you think Houston kept moving his troops instead of fighting?

____

____

____

____

____

Name ______________________ Date ______________ Class ______________

Chapter 11-2

For use with textbook pages 252–259

Victory at San Jacinto

Key Terms

cavalry Mounted horse soldiers *(page 253)*

flank The right or left side of a military formation *(page 255)*

infantry Foot soldiers *(page 255)*

★ DRAWING FROM EXPERIENCE

Have you ever visited a former battle site? In this section, you will learn about the Battle of San Jacinto and how the Texan army was able to overcome Santa Anna's army. You will also learn about the treaty that was signed at the end of the conflict.

★ ORGANIZING YOUR THOUGHTS

Use the diagram below to help you take notes as you read the summaries that follow. Examine the effects of the Treaty of Velasco.

Effects of the Treaty of Velasco	
1.	4.
2.	5.
3.	6.

(continued)

Name ______________________ Date ______________ Class ______________

Reading Essentials and Study Guide

Chapter 11-2

★ **READ TO LEARN** *Write in complete sentences to answer the following questions. Use correct spelling, punctuation, and grammar.*

The Eve of Battle *(pages 252–253)*

On April 20, 1836, the Texan troops were in place along the San Jacinto River. Santa Anna's troops were less than a mile away. Santa Anna's men complained that their position wasn't good because of the swamps and marshland. Santa Anna was sure that the Texans would not attack first. On the afternoon of April 20, a small skirmish occurred between the Mexican army and the Texan **cavalry,** or mounted horse soldiers.

7. Why did Santa Anna's troops complain about their position?

____

____

____

____

San Jacinto Soldiers From Varied Backgrounds *(page 253)*

Only 20 to 30 of the soldiers in Houston's army were native Texans, or Tejanos. Houston was afraid they might be mistaken for the enemy and be shot. At first, Houston had the Tejano soldiers guard the camp. The Tejano soldiers, however, wanted to fight. Houston admired their courage and changed his order. The Tejanos wore cardboard hatbands so they would not be mistaken for Mexican soldiers. The other members of Houston's army came from the United States.

Many other soldiers had come to Texas in the weeks just before the battle. One soldier reported seeing English, Irish, Scots, Mexicans, French, Germans, Italians, and Poles in Houston's army.

8. What did the Tejano soldiers do so they wouldn't be mistaken for the enemy?

____

____

____

____

____

(continued)

Reading Essentials and Study Guide

Houston Calls a Council of War *(page 254)*

By late March, 1836, Santa Anna had an army of about 1,400 men. Many of these soldiers were inexperienced. Some were tired after marching all night to get to the river. They took time to eat and rest.

Houston and his troops were busy. Houston ordered his scouts to destroy a bridge at Vince's Bayou. This would cut off a path of retreat so the Mexican army could not escape. At noon, Houston called a council of war with his officers. They tried to decide if they should attack right away or set up a defense and wait for the enemy to attack.

9. Why did Houston call for a council of war?

____

____

____

____

____

"Remember the Alamo" *(pages 254–255)*

At 3:30 that afternoon, General Houston ordered an immediate attack. A battle line was formed with regiments on the left and right **flanks,** or sides. The "Twin Sisters" were in the center, attended by 30 men. Both the **infantry,** or foot soldiers, and the cavalry lined up.

Houston drew his sword and ordered the troop to advance. The men moved out of the woods and across the open prairie. Since many of Santa Anna's troops were resting, the Texans arrived at the enemy camp and surprised the Mexican army.

"Remember the Alamo! Remember Goliad!" was the battle cry. The Twin Sisters blew a hole in the Mexican lines. The Texans stormed through the enemy lines. They seized the Mexican artillery. The Mexican army was in total confusion. Some tried to escape across Vince's Bayou but found the bridge was gone. Many tried to flee across the prairie. The Mexican army fought back in an organized way for only 18 minutes, but fighting went on until dark.

(continued)

Reading Essentials and Study Guide

10. Why did the Texan troops use "Remember the Alamo! Remember Goliad!" as a battle cry?

____

____

____

____

____

Mexicans Suffer Heavy Losses *(page 256)*

Fewer than 10 Texans were killed or fatally wounded at the Battle of San Jacinto. About 30 others, including General Houston, were injured. The Mexicans suffered heavy losses. According to Houston, 630 Mexicans were killed and 730 were taken prisoner. Santa Anna disappeared during the fighting. He was found the next day and taken to meet Houston. He introduced himself as "General Antonio Lopez de Santa Anna . . . a prisoner of war at your disposition."

11. Why were so few Texans killed in this battle although they were outnumbered?

____

____

____

____

____

Comparing Reports *(pages 256–257)*

In Houston's report, he told about the battle and the courage of his men. Santa Anna also reported about the battle. He blamed his loss on the inexperience of his men, a lack of supplies, and the belief that the enemy would not attack.

The capture of Santa Anna helped the Texans. As a prisoner, he could not continue the war. At Houston's request, Santa Anna signed an order to withdraw all Mexican troops to south of the Rio Grande.

(continued)

Name ______________________ Date ______________ Class ______________

12. How did Santa Anna explain the Mexicans' defeat in the Battle of San Jacinto?

____

____

____

____

The Texan Navy Controls the Coast *(page 257)*

The small Texas navy played an important role, even though it had only four ships. The navy brought supplies to the Texan armies and cut off supplies to the Mexican troops. The Mexican troops that stayed in Texas after the Battle of San Jacinto were forced to leave because of the shortage of supplies.

13. What did the Texas navy do to help the Texan armies?

____

____

____

____

Treaties of Velasco *(page 257)*

The capital of Texas was moved to Velasco for several months. Santa Anna was taken there to sign two treaties with the Texas government. In the public treaty, Santa Anna agreed never to fight against the Texans again. He also agreed to remove all Mexican troops from Texas and exchange prisoners. In the secret treaty, Santa Anna agreed to work for Mexican recognition of Texas independence and to set the boundary at the Rio Grande. The Texas government released Santa Anna and escorted him back to Mexico.

14. What did Santa Anna promise in the secret treaty?

____

____

____

____

(continued)

Name ______________________ Date ______________ Class ______________

Many Texans Wanted Revenge *(page 258)*

Many Texans wanted to hang Santa Anna for the deaths of those at the Alamo and Goliad. Texas President Burnet, however, wanted to follow the Treaty of Velasco. A group of angry Texan army officers prevented Santa Anna from leaving Texas. They wanted him to be turned over to the army to be killed. Burnet stopped the officers from killing Santa Anna. He was kept captive for several months and then allowed to return to Mexico.

15. Why didn't President Burnet agree to execute Santa Anna?

____

____

____

____

____

Victory's Consequences *(pages 258–259)*

Once word of victory spread, many Texans returned home. Some found their homes had been burned, and their possessions were gone. Houston went to New Orleans to get medical treatment for his wounds. The Mexican troops went back to Mexico. Texas leaders now faced many problems. Texans returned to their homes not as Mexican citizens but as citizens of the new Republic of Texas.

16. What were some of the results of the Texans' victory in their war for independence?

____

____

____

____

____

Name ______________________ Date ______________ Class ______________

Reading Essentials and Study Guide

Chapter 12-1

For use with textbook pages 270–274

Sam Houston's Government

Key Terms

capitol A building in which a legislative body meets *(page 271)*

annexation Incorporating a country or territory into another country or territory *(page 271)*

expenditure Money paid out *(page 274)*

revenue Money received *(page 274)*

tariff A tax on imported goods *(page 274)*

★ DRAWING FROM EXPERIENCE

Have you ever wanted to become part of a particular group? Did the group welcome you as a member? Why or why not? In this section, you will read about some of the challenges Texas faced as an independent nation. You will learn that many people wanted Texas to become part of the United States. You will also learn why the United States government was not eager to make Texas a state at this time.

★ ORGANIZING YOUR THOUGHTS

Use the diagram below to help you take notes as you read the summaries that follow. Compare and contrast reasons why most Texans wanted Texas to become a state with reasons why some Americans did not want Texas to become a state.

Should Texas Become Part of the United States	
Texans–Yes, because	**Americans–No, because**
1. ______________________	4. ______________________
2. ______________________	5. ______________________
3. ______________________	

(continued)

Name ______________________ Date ______________ Class ______________

Chapter 12-1

★ **READ TO LEARN** *Write in complete sentences to answer the following questions. Use correct spelling, punctuation, and grammar.*

Houston Forms a Government *(pages 270–271)*

In September 1836, Sam Houston was elected the first president of Texas. Mirabeau B. Lamar was elected the first vice president. Texans also approved the Constitution of 1836 and voted to join the United States.

The town of Houston was chosen to be the temporary capital of Texas. The government was located in a building in Houston. This building was called the **capitol.**

6. What was the temporary capital of Texas?

____

____

____

Houston Faces Trouble with the Army *(page 271)*

Houston faced serious problems with the military. Soldiers who had arrived in Texas too late for the revolution wanted action. Their leader, Felix Huston, called for an invasion of Mexico. Houston did not want to invade Mexico. It would be costly and would probably mean the end of the new republic. He sent all but 600 soldiers home and never called them back. The threat from the army disappeared.

7. Who wanted to invade Mexico, and why?

____

____

____

The United States Delays Annexation *(pages 271–272)*

Texans had voted to join the United States. Most Texans had come to Texas from the United States. They wanted U.S. protection. In addition, Texas and the United States had strong business ties.

Several problems had to be solved before **annexation** of Texas could take place. Annexation is when a country or territory becomes part of another country or territory. One problem was that the Mexican government did not recognize Texas as an independent country. The

(continued)

Name ______________________ Date ______________ Class ______________

Reading Essentials and Study Guide **Chapter 12-1**

United States did not want to annex Texas if it would cause problems with Mexico. Slavery was also a problem. Slavery was legal in Texas. Many people in the United States were against slavery and stopped annexation.

8. What part did Mexico play in stopping annexation of Texas?

____

____

____

Recognition as a Nation *(pages 272–273)*

At first, the United States government did not recognize Texas as a nation. U.S. officials did not think that Texas would be able to remain independent of Mexico. The U.S. government thought Mexican soldiers might invade Texas again. Houston kept pushing for recognition, however. In 1837, President Jackson officially recognized Texas as an independent nation.

President Houston moved to open political negotiations with European powers. He sent J. Pinckney Henderson to get recognition with France and Great Britain. Finally, France extended recognition and a treaty was negotiated in 1839. Great Britain followed a year later. Houston hoped that the United States would move quickly to annex Texas if the European countries showed interest in Texas.

9. Why didn't the United States recognize Texas as a nation at first?

____

____

____

Native American and Texan Conflicts *(pages 273–274)*

More and more Anglo American settlers moved to central Texas. Some settlers treated the Native Americans unfairly and stole from them. Some Native Americans attacked and killed the settlers. President Houston stressed that friendship between the settlers and the Native Americans was very important.

During the fight for independence from Mexico, the Texas government had reached an agreement with the Cherokees. The Cherokees had promised not to fight against the Texans during their fight for freedom. In return, Texas promised to give the Cherokees title to

(continued)

their land. After Texas became independent, however, the Cherokees did not receive title to their land. More settlers kept moving onto land claimed by Native Americans.

10. What did the Texans promise to give the Cherokees? Did they keep their promise?

____

____

____

Texas Debt Soars *(page 274)*

The new nation of Texas had money problems. Money it paid out, **expenditures,** was greater than money received, **revenue.** Texas could not pay its bills for supplies and equipment used during the revolution.

Congress tried to get the money Texas needed. It put a **tariff,** or tax, on goods imported into Texas. The government also taxed the citizens on their property and businesses and collected land title fees. Even with these new taxes, the government was still spending more money than it collected.

11. Why did Texas have money problems?

____

____

____

The Release of Santa Anna *(page 274)*

Santa Anna visited the United States after his release in 1836. When he returned to Mexico, he said he would not keep the promises he had made in Texas. He also said he was leaving politics. In a few years, however, he returned to power. Texas–Mexico relations did not improve. Mexico still did not recognize Texas as an independent nation.

12. Why didn't Texas–Mexico relations improve after Santa Anna came to power a second time?

____

____

____

Name ______________________ Date ______________ Class ______________

Chapter 12-2

For use with textbook pages 275–279

Lamar Becomes President

Key Terms

endowment fund Money saved to support education *(page 276)*

cabinet A group of advisers *(page 276)*

redback Paper money of little value issued by the Republic of Texas *(page 279)*

★DRAWING FROM EXPERIENCE

Have you ever noticed that people can have very different points of view about the same situation? Have you ever disagreed with someone about an important issue? What was the issue? What was your point of view? How did the other person see the issue? In this section, you will read about life in Texas during Mirabeau Lamar's term as president. You will learn about Mirabeau Lamar's hopes for Texas. You will discover how Lamar's ideas differed from those of Sam Houston.

★ORGANIZING YOUR THOUGHTS

Use the diagram below to help you take notes as you read the summaries that follow. Think about Lamar's successes and failures as president of Texas.

Lamar's Term as Texas President

Successes	Failures
1.	4.
2.	5.
3.	6.

(continued)

Name ______________________ Date ______________ Class ______________

Reading Essentials and Study Guide

Chapter 12-2

★**READ TO LEARN** *Write in complete sentences to answer the following questions. Use correct spelling, punctuation, and grammar.*

Mirabeau Lamar Becomes President *(pages 275–276)*

Houston could serve only one term as president of Texas under the Constitution of 1836. In 1838, Texas vice president Mirabeau Lamar was elected president. Lamar believed that one day Texas would become a powerful country that stretched all the way to the Pacific Ocean.

Improving Texas's schools was important to Lamar. He believed that all citizens of a republic needed a good education to make intelligent decisions. The Texas Congress set aside land in each Texas county to support public schools. It also reserved public land in central Texas to provide income for two universities. Later, land in West Texas replaced this land. Oil discovered on these lands helped increase the **endowment fund,** or money saved to support education. Lamar's efforts to improve schools earned him the name "Father of Education in Texas."

7. Why is Lamar called the "Father of Education in Texas?"

____

____

____

____

____

The Capital Is Moved to Austin *(page 276)*

Houston was only a temporary capital. In 1839, a location on the Colorado River was selected for a new capital. Lamar was pleased with this choice because he wanted Texas to spread farther west.

Streets were laid out, and a capitol was built. President Lamar and his **cabinet** (group of advisers) moved to the new capital in October 1839. The capital was named Austin after Stephen F. Austin.

(continued)

Name ______________________ Date ______________ Class ______________

8. Why was Lamar pleased about the location of the new capital?

____

____

____

____

____

Lamar's Policy Toward Native Americans *(pages 276–277)*

Lamar had a different policy toward Native Americans than Houston. Lamar did not believe the Cherokees who had settled in northeastern Texas had a fair claim to the land there. He believed white Texans and the Native Americans could not live together peacefully.

Lamar heard that the Mexicans were trying to get the Cherokees to rise up against Texas. He wanted the Cherokees to be removed from Texas. The Texas army attacked the Cherokees near present-day Tyler. Nearly 100 Cherokees were killed, and villages and farms were burned. The Cherokees were forced to move across the Red River, out of Texas.

9. What was Lamar's policy toward the Cherokees in Texas?

____

____

____

____

____

____

Raids Lead to Council House Fight *(pages 277–278)*

The Texas government held peace talks with the Comanches in San Antonio in 1840. Hopes of peace disappeared, however, when the Comanches brought with them only one of their Anglo captives, a young girl. When they saw how bruised and sick the girl looked, the Texans became angry. They tried to hold the Comanches who had come to the meeting until they released other captives. A fight broke out. Seven Texans and 35 Comanches died. This struggle was known as the Council House

(continued)

Fight. The Comanches would not make treaties with the Texans. They were angry about the deaths of their people. This caused years of bitter warfare and many lives lost.

The Comanches also raided more settlements. Texas Rangers, along with other Texans, attacked a group of Comanches returning from a raid. Nearly 100 Comanches were killed.

10. What caused the Council House Fight?

____

____

____

____

____

Texas Rebuilds Its Navy *(page 278)*

President Lamar thought a strong military would make Mexico recognize Texas as independent. He ordered the newly rebuilt navy into Mexican waters. The navy helped some Mexican rebels. Lamar thought the Mexican government would recognize the Republic of Texas if he promised that the navy would not invade Mexico. When Sam Houston became president again, he called the navy home.

11. Why did Lamar rebuild the navy and send it into Mexican waters?

____

____

____

____

____

The Santa Fe Expedition *(pages 278–279)*

The Nueces River was the traditional boundary between Texas and Mexico. Texans, however, claimed the Rio Grande as a border after the revolution. They wanted to control Santa Fe, an important trading town on the upper Rio Grande.

(continued)

Reading Essentials and Study Guide

Lamar sent a group of people to Santa Fe to control the region and trade there. This group of soldiers, merchants, wagon drivers, and adventurers was called the Santa Fe expedition. It set out from Austin on June 19, 1841. The Santa Fe expedition had many problems on its trip. There was not enough food and water, and it was very hot. The group was also attacked by Native Americans.

As the group got close to Santa Fe, they met some Mexican soldiers. The soldiers forced the group to surrender. The Texans were forced to walk more than 1,000 miles from Santa Fe to Mexico City. Many died along the way. Others died in prison in Mexico City.

The Santa Fe expedition was a failure in many ways. It angered the Mexicans and resulted in the loss of many lives. It cost a great deal of money and failed to take control of Santa Fe.

12. What was the purpose of the Santa Fe expedition?

____

____

____

____

____

Financial Difficulties *(page 279)*

Lamar's campaigns against Native Americans and the expedition to Santa Fe cost a great deal of money and many lives. Lamar wanted to borrow money from the United States and European countries, but they would not give money to Texas. To help pay its bills, Texas issued more paper money. This money was known as **redbacks.** The redbacks quickly decreased in value. By the time Lamar's presidency ended, Texas had a huge public debt.

13. How did Lamar try to solve Texas's money problems?

____

____

____

____

____

Name ______________________ Date ______________ Class ______________

Chapter 12-3

For use with textbook pages 281–284

Houston Regains Presidency

Key Terms

archives Official documents *(page 282)*

★ DRAWING FROM EXPERIENCE

What do you know about the current president of the United States? How do this president's ideas differ from those of presidents before him? In this section, you will learn how Houston's ideas about money problems and policies toward Native Americans differed from Lamar's.

★ ORGANIZING YOUR THOUGHTS

Use the diagram below and on the next page to help you take notes as you read the summaries that follow. Think about the outcome of each event during Houston's second term as president.

Event	Outcome
Houston cut government positions and the size of the army.	1.
Texas made treaties with Native Americans.	2.
Houston tried to move the government archives to the city of Houston.	3.

(continued)

Name ______________________ Date ______________ Class ______________

Event	Outcome
General Woll invaded Texas with Mexican troops.	**4.**
A group of Texan soldiers attacked the Mexican town of Mier.	**5.**
Houston traveled to East Texas to stop fighting between two groups of settlers.	**6.**

★**READ TO LEARN** *Write in complete sentences to answer the following questions. Use correct spelling, punctuation, and grammar.*

A Policy of Economy *(page 281)*

Sam Houston became president again in 1841. President Houston knew that Texas was in debt. To balance the budget, he got rid of many positions in government and cut the size of the army. He also tried to sell navy ships. The debt still increased because of the high interest that had to be paid on it.

7. What did President Houston do to try to reduce Texas's debt?

____

____

____

____

____

(continued)

Name ____________________ Date ______________ Class ______________

Reading Essentials and Study Guide

Chapter 12-3

A Temporary Peace *(page 282)*

Houston wanted to treat Native Americans fairly and have peaceful relations with them. Houston stated that white people should respect the land, lives, and property of Native Americans. He believed that crimes against Native Americans should be punished by the laws of the republic. The Texas government signed treaties with Native Americans during this time. The treaties brought calm to Texas for several years.

8. What helped create peace between Native Americans and Texans for several years during Houston's presidency?

____

____

____

____

____

Invasion Triggers the Archives War *(page 282)*

The Santa Fe expedition had made Mexico angry. In March 1842, hundreds of Mexican soldiers invaded Texas. Though they stayed in Texas only a few days, Texans were frightened. President Houston was afraid the government **archives,** or official documents, might be destroyed. Houston wanted to move the archives from Austin to the city of Houston. Many Austin residents thought Sam Houston wanted to make Houston the capital of Texas. These people fought with the government officials who were trying to move the archives, and won. The archives and the capital remained in Austin. This skirmish was called the Archives War.

9. Why did people in Austin fight with government officials in charge of the archives?

____

____

____

____

____

(continued)

Name ________________ Date ________________ Class ________________

Reading Essentials and Study Guide **Chapter 12-3**

Woll Invades Texas *(page 282)*

Later in 1842, Mexican troops invaded Texas again. This time more soldiers came. Their leader was General Adrián Woll. Woll's troops took over San Antonio. The Texas militia and Texas Rangers rushed to San Antonio to fight the Mexicans. They forced them to leave Texas.

10. What did the Texans do when General Woll's soldiers invaded Texas?

____

____

____

____

____

The Mier Expedition *(pages 282–283)*

Texans were upset about Woll's invasion of Texas. They wanted President Houston to take action to protect the republic. Houston wanted to settle the problems peacefully.

In November 1842 Houston ordered a group of Texan soldiers to check the area from San Antonio to Laredo. When no Mexican soldiers were found in this area, the soldiers were ordered back to Gonzales. A small group of soldiers did not want to go back and split off from the others. This smaller group attacked the Mexican town of Mier. They expected an easy victory, but were beaten by a much larger army of Mexicans who came to defend the town. Outnumbered and low on supplies, the Texans finally surrendered.

11. Why were Texan soldiers sent to check the area from San Antonio to Laredo?

____

____

____

____

____

(continued)

Name ______________________ Date ______________ Class ______________

The Drawing of the Black Beans *(pages 283–284)*

Mexican soldiers began marching the Texans to Mexico City. Some of the Texans escaped. They fled to the mountains. Some became lost and died. Others were caught again by the Mexicans.

The Mexican leader, Santa Anna, said that every 10th captured Texan should be killed. Of the 176 captured Texans, 17 were to be killed. The Texans were forced to pick beans from a jar. If they picked a black bean, they were shot. If they picked a white bean, they were forced to march to prison in Mexico City.

12. Why do you think Santa Anna told his soldiers to kill every 10th captured Texan?

____

____

____

____

____

Feuds Lead to Unrest in East Texas *(page 284)*

Late in his term, Houston had to deal with unrest in East Texas. Two groups of settlers—the Regulators and the Moderators—had been fighting there for several years. President Houston sent soldiers to stop the fighting. Then he went to the area. He told the settlers that they were all Texans and should not fight each other. He talked the two groups into ending their fighting.

13. What reason did President Houston give the Regulators and Moderators for not fighting?

____

____

____

____

____

Name ______________________ Date ______________ Class ______________

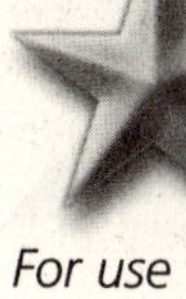

Reading Essentials and Study Guide — Chapter 12-4

For use with textbook pages 286–289

Texas Becomes a State

Key Terms

manifest destiny The view that the United States was destined to expand from coast to coast *(page 288)*

joint resolution A statement passed by both houses of the U.S. Congress that has the force of law and requires only a simple majority of votes in each house *(page 288)*

★ DRAWING FROM EXPERIENCE

Have you ever waited a long time for something? How do you feel when an important day, such as your birthday, a holiday, or the first day of school, finally arrives?

In this section, you will discover how Texans felt when Texas finally became part of the United States. You will learn about changes that took place in the United States that made it possible for Texas to join the other states. You will also read about the steps involved in becoming a state.

★ ORGANIZING YOUR THOUGHTS

Use the diagram on the next page to help you take notes as you read the summaries that follow. Then, place the letter of the following events on Texas's road to statehood in the proper order in the boxes.

A. Delegates to convention in Austin write a constitution.

B. President Polk signs resolution making Texas a state.

C. U.S. Congress passes a joint resolution for annexation.

D. Jones turns Texas government over to J. Pinckney Henderson.

E. Texas voters approve annexation.

F. U.S. Congress approves the Texas Constitution.

(continued)

Name ______________ Date ______________ Class ______________

Reading Essentials and Study Guide

Chapter 12-4

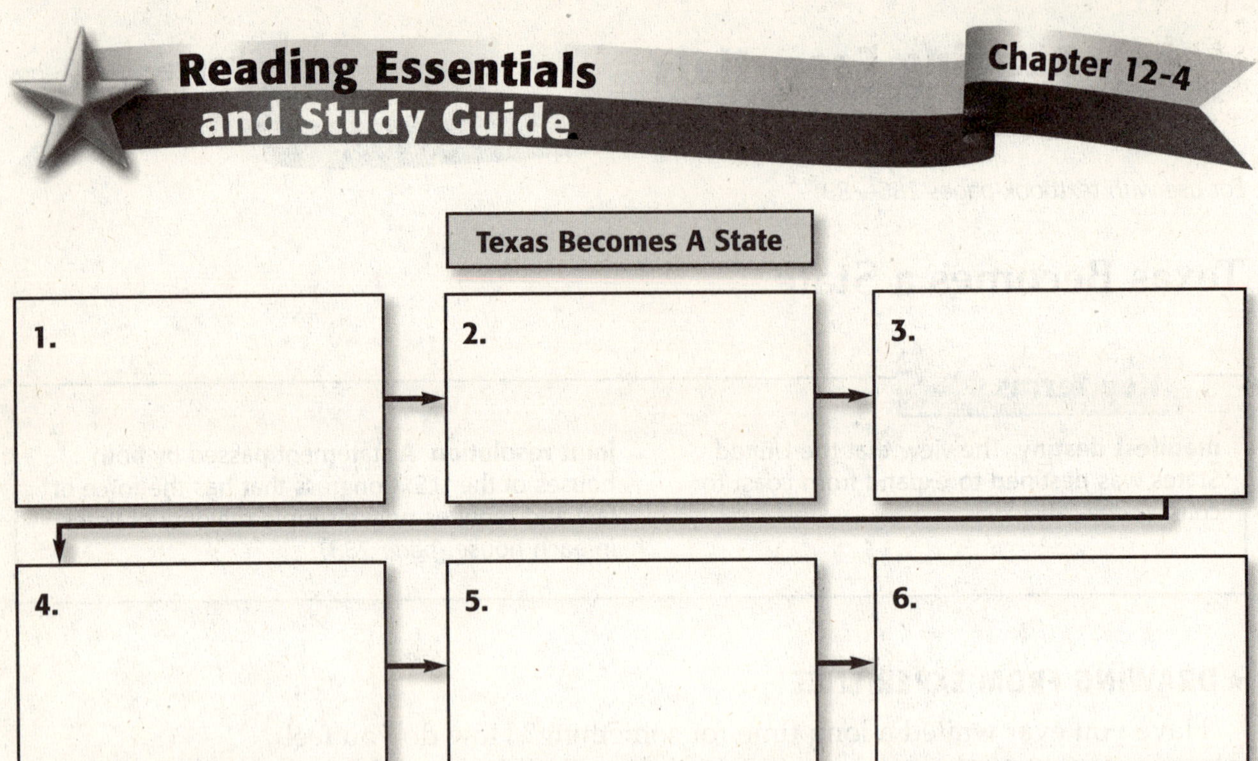

★ **READ TO LEARN** *Write in complete sentences to answer the following questions. Use correct spelling, punctuation, and grammar.*

The Texas Question *(pages 286–287)*

The "Texas Question" had become an important issue in the United States. People in the United States still disagreed about whether Texas should become a state. Some people believed that annexing Texas would benefit people in the South who owned slaves. They also were afraid that it would mean war with Mexico. However, more and more people wanted to annex Texas. Thousands of Americans had immigrated to Texas. Ties between Texas and the United States were strong.

In April 1844, representatives from the United States and Texas signed a treaty. The treaty made Texas a territory of the United States. Texas agreed to give its public lands to the United States. The United States agreed to pay all of Texas's debts.

Texas expected the United States to accept the treaty. However, the U.S. Senate did not approve the treaty. Some senators did not want Texas to join the United States as a slave state. Others did not want to anger Mexico. Still others did not want to stir up bad feelings among Americans because it was an election year.

7. What was the "Texas Question"?

____

____

____

(continued)

Name ______________________ Date ______________ Class ______________

Reading Essentials and Study Guide

Polk Wins Election *(page 288)*

The United States held a presidential election in 1844. One of the candidates, James K. Polk, wanted Texas to become a state. The other candidate, Henry Clay, was against Texas becoming a state immediately. Polk won the election. This showed that most of the voters wanted Texas to be annexed.

Many Americans believed that the United States should expand. They believed that it was the destiny of the United States to include all the land from the Atlantic Ocean to the Pacific Ocean. This idea was known as **manifest destiny.** The idea of manifest destiny strengthened the case for the annexation of Texas.

8. How did the idea of manifest destiny support the annexation of Texas?

____

____

____

____

____

Congress and Texas Approve Annexation *(pages 288–289)*

Some members of the U.S. Congress said that Congress should pass a **joint resolution** that Texas should be annexed. A joint resolution is a statement passed by both houses of Congress (the Senate and the House of Representatives). It has the force of law. Unlike a treaty, which requires approval by two-thirds of the Senate, a joint resolution needs only a simple majority in each house to become law.

On February 28, 1845, the joint resolution was passed. Texas could join the United States as soon as the people of Texas approved the annexation and wrote a constitution. Texas would have to sell some of its public lands. The money from the sale of these lands would be used to pay Texas's debts.

The Texas Congress met to consider these terms. It quickly approved them. Then Texans sent representatives to a convention to approve annexation and write a constitution. On October 13, 1845, Texas approved the annexation and constitution. The U.S. Congress approved the Texas Constitution. On December 29, 1845, President Polk signed the resolution, and Texas became a state.

(continued)

Name ______________________ Date ______________ Class ______________

9. According to the joint resolution, what did Texas have to do to become a state?

____

____

____

____

Mexico Offers Recognition *(page 289)*

Mexico would not recognize Texas independence until the United States and Texas finally agreed on annexation in 1845. Britain and France wanted Texas to remain an independent nation. For this reason, they tried to persuade Mexico to recognize Texas independence. Mexico agreed to do so if Texas would reject the idea of becoming part of the United States. Texas, however, was not interested in the Mexican offer. The Texas Congress rejected what the Mexicans wanted. It voted instead to accept annexation by the United States.

10. What was Mexico's offer to Texas?

____

____

____

____

"The Republic of Texas Is No More" *(page 289)*

On February 19, 1846, a ceremony was held in front of the Texas capitol. Anson Jones, the last president of the republic, turned the government of Texas over to J. Pinckney Henderson. Henderson became the first governor of the state of Texas. As Jones said farewell, he said, "The Republic of Texas is no more." The Lone Star flag was lowered and the Stars and Stripes was raised. Texas became the twenty-eighth state in the United States.

11. Why did President Jones say, "The Republic of Texas is no more"?

____

____

____

Name ______________________ Date ______________ Class ______________

Reading Essentials and Study Guide

Chapter 13-1

For use with textbook pages 296–300

Population Growth

Key Term

immigrant agent A person paid in land or money to relocate settlers to an area *(page 297)*

★DRAWING FROM EXPERIENCE

Did you or someone you know move to the United States from another country? How do people keep the culture of their old country? Have you ever witnessed prejudice against people from other countries?

In this section, you will learn about the growing number of immigrants who came to Texas from the United States, Europe, and Mexico. You will learn about their reasons for coming and problems some of them faced.

★ORGANIZING YOUR THOUGHTS

Use the diagram below to help you take notes as you read the summaries that follow. Identify the three most successful immigrant agents and where the relocated settlers came from.

Immigrant Agents	Where Settlers Came From
1.	4.
2.	5.
3.	6.

(continued)

★ **READ TO LEARN** *Write in complete sentences to answer the following questions. Use correct spelling, punctuation, and grammar.*

The Republic Attracts Immigrants *(pages 296–297)*

The Republic of Texas grew quickly. Thousands of people from the United States moved to Texas each year. In ten years, the population nearly tripled. In 1836, about 35,000 Anglos and Tejanos lived in Texas. By 1846, the population had grown to more than 125,000. The enslaved population increased even faster, from about 5,000 in 1836 to about 38,000 in 1846.

Settlers did not have to live on the land. Sometimes they sold it to speculators. The Texas Congress passed the Homestead Act. This law protected a family from losing its home, tools, and 50 acres of land for not paying its debts.

7. How many more Anglo and Mexican settlers lived in Texas in 1846 than in 1836?

____

____

____

Immigrant Agents Bring Settlers *(pages 297–298)*

Congress granted contracts to **immigrant agents.** They were people who were paid in land or money to bring settlers to an area. An agent received 10 sections of land for every 100 families. Often, the agent also charged the colonists for his services. W. S. Peters and Associates, Henri Castro, and the German Emigration Company were the most successful agents.

W. S. Peters got a contract to settle colonists in an area from the Red River to slightly south of present-day Dallas. Peters's company settled more than 2,000 families here between 1841 and 1848. Most settlers came from Illinois, Missouri, and Tennessee.

Henri Castro, a French Jew, received two grants in southwestern Texas. In 1844, he established the town of Castroville on the Medina River near San Antonio. He brought more than 2,000 colonists to Texas between 1844 and 1847. Most came from France, Germany, and Switzerland.

German nobles started the German Emigration Company in 1842. They wanted to bring Germans to Texas. They set up colonies north of San Antonio.

(continued)

Name ______________________ Date ______________ Class ______________

8. How were immigrant agents paid?

____

____

____

____

Slavery Continues in Texas *(pages 298–299)*

Not all who came to Texas came freely. The Mexican government had discouraged slavery. However, the government did little to stop its spread. Slavery increased during the days of the republic and early statehood. Plantations were started in East and central Texas. Planters brought slaves, sometimes in chains, to work their fields. Farmers also used slaves, though in fewer numbers. One out of every four families in Texas had at least one slave.

Even people who did not own slaves, such as merchants, were dependent on them. This was because the slaves worked to produce the cotton crop. Some slaves worked in towns as blacksmiths, carpenters, bricklayers, and in other crafts. Other slaves worked on ranches, tending cattle and breaking in horses.

By the mid-1840s, African Americans made up almost 30 percent of the Texas population. Brazoria, Harrison, Montgomery, Nacogdoches, Red River, San Augustine, and Washington Counties had the most enslaved people.

Although their lives were harsh, slaves were able to keep a rich culture. Family life, artistic expression, and religion were important to their culture. Slaves also found ways to resist their owners. Some slaves would not cooperate. They would break their tools or pretend to be sick. Some slaves ran away. Most runaway slaves were captured, although some found freedom.

9. Why were people who did not own slaves dependent on them?

____

____

____

____

____

(continued)

Name ______________________ Date ______________ Class ______________

Chapter 13-1

Free African Americans Build Lives *(pages 299–300)*

Hundreds of free African Americans lived in Texas before the Civil War. African Americans served in the Texas armies during the revolution. They were given land for their service. Most African Americans lived as farmers in rural areas. William Goyens served as an interpreter of Native American languages during the revolution. He started a freight line, bought and sold land, and ran an inn and two mills. In 1840, the Texas Congress passed a law allowing free African Americans to ask for the right to remain in Texas. Mary Madison was a nurse and a free African American. She was one of the few African Americans given official permission to stay in Texas. However, many free people stayed in Texas without official permission.

10. What was the main occupation of most free African Americans?

____

____

____

____

____

Mexican Texans Face Tensions *(page 300)*

Mexican Texans faced many difficulties in the new republic. Many new Anglo settlers thought that all Tejanos had opposed the war for independence. Anglo settlers held racial and religious prejudices against Tejanos. Some used force to take land away from Mexican settlers. However, Mexicans continued to settle in Texas. Between 1838 and 1841, more than 500 Mexicans received land in Texas.

11. Why did the new Anglo settlers dislike the Mexican Texans?

____

____

____

____

____

____

Name ______________________ Date ______________ Class ______________

Reading Essentials and Study Guide

Chapter 13-2

For use with textbook pages 302–305

Texans on Farms and Ranches

Key Terms

subsistence crop A crop used on the farm where it was raised *(page 303)*

★DRAWING FROM EXPERIENCE

Do you live near factories or farms? How old is your town? As the Texas population grew, so did the farms, ranches, and towns throughout Texas. In this section, you will learn about the importance of rural life as well as the development of new towns all over Texas.

★ORGANIZING YOUR THOUGHTS

Use the diagram below to help you take notes as you read the summaries that follow. Think of examples of the two types of crops Texas farmers raised.

	Subsistence Crops		Cash Crops
What are they?	1.		2.
Examples	3. 4. 5.		6. 7.

(continued)

Name ______________________ Date ______________ Class ______________

Chapter 13-2

★ **READ TO LEARN** *Write in complete sentences to answer the following questions. Use correct spelling, punctuation, and grammar.*

Texas Life Centers Around Farming *(pages 302–303)*

Most Texans farmed or raised livestock. Farmers grew both cash crops and subsistence crops. Farmers sold cash crops to get money to buy things they could not make for themselves. **Subsistence crops** were crops used on the farm where they were raised. Corn was the main subsistence crop. It was eaten in cornbread, tortillas, and hominy. Horses, mules, and oxen also ate corn. Sugarcane was an important cash crop along the Colorado and Brazos Rivers. The most important cash crop was cotton. Most of the cotton went to Europe and the northeastern United States. It was shipped by boat. In 1849, Texas produced 58,000 bales of cotton. In 1869, it sold 350,000 bales.

Both men and women worked hard on the farms. Women took care of the animals and gardens. Alongside the men, women helped clear the land, cut wood, build fences, and pick corn.

8. What was the main subsistence crop, and how was it used?

____

____

____

Ranches Flourish *(pages 303–304)*

Some Mexican ranchers in the Goliad–Victoria area lost their land after independence. However, many Tejanos continued to raise cattle. Doña María del Carmen Calvillo of Floresville was one of the most successful Tejano ranchers. She inherited a ranch from her father and increased the number of livestock on it.

It was easy for new settlers to get into the cattle business. Herds of wild cattle roamed much of South and East Texas. The climate was good for cattle. There was a lot of grass for the cattle to eat.

Women owned and managed plantations, too. Mildred Satterwhite Littlefield, Sarah Mims, and Rebecca Hagerty owned their own plantations.

9. Why was it easy to raise cattle in South and East Texas?

____

____

____

(continued)

Name ______________________ Date ______________ Class ______________

Reading Essentials and Study Guide

Chapter 13-2

Settlers Establish New Towns *(pages 304–305)*

More settlers from the United States came to Texas after independence. Some older settlements became less important as new towns grew. San Felipe and Harrisburg were burned during the revolution. They never regained the same importance.

During the revolution, the only towns in northeastern Texas were Clarksville, Jonesborough, and Pecan Point. Settlers from Arkansas, Missouri, and Tennessee set up new towns. Some towns, like Marshall and Jefferson, were built along transportation routes. Before railroads, Jefferson was the outlet for cotton grown in northeastern Texas. Steamboats traveled from Jefferson by way of Cypress Bayou, Caddo Lake, and the Red River into Louisiana.

Other towns were built to serve as seats of government for new counties. Some towns were founded because of a natural resource there. Grand Saline was founded for its salt mines.

In southeastern Texas, towns were often located along rivers. Houston's site was chosen because the Allen brothers thought that steamboats could not go up Buffalo Bayou any farther than Houston. They would have to stop there to load and unload cargo.

Anglos did not settle in the Brazos Valley until the early 1840s. This was because of conflicts with Native Americans.

The Hill Country was rugged. However, settlers moved up the valleys of the Blanco, Guadalupe, and Pedernales Rivers. Kerrville was established by a group of cypress shingle makers in 1856.

South Texas grew slowly. The area often had Native American and Mexican raids. However, new towns sprang up. At the mouth of the Nueces River, H. L. Kinney built a trading post that became Corpus Christi.

Laredo was the oldest settlement in Texas along the Rio Grande. Tomás Sánchez founded it in 1755. Upstream from Laredo, Eagle Pass, Texas, and Piedras Negras, Mexico, formed near crossings of the Rio Grande.

10. What purpose did the town of Jefferson serve for the people of North Texas?

____

____

____

____

Name ______________________ Date ______________ Class ______________

Chapter 13-3

For use with textbook pages 306–311

Commerce and Transportation

Key Terms

raft A driftwood tangle *(page 308)*
charter Establish by a state contract *(page 309)*
fiesta A festival or religious celebration *(page 310)*

★ DRAWING FROM EXPERIENCE

Have you ever taken a trip to visit relatives or friends? Have you ever traveled by train or boat? How do you get around in your daily life?

In this section, you will learn about advances in commerce, transportation, and education as the population of Texas grew.

★ ORGANIZING YOUR THOUGHTS

Use the diagram below to help you take notes as you read the summaries that follow. Name four methods of transportation Texans used to travel and to ship goods.

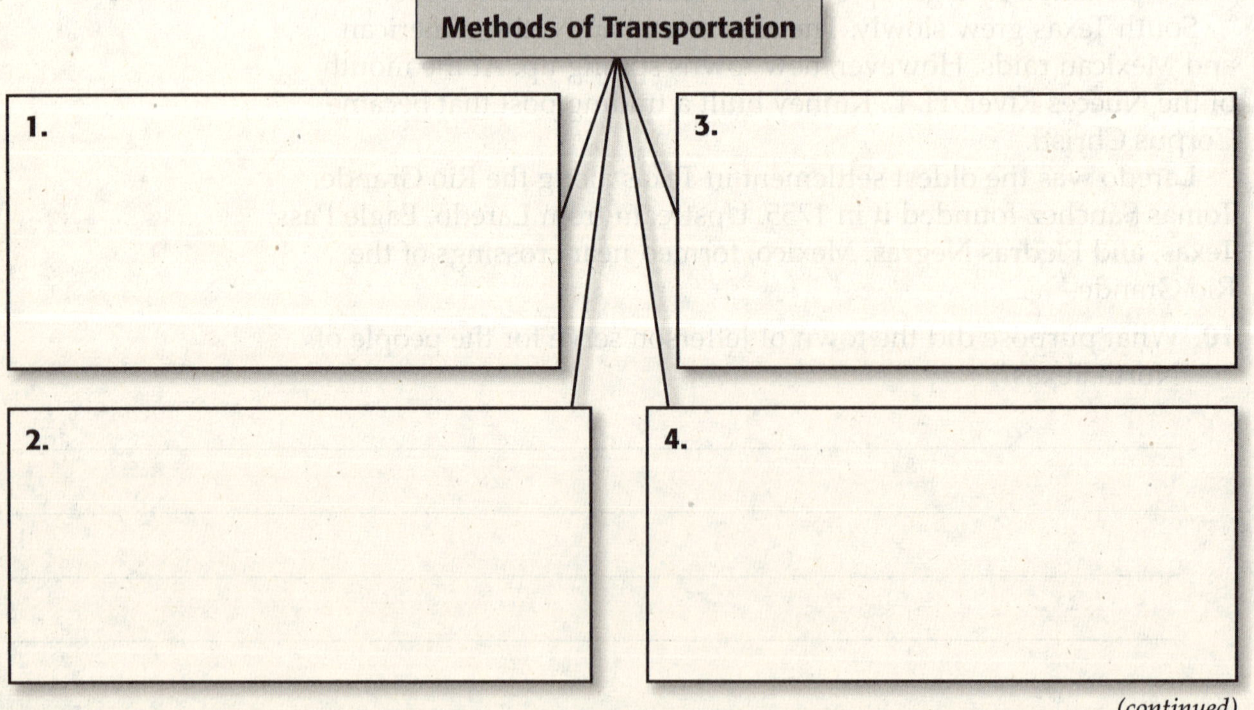

(continued)

Name ________________ Date ________________ Class ________________

Reading Essentials and Study Guide

★ **READ TO LEARN** *Write in complete sentences to answer the following questions. Use correct spelling, punctuation, and grammar.*

Trades and Professions *(pages 306–307)*

Some Texans worked in trades, including brick masons, blacksmiths, carpenters, and wheelwrights. Others worked as professionals in law, medicine, the ministry, and teaching.

As the population grew, there were more skilled people in Texas. Doctors, ministers, and lawyers were often also farmers. Ashbel Smith was a diplomat, soldier, educator, planter, scientist, and doctor. John S. "Rip" Ford was a Texas Ranger and frontiersman. He was also a doctor, a newspaper editor, lawyer, politician, and playwright. Frances Cox Henderson ran her husband's law office when he was out of town. Some doctors made extra money selling medicines, hair tonics, and perfumes. A New Braunfels doctor was also a baker and a druggist. A Houston doctor also worked as a barber. Midwives, women who helped deliver babies, performed valuable services.

5. What were common trades and professions of pioneer Texans?

____

____

____

Industry and Commerce Fuel Growth *(page 307)*

The few industries in Texas were located in towns or along roads or rivers. Most communities had a sawmill for cutting wood and a gristmill for grinding grain. Texans also built brickyards, tanneries, iron factories, cotton gins, soap factories, carriage factories, and textile mills.

Able and creative leaders helped the growth of business. Gail Borden, Jr., moved to Galveston in 1837. He was a customs collector and inventor. He also developed a way to make condensed milk. He eventually moved his factory to New York to sell his products to a larger market.

6. Where were industries in Texas located?

____

____

____

____

(continued)

Name ______________________ Date ______________ Class ______________

Better Transportation Is Needed *(page 307)*

Travel in Texas was difficult. Most people traveled by road. Some roads had been Native American trails. Other roads had been built when Texas was a part of Spain and Mexico. The roads were not paved. Rain made them muddy and slushy. Crossing streams was very dangerous. Most goods were carried by freight wagons pulled by oxen or mules. In South Texas, Mexican Americans played an important part in moving goods from one part of Texas to another.

7. Why was travel in Texas difficult?

____

____

____

____

Stagecoaches and Steamboats *(pages 307–308)*

The stagecoach was a popular but expensive way to travel. The Butterfield Overland Line crossed Texas from the Red River to El Paso. It provided transportation and carried mail to St. Louis and Memphis on the east and San Francisco on the west. In 1857, mail and passenger service began between San Antonio and San Diego, California. The trip took about 30 days and it cost $200.

Steamboats carried passengers and freight on Texas's rivers. Steamboat travel was comfortable and cheap but had problems. The rivers were crooked and difficult to steer. Driftwood tangles, or **rafts,** and sandbars blocked parts of the waterways. The Colorado River could not carry a lot of traffic because of a raft near its mouth.

Buffalo Bayou connected Houston with the port of Galveston. It was the most traveled waterway in Texas. The bayou was narrow and surrounded by overhanging tree limbs. However, it was a good passageway for boats that carried cotton from Texas's interior to Galveston.

8. How did stagecoaches improve life in Texas?

____

____

____

____

(continued)

Name ______________________ Date ______________ Class ______________

Reading Essentials and Study Guide

Chapter 13-3

Railroads Aid Business *(pages 308–309)*

The first railroads in Texas were built after it became a state. In 1852, work began on the Buffalo Bayou, Brazos, and Colorado Railroad, usually called the Harrisburg Railroad. Sidney Sherman, a war veteran and business leader in Harrisburg and Houston, organized the railroad.

The state gave land and loaned money from the school fund to railroad companies to extend the rail lines. By 1860 several railroads connected Houston with other communities. The railroads carried many kinds of products in and out of Houston. This helped make Houston one of Texas's most important and busiest cities.

9. How did railroads help business in Houston?

____

____

____

____

Telegraph and Newspapers *(pages 309–310)*

One of the first telegraph lines in Texas connected Houston with Galveston. The Texas and Red River Telegraph Company was **chartered,** or set up by a state contract, in 1854. The company opened the first telegraph office in Marshall and extended lines to other communities, including Houston and Galveston.

Newspapers were an important way to get information. The *Telegraph and Texas Register* and *Galveston Daily News* were influential papers. Simon Mussina, a Jewish attorney, published the *American Flag*. After Texas became a state, many newspapers opened. By 1860, there were more than 70.

10. How was the first telegraph line in Texas started?

____

____

____

____

____

(continued)

Name ______________________ Date ______________ Class ______________

Reading Essentials and Study Guide

Texans Gather for Social Life *(page 310)*

During the 1850s, most Texans lived on farms far from each other. They rarely visited with their neighbors. They often combined social activities with work. Log rollings, shooting matches, husking bees, quilting parties, house raisings, church dinners, and cotton choppings were activities that made work more fun. Hunting and fishing were sports that provided food for the family.

Dancing was popular. The fandango, a Spanish dance, was a favorite with Hispanic residents. The *baile* was a festive occasion for dancing. It was held in a hall or outside. It was popular with Mexican Americans. There were other occasions for dancing, such as the San Jacinto balls in Houston. At these, Texans wore fine clothes and danced waltzes and reels. In the slave quarters, people enjoyed "ring" dances.

The **fiesta,** a festival or religious celebration, was part of the Hispanic culture. It included dancing, games, exhibitions of art, and foods.

11. Why didn't Texans socialize with each other very often?

____

____

____

____

Formal Education Advances Slowly *(pages 310–311)*

The Texas Congress had set aside land for public schools, but no public school system was established. There were many private schools. Only Houston had a public school. In 1839 the Houston city council hired the first public school teacher in the republic.

In rural areas, mothers often taught their children reading, writing, and arithmetic. Some rural families hired teachers. They paid the teachers in food, not money. Almost every town had a private elementary school.

In 1854, Governor Elisha M. Pease and the legislature set aside $2 million as a school fund. Money was given out based on the number of school-age children in each county. Even with the money from this fund, Texas built few public schools.

(continued)

Reading Essentials and Study Guide

Some colleges were founded by churches. Methodists started Rutersville College in 1840. Baylor University was a Baptist school chartered in 1845. Presbyterians founded Austin College. Other colleges were founded in Chappell Hill, Clarksville, Galveston, and San Augustine.

12. What were two ways children in rural areas were educated?

____

____

____

____

____

Religious Diversity Flourishes *(page 311)*

Before the Texas Revolution, the Mexican government recognized only the Roman Catholic faith. The Constitution of 1836 gave people in Texas freedom of religion after independence. Protestant groups grew. The Baptist, Methodist, and Presbyterian faiths gained many members. Rosanna Osterman helped get Jewish services in Galveston. The Roman Catholic Church continued to be a strong force. The churches provided a place for religious services and social activities.

13. Why did Protestant groups grow after Texas became independent from Mexico?

____

____

____

____

____

Name ______________________ Date ______________ Class ______________

Reading Essentials and Study Guide **Chapter 14-1**

For use with textbook pages 322–325

A New State Government

Key Terms

legislature A body of elected members that makes laws *(page 323)*

amend Change, such as make changes in a constitution or laws *(page 323)*

convention A political meeting held to choose candidates to run for office *(page 324)*

★ DRAWING FROM EXPERIENCE

Does your school have a student council or class officers? Have you ever voted in a school, class, or club election? Do you know anyone who belongs to a political party?

In this section, you will learn about the new constitution that was written for Texas and how the early state government worked. You will also learn about the development of political parties in Texas.

★ ORGANIZING YOUR THOUGHTS

Use the diagram below to help you take notes as you read the summaries that follow. Identify solutions to problems facing the new state.

Problem	Solution
New state needs government.	1.
Free African Americans need to protect their freedom.	2.
Conflict between settlers and Native Americans continues.	3.

(continued)

Name ____________________ Date ____________________ Class ____________________

Reading Essentials and Study Guide

Chapter 14-1

★ **READ TO LEARN** *Write in complete sentences to answer the following questions. Use correct spelling, punctuation, and grammar.*

A New Constitution *(pages 322–323)*

The first task of the new state government was to write a new constitution for Texas. The document was based on other states' constitutions.

The Texas Constitution of 1845 provided for a governor. There was also a **legislature,** or body of elected members that makes laws. Its two houses were the House of Representatives and the Senate. The constitution also created a supreme court and district and county courts. At first, the governor chose all the judges. In 1850, the constitution was **amended,** or changed, to allow voters to choose the judges. Slavery was protected under the new constitution.

4. What change was made in the Texas constitution in 1850?

____

____

____

____

____

Texas Legislators at Work *(pages 323–324)*

Members of the legislature stayed busy trying to solve the problems of the young state. The governor was allowed to serve for two years. The first elected governor of Texas was J. Pickney Henderson. Sam Houston and Thomas J. Rusk were the first Texans elected to the U.S. Senate. David Kaufman and Timothy Pillsbury were Texas's first members of the U.S. House of Representatives.

5. What was the main focus of members of the legislature?

____

____

____

____

____

(continued)

Reading Essentials and Study Guide

Chapter 14-1

Political Parties *(pages 324–325)*

Texas politics centered around strong leaders. Political parties developed in Texas by the 1850s. Most of the leaders of early Texas were members of the Democratic Party. The Democratic Party was strong in the South and had supported the annexation of Texas. The party generally represented farmers and laborers.

The other major party in the United States was the Whig Party. The Whigs generally represented business and commercial interests. The Whig Party had little support in Texas. The party had been against annexation. It also was against slavery in territories of the United States.

In the mid-1850s some Texans joined the American, or Know-Nothing, Party. The American Party wanted to keep new immigrants from voting or holding office. It was called the Know-Nothing Party because when asked about the party or its activities its members would say, "I know nothing." The American Party was part of Texas politics for only a few years. It influenced the Democratic Party in the state. The Democratic Party took the practice of nominating candidates at political **conventions** from the American Party. A convention is a political meeting held to choose candidates for office.

None of the major political parties in this period represented African Americans. Although some African Americans were free, they were not allowed to vote or join political parties in Texas. Some filed petitions with the legislature to remain free. Others went to court.

6. Which political party had few members in Texas, and why?

____

____

____

____

____

(continued)

Name ______________________ Date ______________ Class ______________

Federal Aid for Reservations *(page 325)*

To prevent clashes between settlers and Native Americans, the federal government stationed troops in western Texas. By 1851, though, the line of settlements had moved beyond the line of new forts. As a result, the federal government built a new string of seven forts. These forts were located about 100 miles to the west.

As more and more settlers moved farther west, the fighting with Native Americans increased. The U.S. government made plans to relocate the Native Americans on reservations. The Wacos and Tonkawas were moved to a reservation near present-day Graham. The Comanches were sent to a reservation on the Brazos River.

The reservation system in Texas was never a success. The Native Americans were not given enough land in the reservations. Others could not adopt the limited way of life.

Many settlers did not like the system because they thought the Native Americans made their raids from the reservations. To end the conflict, the government decided to move Native Americans to the Indian Territory north of the Red River. Some Native American groups continued their raids.

7. What was the government's solution to the conflict between settlers and Native Americans in the west?

____

____

____

____

____

Name ______________________ Date ______________ Class ______________

Chapter 14-2

For use with textbook pages 326–330

War With Mexico

Key Terms

cede Give up something, such as territory *(page 327)*

abolitionist A person who works to end slavery *(page 328)*

★ DRAWING FROM EXPERIENCE

Have you ever had a disagreement with a friend or family member? Were you able to work out your problems without having a fight? Have you ever settled a disagreement by giving up part of what you wanted?

In this section, you will learn about the disagreements that led to war between the United States and Mexico. You will also learn about how the conflict was settled through a compromise, or agreement that each side would give up something.

★ ORGANIZING YOUR THOUGHTS

Use the diagram below to help you take notes as you read the summaries that follow. Think about causes of the war with Mexico.

Cause	Cause	Cause	Cause	Cause
1.	2.	3.	4.	5.

War With Mexico

(continued)

Name ______________________ Date ______________ Class ______________

Reading Essentials and Study Guide

★ **READ TO LEARN** *Write in complete sentences to answer the following questions. Use correct spelling, punctuation, and grammar.*

Causes of the War *(pages 326–328)*

The Mexican government never recognized the Republic of Texas. It also did not accept Texas as part of the United States. Even Mexicans who recognized Texas independence could not accept the Rio Grande as the boundary between Texas and Mexico. Mexico insisted that the Nueces River was the boundary.

Trade and business created by the United States spreading west also caused conflict between the United States and Mexico. American merchants in Texas had expanded trade into Mexico. American merchants were also trading with China and other countries in the Pacific and East Asia. To help this trade, the United States wanted the port of San Francisco in California, which was part of Mexico.

In addition, Mexico's army had destroyed much American property in the Texas Revolution. The United States demanded that the Mexican government pay the victims of this damage. The United States was going to pay all the debts and give $30 million to Mexico. In return, the United States wanted the Mexico-Texas boundary set at the Rio Grande. The United States also wanted Mexico to **cede,** or give up, California and part of New Mexico. The Mexican government, however, refused to talk, so in March 1846, President Polk ordered General Zachary Taylor to move U.S. troops across the Nueces River to the Rio Grande.

6. Why did the United States want California?

____

____

____

____

____

War Declared *(pages 328–329)*

In May 1846, Mexican and American soldiers clashed near the Rio Grande. Some Americans were killed, so on May 13, the U.S. Congress declared war. Some members of Congress questioned the reasons for going to war. **Abolitionists**—people who worked to end slavery—thought war was an excuse to increase slavery.

(continued)

Name ______________________ Date ______________ Class ______________

Chapter 14-2

More than 5,000 Texans signed up to fight in the war. Various Texas leaders commanded troops. These leaders included Mirabeau B. Lamar and J. Pinckney Henderson. Several companies of Texas Rangers served as scouts for the American army as it marched into Mexico. Unfortunately, some Texans were so anti-Mexican that they took out their anger on Mexican civilians.

7. Why did the abolitionists question the motives for going to war?

____

____

____

____

____

United States Victory *(pages 329–330)*

The United States Army was better equipped than the Mexican army. The United States also had better military leaders. By September 1846, General Zachary Taylor's army had moved south to Monterrey, Mexico. In 1847, Taylor and his men defeated Santa Anna at Buena Vista, and General Winfield Scott captured Mexico City. Other troops moved west to occupy California.

Women also played an active role in the war. Sarah Borginnis cooked, washed, loaded cartridges, and cared for the wounded in Taylor's army. Mexican women nursed the American army's sick and wounded.

On February 2, 1848, representatives from the United States and Mexico met at the Mexican town of Guadalupe Hidalgo to sign a treaty. The Treaty of Guadalupe Hidalgo set the Texas boundary at the Rio Grande. Mexico gave up its claims to Texas and all the land between western Texas and the Pacific Ocean. This territory included Arizona,

(continued)

Name ______________________ Date ______________ Class ______________

Reading Essentials and Study Guide

California, Colorado, New Mexico, and parts of Nevada, Utah, and Wyoming. The United States paid $15 million for the land and another $3.5 million for other expenses. The Mexican citizens who lived in the lost territory had one year to decide if they wished to become American citizens.

8. What helped the United States win the war?

____

____

____

____

____

The New Mexico Boundary Dispute *(page 330)*

The Treaty of Guadalupe Hidalgo ended the dispute between the United States and Mexico concerning Texas. The people in Santa Fe, New Mexico, however, did not want to become part of Texas. They wanted to be a separate territory or state.

People in the northern United States did not want slavery to expand from Texas to New Mexico. Members of Congress, led by Henry Clay, worked out a solution. Under the Pearce Act, part of the Compromise of 1850, Texas agreed to give up part of the disputed territory in exchange for $10 million from the United States.

9. What did the people of Santa Fe, New Mexico, want?

____

____

____

____

____

Name ______________________ Date ______________ Class ______________

Chapter 14-3

For use with textbook pages 332–337

Immigrants Come to Texas

Key Terms

census A count of the population *(page 332)*

teamster An animal driver *(page 333)*

descendant Offspring *(page 337)*

★DRAWING FROM EXPERIENCE

Are you from another country? Do you know someone from another country? What do you think it would be like to move to another country to live? What would you try to save from your culture as you tried to fit into a new culture?

In this section, you will learn how Texas's population grew after statehood. You will read about groups that migrated to Texas, including European immigrants. You will also learn more about the Native Americans who already lived in Texas.

★ORGANIZING YOUR THOUGHTS

Use the diagram below to help you take notes as you read the summaries that follow. Think about the European immigrants who came to the new state of Texas and what they contributed to its culture.

European Immigrants

3.

4.

5.

2.

6.

1.

8.

7.

9. Contributions

(continued)

Name ______________________ Date ______________ Class ______________

Reading Essentials and Study Guide

★ **READ TO LEARN** *Write in complete sentences to answer the following questions. Use correct spelling, punctuation, and grammar.*

Texas Population Booms *(pages 332–333)*

After statehood, Texas's population grew quickly. The **census,** or count of the population, taken by the U.S. government in 1850 counted 212,592 Texans. This was almost a 50 percent increase since 1847. In the next 10 years, the population grew to 604,215, nearly triple what it was in 1850.

Many people came to Texas because it was now part of the United States. Land was cheap and slavery was legal. Under the Homestead Act settlers could claim land just by living on it and improving it. They could purchase more for a small amount of money. Many settlers came from other Southern states.

New counties were needed because of the increase in population. The counties were needed to take care of collecting taxes and holding elections. Texas had 36 counties when it joined the Union in 1845. By 1860 there were 122 counties. One of the first things the state legislature did was create 26 new counties.

10. What brought new settlers to Texas?

____

____

____

____

____

Mexican Texans *(page 333)*

Many people from Mexico also moved to Texas. Most Mexican Americans lived in one of three areas: the area between the Nueces River and the Rio Grande, the San Antonio-Goliad area, and the area along the Rio Grande from Del Rio to El Paso. South Texas towns like Laredo, Corpus Christi, and Brownsville grew rapidly. Many Mexican Americans worked as farmers and ranchers. Some owned ranches, but others worked as cowhands and ranch laborers. Mexican Americans living in towns were business owners, **teamsters** (animal drivers), servants, laborers, and craftworkers.

(continued)

11. Where did most Mexican Americans live?

____

____

____

____

____

Politics and Bias *(pages 334–335)*

Some Mexican Americans became active political leaders. José Antonio Navarro held offices in the republic and later became a state senator. Other Mexican Americans faced hostility and prejudice. Juan Cortina was a protector of the rights of Mexicans and Tejanos and a hero to people living on the Texas-Mexico border. Government authorities saw him as an outlaw and believed he was responsible for much violence along the Rio Grande. The Texas Rangers and Mexican army watched over the border, but peace did not come easily.

Some of the negative feelings against Mexican Americans were left over from the battles of the Alamo and Goliad. Bitterness also developed because Tejanos held land Anglos wanted. In spite of prejudice and discrimination, Mexican Texans held onto their culture. As time went by, the Mexican culture mixed with Anglo American culture. Today many Mexican Americans are bicultural and bilingual.

12. Why were there negative feelings against Mexican Americans?

____

____

____

____

____

(continued)

Name ______________________ Date ______________ Class ______________

Reading Essentials and Study Guide

Chapter 14-3

German Texans *(page 335)*

Thousands of people came to Texas from Europe. German immigrants began to come during the days of the republic. German communities such as Fredericksburg and New Braunfels continued to grow. Some settled in the larger cities, including Galveston, Houston, and San Antonio. Poor potato harvests and other hardships drove many Germans from their homeland. Germans contributed to medicine and science in Texas.

13. Why did some of the Germans leave Europe?

____

____

____

____

____

Other European Arrivals *(pages 335–337)*

Immigrants from Ireland, England, and France also came to Texas. They settled in major cities and became artisans, merchants, and laborers. Many Poles, Czechs, and Norwegians came to Texas in the late 1840s and the 1850s. Jewish immigrants had been active in Texas since the days of colonization.

Immigrants did more than just increase the Texas population. They brought music, languages, arts, literature, and traditions. They also brought new skills, crafts, and ideas. These elements became part of a diverse Texas culture.

14. What European immigrant groups contributed to Texas culture?

____

____

____

____

____

(continued)

Name ______________________ Date ______________ Class ______________

Reading Essentials and Study Guide

Chapter 14-3

The Alabama-Coushattas *(page 337)*

A few Native Americans lived peaceably in Texas. Before the revolution, the Alabama-Coushattas settled in East Texas. In 1854, the Texas legislature bought land for a reservation for the Alabama tribe. By 1855, more than 300 lived there.

15. In what part of Texas did the Alabama-Coushattas live?

____

____

____

____

____

The Tiguas and the Kickapoos *(page 337)*

The Tiguas have lived near El Paso for more than 300 years. They are believed to be **descendants,** or offspring, of the Pueblos of New Mexico. For years, the Tiguas were considered Mexican Texans. The Kickapoos, also native to Texas, originally lived in Illinois but migrated to East Texas in the 1820s. Forced to leave Texas, some went to Oklahoma and Mexico. In 1989, the Kickapoos were recognized as a nation and officially named the Kickapoo Traditional Tribe of Texas. Besides land in Mexico, they have 125 acres near Eagle Pass, Texas.

16. Which Native Americans are considered descendants of the Pueblos?

____

____

____

____

____

Name ____________ Date ____________ Class ____________

Reading Essentials and Study Guide **Chapter 15-1**

For use with textbook pages 342–346

Texas Secession

Key Terms

states' rights The belief that the federal government should not block the states' use of their constitutional powers *(page 343)*

secede Withdraw *(page 343)*

sovereignty Supreme power of a state or nation *(page 343)*

ordinance A local law *(page 345)*

perpetual Continuing forever *(page 346)*

★DRAWING FROM EXPERIENCE

What do you know about the Civil War? Who fought whom? What were the two sides fighting about? In this section, you will learn about the issues that divided the nation and finally led to war. You will learn about Texas's views on these issues. You will discover what side Texas took in the conflict known as the Civil War.

★ORGANIZING YOUR THOUGHTS

Use the diagram below to help you take notes as you read the summaries that follow. Show the sequence of events before and after the Texas secession.

Texans urge Governor Houston to call a secession convention.

1. ____________

2. ____________

3. ____________

4. ____________

Convention adopts Ordinance of Secession, and Texans vote to secede.

5. ____________

6. ____________

7. ____________

8. ____________

Edward Clark becomes governor of Texas.

(continued)

Name ______________________ Date ______________ Class ______________

Reading Essentials and Study Guide

Chapter 15-1

★ **READ TO LEARN** *Write in complete sentences to answer the following questions. Use correct spelling, punctuation, and grammar.*

Many Issues Divide the Country *(pages 342–343)*

In 1861, Texas and 10 other Southern states withdrew from the United States. They formed the Confederate States of America. Their decision came after many years of differences between the North and the South. The two regions of the country disagreed on many issues. These included tariffs, distribution of public lands, and states' rights. **States' rights** is the belief that the federal government should not block the states' use of their constitutional powers. More than anything else, the North and the South disagreed about slavery.

9. What issues divided the North and the South?

____

____

____

____

The Republican Party Opposes Slavery *(page 343)*

At one time, slavery existed in many Northern states. Over the years, steps had been taken to stop it. The abolitionists wanted slavery to end everywhere. Even people who were not completely against slavery did not want it to spread to new territories or states.

Many Northerners who were against slavery joined the Republican Party. They also blamed the Southern Democrats for the poor state of the economy in the late 1850s. The Republicans thought high tariffs, a home-stead act, and other changes could bring back prosperity. Southerners were against these measures. They believed the rise of the Republicans would mean the end of slavery and the Southern way of life.

10. Why were Southerners concerned about the rise of the Republican Party?

____

____

____

____

(continued)

Name ______________________ Date ______________ Class ______________

Reading Essentials and Study Guide

Chapter 15-1

Southern States Vow to Secede *(pages 343–344)*

Some Southern leaders said that the Southern states would **secede,** or withdraw, from the Union if the Republicans won the presidential election of 1860. They believed that **sovereignty** (supreme power) belonged to the states. After Republican candidate Abraham Lincoln won the election, six Southern states voted to secede. Many Texans wanted Governor Houston to hold a convention to decide whether Texas also should secede.

11. What happened after Abraham Lincoln was elected?

____

____

____

____

____

The Convention Votes on Secession *(pages 344–345)*

Governor Houston was against Texas seceding from the Union. He would not call for a convention. Several Texans called a convention on their own, urging citizens to elect delegates. Many Texans who were against secession thought the convention was illegal and did not take part. As a result, most of the delegates chosen in the election favored secession.

Houston asked the legislature to declare the convention illegal. Instead, the legislature supported the convention. It said it could act for the people.

The Texas Secession Convention met in early 1861. It adopted the Ordinance of Secession. This **ordinance,** or local law, said that Texas was declaring its freedom from the United States. Then the people of Texas voted for secession. Texas became the seventh state to secede.

12. What was the Ordinance of Secession?

____

____

____

____

(continued)

Name ______________________ Date ______________ Class ______________

Reading Essentials and Study Guide

Chapter 15-1

The Confederacy Is Formed *(page 345)*

The states that withdrew from the Union met to form a new nation, the Confederate States of America. The Confederacy wrote a constitution. It was similar to the United States Constitution but had some important differences. The Confederate constitution gave states more power than the federal government and protected slavery. Jefferson Davis was elected president of the Confederacy. The Texas Secession Convention met again and approved the Confederate constitution. It also prepared the Texas Constitution of 1861.

13. How did the Confederate constitution differ from the United States Constitution?

____

____

____

____

Houston Is Removed and War Begins *(pages 345–346)*

The Texas Secession Convention said all Texas officials had to state that they would be loyal to the Confederacy. Governor Houston refused to do this, so Lieutenant governor Edward Clark became the new governor.

The United States government believed that the Southern states had broken the law when they seceded. Lincoln stated that the Union was **perpetual,** continuing forever. Lincoln said he would do anything necessary to keep the Southern states in the Union.

Early in 1861 the Confederate states began taking control of military buildings within their borders. When U.S. troops refused to leave Fort Sumter in Charleston, South Carolina, Confederate soldiers began shooting. The attack on Fort Sumter marked the beginning of the Civil War.

14. How did the Civil War start?

____

____

____

____

Name ______________________ Date ______________ Class ______________

Reading Essentials and Study Guide

Chapter 15-2

For use with textbook pages 347–352

Texans Go to War

Key Terms

conscription The forced enrollment of people into military service *(page 348)*

Unionist A person who supported the Union cause *(page 349)*

vigilante A citizen who acts as the unauthorized police power for an area *(page 349)*

preventive strike An offensive move designed to stop a possible future attack by the enemy *(page 350)*

blockade To cut off, using troops or ships to stop goods and supplies from entering or leaving *(page 350)*

★DRAWING FROM EXPERIENCE

Do you know where the food you eat comes from? Where do you get various items you use every day? What would you do if you could not get goods or supplies you needed? In this section, you will find out how important Texas and its trade routes were for the Confederate economy. You will learn about Union attempts to invade Texas and prevent supplies and goods from entering or leaving. You will also learn how Texans and the Confederate army defended their supply lines.

★ORGANIZING YOUR THOUGHTS

Use the diagram below to help you take notes as you read the summaries that follow. Recall the actions of Confederate troops at each location in or near Texas and the outcome of their efforts.

Location	Confederate Actions	Outcome
Galveston	1.	2.
Sabine Pass	3.	4.
Laredo	5.	6.
Red River	7.	8.

(continued)

Name ______________ Date ______________ Class ______________

Reading Essentials and Study Guide

Chapter 15-2

★ **READ TO LEARN** *Write in complete sentences to answer the following questions. Use correct spelling, punctuation, and grammar.*

Many Texans Become Soldiers *(pages 347–348)*

As soon as the Civil War started, thousands of Texans joined the Confederate army. By the end of the first year of the war, more soldiers were needed, so the Confederate Congress passed the Conscription Act. **Conscription** is the forced enrollment of people into military service. This act required all men between 18 and 35 to serve in the Confederate army. It also excused some and allowed the hiring of substitutes.

9. Why did the Confederate Congress pass the Conscription Act?

____

____

____

____

Most Texans Support the South *(page 348)*

Before the war began, about one-fourth of Texans were against secession. Once the Civil War began, however, most Texans supported the Confederacy.

More than 60,000 Texans served in the Confederate forces. Almost one-third of the Texas soldiers were in armies east of the Mississippi River. Others were along the Texas borders and in nearby states such as Louisiana.

Many Civil War officers came from Texas. Albert Sidney Johnson was the second highest ranking general in the Confederate army. He was killed at the Battle of Shiloh in 1862.

10. How did Texans' views about secession change once the Civil War began?

____

____

____

____

____

(continued)

Name ______________________ Date ______________ Class ______________

Reading Essentials and Study Guide

Chapter 15-2

Some Texans Aid the Union *(pages 349–350)*

About 2,000 Texans were **Unionists.** They supported the Union cause and joined the Union army. Approximately 50 of the Texas Unionists were African Americans. Some Mexican Americans also fought on the Union side. Some Unionists did not want to fight for either side. Many hid from conscription officers. Some were captured and arrested. Others were forced to join the Confederate army. Still others were killed. **Vigilantes**—people who act as the unofficial police power for an area—hanged people they thought were Unionists.

11. What happened to the Unionists in Texas?

____

____

____

____

____

Texans on the Attack *(page 350)*

The first job of the Confederate army was to take over the forts and other military locations that belonged to the Union. The Confederate army needed the supplies and equipment kept at these places.

Near the end of 1861, Texan soldiers attacked Union soldiers in New Mexico. This was a **preventive strike.** It was designed to prevent any future attack by the Union army. The Texans hoped to capture Santa Fe and New Mexico.

12. Why did the Confederate army want to take over Union forts?

____

____

____

____

____

(continued)

Name ______________________ Date ______________ Class ______________

Reading Essentials and Study Guide **Chapter 15-2**

Fighting for Galveston *(pages 350–351)*

Texas was an important link in the Confederate chain of supplies. The Union navy used its ships to **blockade,** or cut off, Texas ports so that goods and supplies could not enter or leave Texas by water.

In 1862, Union soldiers captured Galveston. They were able to take the seaport because it was poorly defended. Many of the large guns from its forts had been removed for use in other places.

Confederate leaders did not want Galveston to remain under Union control. In 1863 the Confederate army sent two ships and many soldiers to Galveston and regained the port.

By 1864 Galveston was one of the few ports still open to the Confederacy. Ships called blockade runners carried much-needed supplies. These blockade runners played an important part in the war effort.

13. Why was it easy for the Union navy to capture Galveston?

____

____

____

Texans Defend Sabine Pass *(page 351)*

In 1863, Union soldiers tried to invade Texas by sailing up the Sabine River. Union ships carrying 4,000 soldiers and 4 gunboats sailed from New Orleans. The Union commander planned to land his troops near the Sabine Pass. He would then march overland to capture Beaumont and Houston.

Any vessel sailing up the Sabine Pass had to travel past Fort Griffin. Dick Dowling and 47 soldiers called the Davis Guard were at the fort. When the Union boats got near Fort Griffin at Sabine Pass, the Confederate soldiers attacked. The Guards took 350 prisoners and captured 2 boats.

The Battle of Sabine Pass was a major victory for the Confederacy. President Davis praised the courage of the Davis Guards. They were all awarded medals.

14. How did the Confederates win the Battle at Sabine Pass?

____

____

____

(continued)

Reading Essentials and Study Guide

Chapter 15-2

Forces Battle Near Brownsville *(page 351)*

Union forces continued the blockade of Texas cotton by patrolling the Gulf of Mexico. Traders used foreign ships out of Matamoros. Wagon trains also carried supplies across South Texas from Brownsville. In 1863, Union forces captured Brownsville in order to cut off the overland supply line. They then moved up the Rio Grande until it was stopped near Laredo. Eight months later, Confederate soldiers drove the Union troops back and were able to recapture Brownsville.

15. Why did the Union want to capture Brownsville?

____

____

____

____

____

Red River and Beyond *(page 352)*

In the spring of 1864, a large army of Union soldiers marched up the Red River in Louisiana and overland to invade northeastern Texas. Confederate leaders quickly called out troops to block the Union army. Even though the Confederate army had fewer soldiers, they beat the Union army.

Many Texas military units fought far from the boundaries of their state. Hood's Texas Brigade and Terry's Texas Rangers were the best known. They were named for their courage and bravery. General Robert E. Lee called Hood's men his "finest soldiers." Terry's Texas Rangers, called the Eighth Texas Cavalry Regiment, fought in more battles than any other regiment.

16. Why was it surprising that the Confederate army defeated the Union army?

____

____

____

____

____

Name ______________________ Date ______________ Class ______________

Chapter 15-3

For use with textbook pages 354–358

Home Front Hardships

Key Terms

homespun A coarse, loosely woven, homemade fabric *(page 355)*

quinine An imported drug for fighting malaria and other fevers *(page 356)*

★ DRAWING FROM EXPERIENCE

Have you ever had to live without a family member for a time? Have you ever had to make sacrifices, or give up certain things, to get through a difficult time? What was the experience like? In this section, you will learn about the war's effect on the lives of Texans at home. You will discover how Texans handled the hardships they faced.

★ ORGANIZING YOUR THOUGHTS

Use the diagram below to help you take notes as you read the summaries that follow. Think about how life changed for Texans at home during the war.

Changes on the Home Front		
1.	3.	5.
2.	4.	6.

(continued)

Name ________________ Date ________________ Class ________________

Chapter 15-3

★ **READ TO LEARN** *Write in complete sentences to answer the following questions. Use correct spelling, punctuation, and grammar.*

Texas Confederates Take Charge *(pages 354–355)*

Texas's government was now completely controlled by those who supported the Confederacy. In 1861, Frances R. Lubbock became governor. Two years later, Pendleton Murrah became governor. Murrah served as governor until the last days of the war. Both Texas leaders worked hard for the Confederate war effort.

7. Who served as governor of Texas during the Civil War?

____

____

____

____

____

War Changes Women's Roles *(page 355)*

Because few battles were fought in Texas, it suffered less damage than other Confederate states. Life on the large plantations was much the same as before the war. Slaves continued to do most of the work, just as they always had. On small farms, however, there were no men to do the work. Most of the men were away fighting in the war. Women, children, and slaves did most of the work.

Women also served as nurses during the Civil War. They took care of the sick and wounded.

8. How did life on small farms change during the Civil War?

____

____

____

____

____

(continued)

Name ______________________ Date ______________ Class ______________

Chapter 15-3

War Changes the Economy *(page 355)*

The war brought economic changes. The farmers were asked to grow more corn and wheat for the war effort. Less cotton was grown during the Civil War. Small factories opened in Texas to make cannons and ammunition. Other factories made items such as blankets, shoes, and tents. These supplies were needed for the soldiers. Women made uniforms and other clothing for the soldiers. Many of them worked very long hours making clothing. Women also became teachers, shopkeepers, and drivers. Before the war, men did these jobs.

9. Why did the Confederate government want farmers to grow more corn and wheat and less cotton during the Civil War?

____

____

____

Shortages Make Life Difficult *(pages 355–356)*

During the war Texans made many sacrifices. Because of the Union blockade of Confederate ports, many goods could not reach the South. Clothes, made in the North, were no longer in Southern stores. Many Texans wore **homespun,** a coarse, loosely woven, homemade fabric.

Other items, such as coffee, tea, salt, baking soda, and pepper, were very hard to get. Several newspapers had to stop publishing because they had no paper. Most medicine went to the soldiers. There was no **quinine.** Quinine was an imported drug used to fight malaria and other fevers. The shortages of various goods became worse as people from neighboring states came to Texas to escape the Union armies.

10. Why did shortages in Texas become worse?

____

____

____

The Civil War Ends *(page 357)*

The Confederacy fought the Union for four years. The Union had many advantages. It had more soldiers and more money to pay for the war. It also had more factories to make war materials. In April 1865, the Army of Northern Virginia surrendered. This was the largest army

(continued)

of the Confederacy. Other Confederate armies quickly surrendered. The last battle of the Civil War was fought in May 1865 at Palmito Ranch near Brownsville, Texas. Now the United States had to begin rebuilding. More than 600,000 people had died in the Civil War.

The North's victory meant that the Union had been preserved and that slavery had ended. During the war, President Lincoln had issued the Emancipation Proclamation. It freed all slaves in the Confederate states. After the war was over, officials made sure the proclamation was enforced. Lincoln did not live to see all the slaves freed. The Thirteenth Amendment, which did away with slavery, was not approved until late 1865. Lincoln was shot and killed by John Wilkes Booth just a few days after Confederate armies surrendered. Booth believed he was helping the Confederacy by killing Lincoln.

The government of Texas fell apart as Southern armies surrendered. Many government officials fled to Mexico. They wanted to leave Texas before Union soldiers arrived. For a while, outlaws roamed Texas. Then President Andrew Johnson appointed a temporary governor. Texans had to begin working to rejoin the Union.

11. What was the outcome of the North's victory in the war?

____

____

____

____

A Texas Story Continued *(page 358)*

Lucy Pier Stevens was a young woman who was trapped in Texas when the Civil War broke out. Lucy decided she had to go home. She had a long, hard trip back to New York but finally made it. Her journey was an example of the difficulties many people suffered during the war.

12. Why was Lucy Stevens trapped in Texas?

____

____

____

____

Name ______________________ Date ______________ Class ______________

Chapter 16-1

For use with textbook pages 366–371

Presidential Reconstruction

Key Terms

Reconstruction The period of rebuilding in which the Southern states were gradually brought back into the Union *(page 366)*

nullify Cancel *(page 368)*

freedman A freed slave *(page 369)*

★ DRAWING FROM EXPERIENCE

Have you ever tried to be more independent from your family? Have you ever made an effort to bring together family members or friends who have grown apart?

In this section, you will read about the period of rebuilding following the Civil War and President Johnson's plan to bring the Southern states back into the Union.

★ ORGANIZING YOUR THOUGHTS

Use the diagram below to help you take notes as you read the summaries that follow. List President Johnson's requirements for states to be readmitted to the Union and the steps Texas took to meet them.

Johnson's Requirements	Steps Taken by Texas
1.	**5.**
2.	**6.**
3.	**7.**
4.	**8.**

(continued)

Name ______________________ Date ______________ Class ______________

Reading Essentials and Study Guide

Chapter 16-1

★ **READ TO LEARN** *Write in complete sentences to answer the following questions. Use correct spelling, punctuation, and grammar.*

Reconstruction *(pages 366–367)*

After the Civil War ended in 1865, the Southern states were slowly brought back into the Union. This period of rebuilding is called **Reconstruction.**

Reconstruction was a difficult time. Money was scarce. Many African Americans, though free, had no food or shelter. The differences between Northerners and Southerners continued.

9. Why was Reconstruction a difficult period for African Americans?

____

____

____

____

____

Juneteenth *(pages 367–368)*

Union troops were placed in Southern states after the Civil War. On June 19, 1865, General Gordon Granger and Union troops landed at Galveston. Granger issued a statement that all enslaved Texans were free under the Emancipation Proclamation.

Many African Americans did not know about the Emancipation Proclamation, which had freed slaves in Confederate states in 1863. June 19, 1865, was the day enslaved Texans celebrated their freedom. The date became a holiday known as Juneteenth.

10. Why was June 19, 1865, an important date for African Americans in Texas?

____

____

____

____

____

(continued)

Two Presidential Plans *(page 368)*

President Lincoln had planned to restore the Union quickly. He had wanted a moderate policy of Reconstruction. Some Republican leaders thought that the Southern states should be treated as conquered territories. Lincoln believed that the Southern states still had all the rights of states. After Lincoln was assassinated, Andrew Johnson, the new president, took on the job of rebuilding the nation.

President Johnson set forth a plan for Reconstruction that was like Lincoln's. He set up a provisional, or temporary, government in each Southern state. He appointed officers and federal troops to protect them. The provisional government would govern until the states were readmitted to the Union.

Johnson had several requirements for a state to be brought back into the Union. The state had to end slavery. It must also **nullify,** or cancel, its ordinance of secession. To have the right to vote, each citizen had to take an oath of loyalty to the United States. Leaders of the Confederacy and people who had $20,000 or more in cash and property would have to get a pardon from the president. Once these requirements were met, the state could write a new state constitution and elect its own representatives.

11. What did President Johnson require of Southern citizens before they could vote?

____

____

____

____

____

Governor Hamilton Works to Restore Statehood *(page 368)*

President Johnson appointed Andrew J. Hamilton provisional governor of Texas. Hamilton had represented Texas in Congress and was against secession. After the war, Hamilton wanted to help Texas return to the Union.

Most Texans thought Hamilton was honest and fair. Some groups promised to work to restore the state. Others, however, were openly hostile to Hamilton.

(continued)

12. Why did Hamilton want to help Texas return to the Union?

____

____

____

____

____

The Freedmen's Bureau Assists Freed Texans *(page 369)*

The Freedmen's Bureau was a federal agency that helped African Americans throughout the South. Former slaves were referred to as **freedmen.** Texas had 18 agents working for the Freedmen's Bureau.

The Freedmen's Bureau was active for almost five years. It helped freed Texans find jobs. It also gave food and clothing to the sick, aged, and poor. The agency set up the first public schools in Texas for African Americans. By 1870, Texas had more than 100 schools for African American children. The Bureau also fought for the rights of freed Texans in court cases.

13. What were three ways the Freedmen's Bureau assisted freed Texans?

____

____

____

____

____

Government Restored in 1866 *(page 370)*

By November 1865, most white males in Texas had taken the oath of allegiance to the Union. Next, Texans elected delegates to a convention to write a new state constitution. Many of the delegates to the convention had supported the Confederacy.

The new state constitution stated that secession was illegal. It also ended slavery. It canceled all of the state's war debts. It provided education for African American children, and it gave some legal rights to African Americans. However, it did not give them full legal rights. For example, African Americans were not given the right to vote. This disappointed Governor Hamilton.

(continued)

In June 1866, Texas voters approved the new state constitution. They also elected officers for the new government.

14. Why was Governor Hamilton disappointed with the new state constitution?

____

____

____

____

____

People on the Move *(page 371)*

During Reconstruction many travelers searched for loved ones separated before emancipation. Although there were many joyful reunions, many searchers never found their loved ones.

Other travelers came to Texas in search of a better life. Because Texas had not experienced as much destruction as more eastern Confederate states, Texas still had public lands available for farming. The Bureau of Immigration in 1873 estimated that some 125,000 persons had come to Texas since 1865. Of these people, 100,000 of them were from former Confederate states.

European immigrants also came to Texas. Germans made up the largest group. It is estimated that a million Europeans landed in Texas by the end of Reconstruction.

Some people emigrated, or moved away, from Texas. Some radical Confederates refused to swear allegiance to the United States. They led others to Brazil, where slavery still existed.

15. Why were there so many travelers on the road after Reconstruction?

____

____

____

____

____

Name ______________________ Date ______________ Class ______________

Chapter 16-2

For use with textbook pages 373–379

Congress Takes Control

Key Terms

ratify Approve *(page 374)*
amendment A change *(page 374)*
black codes Laws limiting the rights of African Americans *(page 374)*
Radical Republican A Republican who believed that Congress should direct Reconstruction *(page 374)*
veto An action refusing to approve a law *(page 374)*
impeach Bring charges of misconduct in office *(page 375)*
scalawag A white Southerner who supported Reconstruction *(page 376)*
carpetbagger A Northerner who came to the South during Reconstruction *(page 376)*
compulsory Required *(page 378)*

★ DRAWING FROM EXPERIENCE

Have you ever felt that someone's rights were violated? What did you do? Have you ever experienced racism?

In this section, you will learn about the Radical Republicans in Congress and their stricter plan for Reconstruction.

★ ORGANIZING YOUR THOUGHTS

Use the diagram below to help you take notes as you read the summaries that follow. Identify actions Texas and other Southern states first took *against* Reconstruction and actions they later took *for* Reconstruction when Radical Republicans came to power.

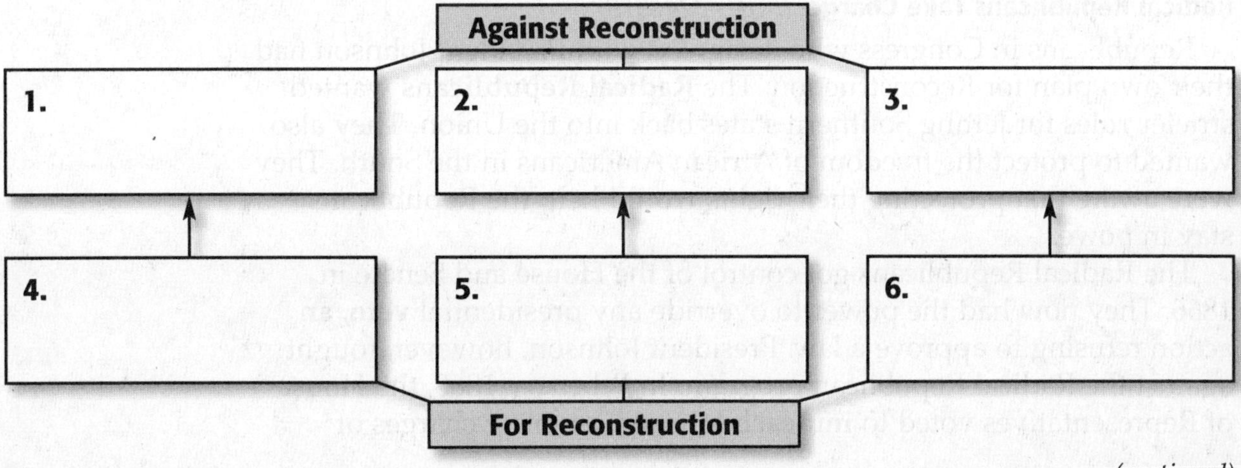

(continued)

Name ______________________ Date ______________ Class ______________

Chapter 16-2

★ **READ TO LEARN** *Write in complete sentences to answer the following questions. Use correct spelling, punctuation, and grammar.*

Texas Elects Ex-Confederates to Office *(pages 373–374)*

Southerners, including Texans, elected many Confederate officials and soldiers to state government. Every Texan elected to the federal House of Representatives had been a secessionist or a Confederate officer. Many Northerners were upset that people who had encouraged secession were now part of the U.S. Congress.

Southern lawmakers took other troubling actions. The Texas legislature would not **ratify,** or approve, changes on two **amendments** to the United States Constitution. The Texas legislature rejected the Thirteenth Amendment, which abolished slavery. It also rejected the Fourteenth Amendment, which gave citizenship to people who had been slaves.

Southern state governments also restricted the rights of African Americans with **black codes.** These were laws that limited the rights of African Americans. African Americans were not allowed to vote. They could not testify against whites in court. They could hold only certain jobs, generally in agriculture.

7. What were the Thirteenth and Fourteenth Amendments?

____

____

____

____

____

Radical Republicans Take Charge *(pages 374–375)*

Republicans in Congress who disagreed with President Johnson had their own plan for Reconstruction. The **Radical Republicans** wanted stricter rules for letting Southern states back into the Union. They also wanted to protect the freedom of African Americans in the South. They were aware that protecting their rights would help the Republicans stay in power.

The Radical Republicans got control of the House and Senate in 1866. They now had the power to override any presidential **veto,** an action refusing to approve a law. President Johnson, however, fought against the Radical Republican program. In February 1868, the House of Representatives voted to **impeach** Johnson, or bring charges of

(continued)

misconduct in office. The Senate failed by one vote to convict him. Johnson finished his term. However, he had lost most of his power.

8. Why did the Radical Republicans want African Americans to vote?

____

____

____

____

____

New Requirements for Statehood *(page 375)*

Congress divided the South into five districts. The army ruled the districts until the states met certain requirements. The states had to write new constitutions that gave African American men the right to vote and hold office. The states also had to ratify the Fourteenth Amendment. Texas also had to ratify the Fifteenth Amendment. States also had to end the black codes.

Under Congress's plan, many voters had to take the *Ironclad Oath*. In the oath, they swore that they had not freely served in the Confederate army or given help to the Confederacy. This oath kept many Southerners from voting.

9. Why did the *Ironclad Oath* keep many Southerners from voting?

____

____

____

____

____

Southerners Oppose Reconstruction *(page 376)*

African Americans and Unionists liked Congress's Reconstruction plan. People who had been Confederates and secessionists thought it was too harsh.

Governor Throckmorton was removed from office because he didn't put the Reconstruction laws into effect. He was replaced by Elisha M. Pease. Pease was well respected by the majority of Texans.

(continued)

Name ______________________ Date ______________ Class ______________

Reading Essentials and Study Guide

Chapter 16-2

Southern whites who supported Reconstruction were called **scalawags.** Northerners who came to the South were called **carpetbaggers.** Some were there to help, but others were there for political or financial gain.

Texans who supported Reconstruction worked to get African Americans the right to vote. However, groups like the Ku Klux Klan used violence and threats to stop African Americans from voting.

10. What two groups liked Congress's Reconstruction plan?

____

____

____

____

____

A New Constitution and Elections *(pages 376–377)*

In February 1868, Texans elected delegates to a new convention. The delegates wrote a new constitution for the state. The Constitution of 1869 stated that no one could be stopped from voting because of race or color. It gave more support for public schools than ever before. It also gave African Americans many rights and protected public lands. It gave more power to the governor and legislature. This constitution was approved in November 1869. The voters also elected a governor and state officials at the same time. Eleven African Americans were elected to the legislature.

Radical Republican candidate Edmund J. Davis narrowly defeated Hamilton in the 1869 election. The new state legislature quickly ratified the Fourteenth and Fifteenth Amendments.

In March 1870, President Ulysses S. Grant signed a proclamation that Reconstruction was ended. Many Texans felt that it wouldn't end until governor Davis and the Radical Republicans were gone.

11. How did the Constitution of 1869 help African Americans?

____

____

____

____

(continued)

Name ______________________ Date ______________ Class ______________

A Republican Governor *(pages 377–378)*

Many thought Davis's term as governor was the darkest period of Reconstruction. Davis was often involved in activities that caused arguments. For example, he claimed he used police to keep law and order. However, those who opposed him said that he used the police to threaten those who disagreed with him.

The government needed to raise more money because of increased spending on police and education. In 1865, the state tax had been 15 cents on every $100 worth of property. By 1872, the tax had grown to $2 on each $100 worth of property. The state debt continued to grow even with the increase in taxes.

Even though Davis was so disliked, he started some important projects. He improved roads, built forts, set up a new Homestead Act, and set up free schools. Attendance in school was **compulsory,** or required. The taxes maintained the schools.

12. Why did some people dislike Davis's use of the police force?

____

____

____

____

____

A Democratic Challenge *(pages 378–379)*

Davis became more and more unpopular. In 1872, anti-Davis Democrats won the majority in the state legislature. The new legislature limited the governor's power and did away with the state police force.

In 1873, Davis ran against Democrat Richard Coke. Coke had been a Confederate officer. Republicans urged African Americans to vote for Davis. Democrats used threats and violence to keep African Americans from voting. Coke received twice as many votes as Davis. Democrats won all other state offices.

(continued)

13. Which political party took control in the 1872 election?

____

____

____

____

____

Reconstruction Ends *(page 379)*

The election caused a crisis in Texas. The Democrats claimed that Coke should take office in January. Republicans claimed that Davis should remain until April. The Texas Supreme Court decided in favor of the Republicans.

Democrats organized a new government anyway. Therefore, on January 15, 1874, Coke took the office of governor. The militia was there in case any violence broke out. Governor Davis asked President Grant to support keeping him in office. The president would not support Davis, and he finally left office on January 17, 1874. Reconstruction in Texas had come to an end.

14. When did Davis finally agree to leave office?

____

____

____

____

____

Name ____________________ Date ____________________ Class ____________________

Chapter 17-1

For use with textbook pages 390–393

West Texas After the Civil War

Key Terms

campaign A military operation *(page 391)*

agent A person acting or doing business for another by that person's authority; a representative *(page 391)*

★ DRAWING FROM EXPERIENCE

Have you ever watched a "western" (movie about the Old West) on television? What ideas did you get about life on the frontier? Did the settlers and Native Americans get along? How true to life do you think the movie was?

In this section, you will read about the continuing conflict between Texans and Native Americans. You will learn about where settlers and Native Americans clashed in the period following the Civil War. You will also learn about attempts by both sides to make peace.

★ ORGANIZING YOUR THOUGHTS

Use the diagram below to help you take notes as you read the summaries that follow. Think about why peace efforts failed.

Failure of Peace Efforts	
1.	3.
2.	4.
5.	

(continued)

Name ______________________ Date ______________ Class ______________

Chapter 17-1

★ **READ TO LEARN** *Write in complete sentences to answer the following questions. Use correct spelling, punctuation, and grammar.*

Native Americans Control the West *(pages 390–391)*

By 1850, nearly all Native Americans had been removed from East Texas. In the western part of Texas, Native Americans fought to keep settlers out. Some settlers moved eastward because they were afraid of attack.

After the Civil War, federal soldiers were stationed in the West. For a time the army could not stop the raids. The soldiers were too few in number and were often untrained or inexperienced. The forts were too far apart and were too far west to protect settlers. There was a shortage of supplies. Sometimes military operations, called **campaigns,** had to be called off because there was not enough food for the soldiers and horses.

The Native Americans were skilled fighters and knew their territory well. Before the invention of Samuel Colt's six-shot pistol, the Comanches had an advantage in warfare. It took a fairly long time to reload pistols and rifles. A Comanche warrior could ride a good distance and shoot many arrows while a soldier reloaded. By the 1870s and 1880s, most Native American warriors had rifles, too.

6. What advantages did Native Americans have over soldiers?

____

____

____

____

____

The Search for Peace *(pages 391–392)*

In 1867, federal **agents,** people doing business for another, and the chiefs of several Native American nations met to sign a peace treaty. The treaty is known as the Treaty of Medicine Lodge Creek. Native Americans agreed to live on reservations in the Indian Territory. This area is now Oklahoma. The government would appoint an agent on the reservation who would get food and supplies for the Native Americans. The army would not be allowed on the reservation. The Native Americans who signed the treaty agreed to stop attacking Anglo American settlers.

(continued)

Name ____________________ Date ____________________ Class ____________________

It was believed that providing kind and fair treatment to Native Americans would stop them from warring with settlers. President Grant tried to choose agents who would treat Native Americans well. Many of the agents were Quakers. Quakers did not believe in violence.

7. Why were many Quakers chosen as agents?

____

____

____

____

____

The Peace Policy Fails *(pages 392–393)*

Peace did not come to western Texas, however. Many Native American leaders did not sign the treaty. Others felt the government broke its promise. They claimed agents cheated them and treated them badly. Many Comanches and Kiowas refused to move to reservations.

Satanta, the most famous Kiowa chief, said West Texas belonged to the Comanches and the Kiowas. He believed that his people could not survive on reservations without the buffalo. He did not want to give up the Kiowa way of life.

Comanche chiefs Wild Horse, Black Horse, and Quanah Parker wanted to continue their fight for independence. Kiowa chiefs Kicking Bird and Striking Eagle advised against war. They argued that their people should accept Anglo ways. Comanche chief Horseback agreed and led his people to a reservation. Still, fighting continued and grew worse.

8. Why did many Native Americans refuse to move to reservations?

____

____

____

____

____

Name ________________ Date ________________ Class ________________

Chapter 17-2

For use with textbook pages 395–400

West Texas at War

Key Terms

paunch The stomach *(page 397)*
sinew A tendon *(page 397)*
bill A law proposed in the legislature *(page 398)*
commissary A storehouse *(page 398)*

★DRAWING FROM EXPERIENCE

Have you ever seen a buffalo? Why did Native Americans on the plains hunt the buffalo? What happened to the huge herds of buffalo that once lived on the plains?

In this section, you will read about the campaigns against the Native Americans. You will learn about the important role the buffalo played in the Native American way of life. You will also learn why the buffalo disappeared from the plains.

★ORGANIZING YOUR THOUGHTS

Use the diagram below to help you take notes as you read the summaries that follow. Tell how each action or activity changed life for Native Americans on the West Texas plains.

Action/Activity	Change for Native Americans
Early Texas campaigns	**1.**
Buffalo hunting by Anglo Americans	**2.**
Red River campaign	**3.**

(continued)

Name ______________________ Date ______________ Class ______________

Reading Essentials and Study Guide

Chapter 17-2

★ **READ TO LEARN** *Write in complete sentences to answer the following questions. Use correct spelling, punctuation, and grammar.*

The Peace Policy Ends *(pages 395–396)*

Quaker agents worked for peace for several years. Many complaints were made about Native American raids. The army sent General Sherman to look into the matter. He didn't believe the stories of the Texas frontier. However, after two weeks in Texas he was convinced the agents were unable to keep peace.

In 1871, while Sherman visited Fort Richardson, a group of Kiowas attacked a wagon train. This became known as the Warren Wagontrain Raid. Several men were wounded or killed. Two Kiowa chiefs were arrested and put on trial. They were found guilty and sentenced to hang.

Federal officials worried about a major war and more attacks. They set the chiefs free. This greatly angered most Texans.

The wagon train raid changed the attitude of the military leaders. The peace policy ended. The army would no longer just defend settlements from attack. Native Americans would be forced onto reservations. The federal government also sent expeditions to locate and destroy Native American camps in northwest Texas.

4. What event changed the army's strategy toward Native Americans?

____

____

____

____

____

Mackenzie Leads the Early Texas Campaigns *(page 397)*

During 1871 and 1872, the army carried out campaigns against the Native Americans on the South Plains. Colonel Ranald S. Mackenzie, commander of the Fourth Cavalry Regiment, led various operations against the Comanches. By 1873, Comanche raids in West Texas had declined. That year Mackenzie and his troops attacked Kickapoo and Apache villages along the Rio Grande. For several years after this, the southern border was more peaceful.

(continued)

5. What happened as a result of Mackenzie's campaign along the Rio Grande?

Native Americans Depend on the Buffalo *(page 397)*

The Plains people depended on open land, the horse, and the buffalo. More and more buffalo hunters were active on the plains. The Native Americans feared the loss of the buffalo would end their way of life. The buffalo provided them with food and other necessities. Water bags were made from the buffalo's **paunch,** or stomach. Hoofs, horns, and bones became ornaments, cups, and utensils. **Sinews** (tendons) and hair were made into bowstrings, rope, and thread. Buffalo hide became clothing, saddles, robes, and covers for tepees.

6. In what ways did the Native Americans use the buffalo?

Buffalo Herds Are Slaughtered *(pages 397–398)*

Charles Rath and brothers John and J. Wright Mooar developed a market for buffalo hides, which could be made into leather goods. By 1873, the buffalo herds north of Texas were gone. Hunters moved onto the Texas plains.

Many Anglo Americans recognized how important the buffalo was to Native Americans. A law to protect the buffalo was proposed in the Texas legislature, but the **bill,** or proposed law, was defeated. General Philip Sheridan favored killing the buffalo as a way of destroying Native American culture. He supported the buffalo hunters because

(continued)

Name ______________________ Date ______________ Class ______________

Reading Essentials and Study Guide

they were destroying the supply of buffalo. He described the buffalo as the Native Americans' **commissary,** or storehouse, because it supplied their needs.

The buffalo hunters continued to slaughter buffalo. They only wanted the hide, which they sold for one or two dollars. Without the buffalo, Native Americans could not continue their way of life. They made plans for war.

7. Why did General Sheridan support the buffalo hunters?

____

____

____

____

____

The Attack on Adobe Walls *(page 399)*

In June 1874, several hundred warriors from five Native American nations attacked a buffalo hunters' camp at Adobe Walls but were unsuccessful. Frustrated by their failure at Adobe Walls, Native American groups of the Plains increased their attacks on West Texas settlements. Many Native Americans left the reservations to join the fighting. They wanted to protect their land and stop the killing of buffalo. The conflict spread across five states and territories.

8. Why did Native American groups of the Plains keep fighting after Adobe Walls?

____

____

____

____

____

The Red River Campaign *(pages 399–400)*

After the attack on Adobe Walls, President Grant put the army in charge of Native American matters in West Texas. Some Native Americans went back to the reservations, but many Comanches,

(continued)

Name ______________________ Date ______________ Class ______________

Kiowas, and Cheyenne did not. They made camps in places they knew in the Texas Panhandle. There, about 1,200 warriors prepared to defend their land.

An army of about 3,000 troops moved against the camps from five directions. This operation, known as the Red River campaign, was fought in late August 1874.

The Frontier Batallion was led by Major John Jones, a former member of Terry's Texas Rangers. Jones protected the West Texas line of defense. The Frontier Battalion fought 21 battles against Native Americans in its first 17 months.

9. What Native Americans groups did the U.S. Army and Texas Rangers fight against in the Red River campaign?

____

____

____

____

The Battle of Palo Duro Canyon *(page 400)*

The Battle of Palo Duro Canyon took place on September 28, 1874. It was the most decisive battle of the Red River campaign. Mackenzie's troops set fire to Comanche, Kiowa, and Cheyenne villages in the canyon. Few lives were lost, but the army captured valuable supplies and more than 1,000 horses. Mackenzie had the horses killed. The Native Americans would not be able to last long without them.

By early November most of the Native American groups were heading back to their reservations. Some held out through a harsh winter. The last bands of Native Americans surrendered in June 1875.

After the Red River campaign, Native Americans were rarely seen in central and West Texas. The Kickapoos and Apaches continued their struggle for a few more years along the Rio Grande.

10. What did most Native Americans do after the Battle of Palo Duro Canyon?

____

____

____

____

Name ______________________ Date ______________ Class ______________

Reading Essentials and Study Guide — Chapter 17-3

For use with textbook pages 402–405

Fighting on the Rio Grande

Key Terms

renegade An outlaw *(page 403)*

★ DRAWING FROM EXPERIENCE

How different do you think Texas or the United States would be if the Native Americans had not been forced off their land? Do you think the settlers and the Native Americans could have worked out their differences? What would life be like now if there were still large herds of buffalo?

In this section, you will learn about the conflicts between Native Americans and the army along the Rio Grande. You will learn about the contributions of the buffalo soldiers and the end of the Native American era in Texas.

★ ORGANIZING YOUR THOUGHTS

Use the diagram below to help you take notes as you read the summaries that follow. Think about how the end of conflict between settlers and Native Americans affected each group.

End of Conflict
Effects
1.
2.
3.
4.

(continued)

Name ______________________ Date ______________ Class ______________

Chapter 17-3

★ **READ TO LEARN** *Write in complete sentences to answer the following questions. Use correct spelling, punctuation, and grammar.*

Buffalo Soldiers End the Wars *(pages 402–403)*

After several years of peace, warfare along the Mexican border began again in 1876. In 1878, Colonel Mackenzie started regular patrols of the border and sometimes crossed into Mexico. With the help of the Mexican army, raids by the Kickapoos were finally stopped. Raids by the Apaches continued.

By the 1870s, most Apaches lived in New Mexico and Arizona. One band of warriors, led by a chief named Victorio, roamed the mountains in West Texas. This band fought in Mexico, Texas, and New Mexico. Colonel Benjamin H. Grierson and the African American troops of the Twenty-Fourth Infantry and the Tenth Cavalry were in charge of fighting Victorio. These troops were experts in warfare against Native Americans.

Native Americans called the African American troops "buffalo soldiers," a title of great respect. Nineteen buffalo soldiers received Congressional Medals of Honor for their army service. The Anglo American settlers, however, gave the buffalo soldiers little respect, even though the African American soldiers defended them.

Grierson and his soldiers followed Victorio through the Mountains and Basins region. They finally forced Victorio across the Rio Grande into Mexico. Mexican soldiers battled Victorio and his Apache warriors when they became trapped in northern Mexico. Victorio was killed. This defeat in 1880 marked the end of the Apache wars in Texas.

5. Why did the Native Americans call the African American troops buffalo soldiers?

____

____

____

____

____

(continued)

Name ____________________ Date ____________________ Class ____________________

Reading Essentials and Study Guide

Chapter 17-3

South Texas Renegades (pages 403–404)

South Texas also experienced conflict and violence. **Renegades,** or outlaws, robbed and raided towns and settlements in the Rio Grande border area. Some ranchers expanded their lands and herds, which also caused problems. Many poorer people, especially those of Mexican heritage, had their lands taken illegally. Some of these people were mistreated in other ways. In many cases, it was difficult to determine who owned the cattle.

The Texas Rangers were sent to the Rio Grande area to help keep the peace. Some people believe they added to the problems by mistreating Mexican Americans. Juan Cortina played a major role in the conflicts in the area. He tried to protect the rights of Mexicans and Tejanos. The authorities saw him as an outlaw. Although the Rangers never captured Cortina, the Mexican army arrested him and had him removed from the area.

Patrolling on either side of the Rio Grande by the Rangers and the Mexican army helped stop lawlessness. Many Mexican Americans, however, were bitter about this period.

6. Why do you think it was difficult to tell who owned the cattle?

____

____

____

____

____

Time of Sadness for Native Americans (page 404)

Native Americans could no longer roam freely, searching for buffalo. The U.S. government wanted Native Americans to become farmers and town dwellers rather than nomadic hunters. Many young Native Americans were taken from their homes. They were placed in schools to learn Anglo ways. They had to wear Anglo clothing, cut their hair, and speak only English. War, disease, and starvation killed many Native Americans. Those who survived saw their lives changed forever.

(continued)

Name ______________________ Date ______________ Class ______________

Reading Essentials and Study Guide

7. In what ways did the government want Native Americans to change their lives?

____

____

____

____

____

A New Era Begins *(pages 404–405)*

As soon as the Native Americans were removed, Anglo American settlers poured into West Texas. Some lived in settlements near old forts. Others settled along transportation routes. Towns quickly sprang up. Colleges were founded. The railroads being built west from Fort Worth brought farming communities. Soon there were farms on land that had been home to Native Americans.

8. What locations did Anglo Americans choose for their settlements?

____

____

____

____

____

Name ______________________ Date ______________ Class ______________

Reading Essentials and Study Guide

For use with textbook pages 412–417

Origins of the Cattle Kingdom

Key Terms

open range Public land that anyone could use *(page 413)*
vaquero A cowhand *(page 413)*
ranchero A rancher *(page 413)*
tallow Cattle fat *(page 413)*
drive Move cattle in large herds to railroad towns, which were connected to the stockyards by rail *(page 414)*
stockyard A holding pen for cattle awaiting shipping or slaughter *(page 414)*
drover A person who moves cattle *(page 414)*
wrangler A ranchhand who takes care of the horses *(page 416)*
quarantine Enforced isolation to prevent the spread of disease or pests *(page 417)*

★DRAWING FROM EXPERIENCE

What do you think it was like to be a cowhand? Would you have liked the job? How do you know what it was like to be a cowhand? Do you trust that information? As you will learn in this section, cowhands worked very hard and their job was often dangerous. You will also learn what changes led to the end of the cattle drive.

★ORGANIZING YOUR THOUGHTS

Use the diagram below to help you take notes as you read the summaries that follow. Tell how each development added to or cut profits for the cattle industry.

Development	How It Increased/Decreased Profits
Demand in North and East	1.
Expansion of Railroads	2.
Costs of Trail Driving	3.
Fences on Farms	4
Quarantines of Cattle	5.
Greater Supply of Cattle	6.

(continued)

Name ______________________ Date ______________ Class ______________

Reading Essentials and Study Guide

Chapter 18-1

★ **READ TO LEARN** *Write in complete sentences to answer the following questions. Use correct spelling, punctuation, and grammar.*

The Spanish Introduce Cattle *(pages 412–413)*

The first cattle to come to America arrived with Spanish explorers in the 1500s. Some escaped, and herds of wild cattle soon grazed throughout Texas. Later Spanish settlers brought more cattle. The Spanish built ranches in South Texas along the Rio Grande, San Antonio, and Nueces Rivers. The climate, water supply, and grass made Texas ideal for cattle.

Cattle were raised on the **open range,** public land, that anyone could use. ***Vaqueros,*** or cowhands, herded the cattle into pens. Then they branded the cattle with a hot iron. The brand showed that the cattle were owned by a particular ***ranchero,*** or rancher.

7. Why were cattle branded?

____

____

____

____

Early Ranchers Use the Open Range *(pages 413–414)*

Anglo American ranchers moved to Texas from other Southern states. These ranchers did not know how to use horses to drive cattle. They were not used to other equipment the Spanish cowhands used. However, they quickly adopted the ways of the vaqueros.

Although the number of cattle continued to increase, ranchers faced many problems. Cattle were stolen. Sometimes there were droughts. The lack of a market for the cattle was a major problem.

Ranchers could sell cattle hides and **tallow,** or fat, which could be shipped easily. However, they did not bring much money compared to what beef was worth in eastern cities.

8. What were some of the problems ranchers had?

____

____

____

(continued)

Name ______________________ Date ______________ Class ______________

Reading Essentials and Study Guide

Trail Driving Opens the Cattle Market *(page 414)*

Several changes made trail driving profitable after the Civil War. Cattle herds had increased in size during the war. Prices for cattle in the North and East were ten times what they were in the Southwest.

The expansion of the railroads after the Civil War played a large role in Texas's cattle industry. Texas ranchers would **drive,** or move, cattle in large herds to railroad towns. The cattle would then be taken by rail to **stockyards,** or holding pens to await shipping or slaughter. There were important stockyards in Chicago and St. Louis.

9. Why did ranchers want to move their cattle to the North and East?

____

____

____

Drovers Follow Major Cattle Trails *(pages 414–415)*

In the spring of 1866 about 260,000 cattle were driven to Sedalia, Missouri. The path became known as the Sedalia or Shawnee Trail.

As time went on, **drovers**—the people who moved cattle—ran into problems. Missouri farmers complained that the cattle drives destroyed their crops. Also, the farmers were afraid the cattle might spread disease to their own animals. Many farmers built fences to keep the cattle herds off their land.

Joseph McCoy convinced the railroads moving west to build towns. The towns would house the drovers and their herds. Drovers turned their herds farther west to avoid Missouri. They used the Chisholm Trail to get to the new towns. Other trails included the Great Western Trail, the Matamoros Trail, and the Goodnight-Loving Trail.

10. Why were farmers in Missouri angry about the cattle drives?

____

____

____

Life Along the Trail Drives *(pages 416–417)*

Days on the cattle drives were long and hard, and often dangerous. Two cowhands rode in front of the herd. Others rode on either side of the herd. Two or three cowhands were behind the herd. They traveled around 10–12 miles a day. At night, the cowhands took turns "riding

(continued)

herd." This meant they guarded the herd against stampedes or raids by Native Americans or rustlers. Eight to 12 cowhands were needed for large herds. A trail boss, cook, and **wrangler,** or ranchhand who took care of the horses, also went along.

Trail driving ended shortly after 1885. The supply of cattle became greater than the demand for them. This made the price of cattle drop. Cattle drives were no longer profitable. Fences often blocked the drovers' path. Cattle could be kept out of certain states by **quarantine,** or enforced isolation, if they were suspected of having a disease. By the late 1800s there were railroads throughout Texas. Long cattle drives were no longer needed.

11. Why did the cattle drives end?

____

____

____

____

____

Ranching Fact and Fiction *(page 417)*

Open range cattle ranching lasted for only a short time. However, the cowboy became an important part of art, literature, music, and movies. There are many stories about ranching, depicting the cowboy's life as glamorous and exciting.

Accounts of ranching based on experience, however, show that the cowhand's life was mainly a lot of hard work and long hours. They sometimes spent 18 hours a day in the saddle. In movies and books, most cowhands were Anglos. In the real world, many of them were Mexican American and African American.

12. What was a cowhand's life like?

____

____

____

____

____

Name ______________________ Date ______________ Class ______________

For use with textbook pages 419–423

The Days of the Big Ranches

Key Terms

mustang A hardy wild horse of the western plains, descended from horses brought by the Spaniards *(page 420)*

felony A serious crime *(page 422)*

★DRAWING FROM EXPERIENCE

What would be on your list of important inventions? Which invention do you think has had the greatest effect on people's lives? Why? In this section, you will learn about an invention that changed ranching in Texas. You will also learn about other developments that changed the lives of ranchers.

★ORGANIZING YOUR THOUGHTS

Use the diagram below to help you take notes as you read the summaries that follow. Identify four reasons for the decline in ranching.

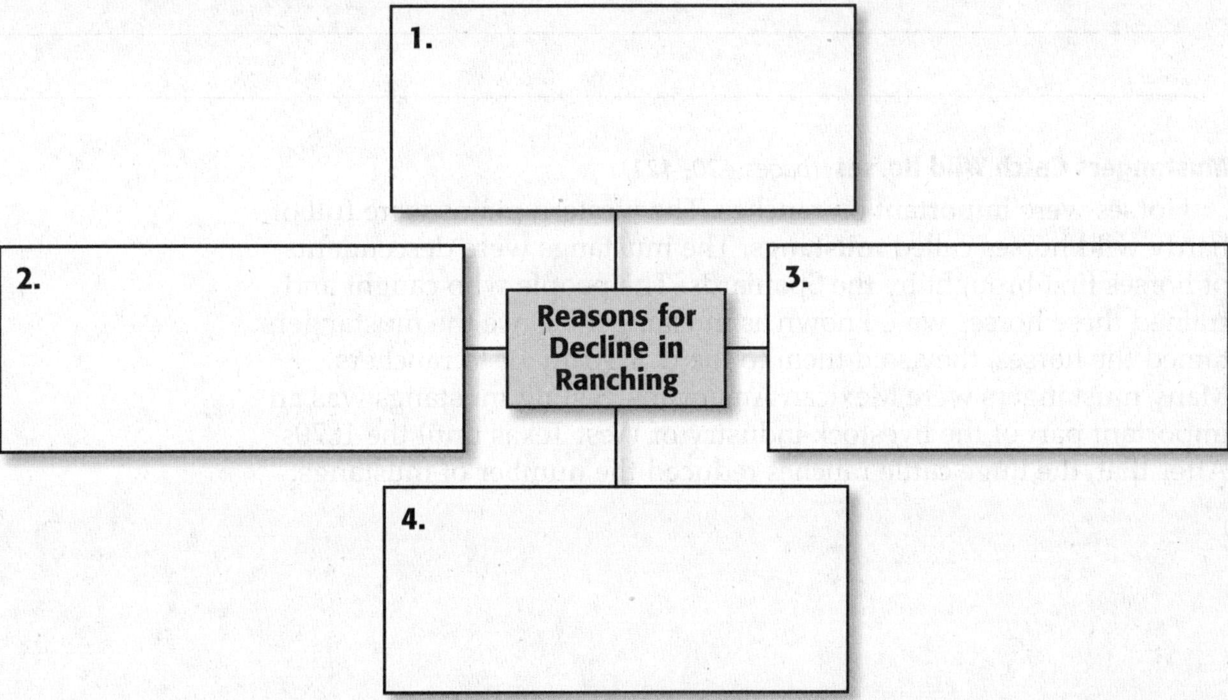

(continued)

Name ______________________ Date ______________ Class ______________

Chapter 18-2

★ **READ TO LEARN** *Write in complete sentences to answer the following questions. Use correct spelling, punctuation, and grammar.*

Big Ranches Bring Big Profits *(pages 419–420)*

South Texas and the rangelands to the north had many huge ranches. The King Ranch alone contained tens of thousands of cattle, horses, mules, and sheep. After the buffalo were wiped out and Native Americans were removed from the Great Plains, ranching moved to West Texas and the Panhandle. Charles Goodnight and John Adair had a ranch of 1 million acres and more than 100,000 cattle. Using crossbreeding, Goodnight raised some of the best beef cattle in the United States.

Ranching was very profitable. People from other countries began to buy ranches. British investors put up money for one of the largest ranches of the period, the XIT. In the 1880s, Texas gave 3 million acres to a Chicago company. In return the company promised to build a new state capitol in Austin.

5. Why did people from other countries want to buy ranches?

____

____

____

____

____

Mustangers Catch Wild Horses *(pages 420–421)*

Horses were important on ranches. The western plains were full of hardy wild horses called **mustangs.** The mustangs were descendants of horses first brought by the Spaniards. The people who caught and trained these horses were known as mustangers. Once the mustangers tamed the horses, they sold them to the U.S. Army or to ranchers. Many mustangers were Mexican Americans. Selling mustangs was an important part of the livestock industry of West Texas until the 1870s. After that, the huge cattle ranches reduced the number of mustangs.

(continued)

6. What did mustangers do with the horses they tamed?

The Sheep Industry Booms *(page 421)*

Sheep had been raised in South Texas for many years. Colonists bred heavy sheep from the East with the lighter Mexican variety. This doubled the sheep's weight and the amount of wool they produced.

The boom started just before the Civil War. George Wilkins Kendall set up a 5,000-acre ranch. He encouraged people to come to Texas to raise sheep, even though there was disease, drought, and trouble with the Native Americans.

After the Civil War, demand for wool grew. More people went into sheep ranching. Cattle ranchers and farmers did not like sheep. Cattle ranchers said sheep cropped the grass too short. According to cattle ranchers, this ruined the grass for cattle. Farmers complained that sheep killed their crops by trampling them. Ranchers and farmers began building fences to protect their lands.

7. Why didn't cattle ranchers and farmers like sheep?

Barbed Wire Ends the Open Range *(pages 421–422)*

By 1873, barbed wire was available for use on ranches. Barbed wire has many sharp pieces of wire (barbs) twisted around the main wires of the fence. These barbs pricked the animals but did not harm them. Barbed wire could be made cheaply and was easy to install.

(continued)

Reading Essentials and Study Guide

Although sales were slow at first, barbed wire began to be used in several Texas counties. Ranchers and farmers clashed during this time. Cattle and sheep raisers enclosed their land. Ranchers cut off the water supply to other ranchers' animals. Fence cutting wars followed between ranchers and farmers.

Restoring law and order was not easy. The Texas Rangers were often called on. Eventually, the state legislature passed a law making fence cutting a **felony,** or serious crime.

By 1883 most ranges in South and Central Texas were fenced. Ranges in other parts of the states were quickly being enclosed. Earlier, cattle had gone to waterholes to get water. Now, windmills became common. They pumped water from wells and helped make fenced pastures possible.

8. Why did farmers and ranchers use barbed wire?

____

____

____

____

____

The Ranching Industry Declines *(page 422)*

Ranching declined rapidly in the late 1880s. There were more cattle than people wanted to buy, and cattle prices dropped. Rangelands were ruined because of overgrazing. There were long droughts in the summers and severe blizzards in the winters. Many ranchers lost all their money. Many large ranches were divided into smaller ones. Some were sold as farmland.

The King Ranch and some other large ranches survived and did well. Ranching became more dependent on scientific techniques. Ranchers began to use modern management techniques. New breeds of cattle replaced the longhorn.

9. What happened to Texas's large ranches?

____

____

____

____

(continued)

Name ____________________ Date ____________________ Class ____________________

Reading Essentials and Study Guide

Chapter 18-2

Cultures Meet in the Ranch Country (pages 422–423)

The people living in West Texas and South Texas came from many cultures. Mexican American *vaqueros* worked the cattle ranches of South Texas. Mexican Americans also raised sheep. Most shepherds were Mexican Americans. African Americans also worked on the cattle ranches and on cattle drives. German, English, Scottish, and Irish people set up ranches in Texas.

10. What cultures did some Texas cattle and sheep ranchers come from?

____

____

____

____

____

Women Ranchers (page 423)

Many women worked with their husbands to build ranches. They worked very hard in the dry, dirty country. A few women owned ranches. Elizabeth Johnson Williams was an experienced rancher. She was widely respected. Henrietta King kept the King Ranch going after her husband's death. Margaret H. Borland owned over 10,000 head of cattle. Many women drove their own cattle to Kansas.

Mexican American women had their own long history of ranching. Men and women of many cultures contributed to the ranching heritage of Texas. They are remembered as pioneers who opened the West.

11. How were women involved in ranching?

____

____

____

____

____

Name ______________________ Date ______________ Class ______________

Chapter 18-3

For use with textbook pages 424–427

Farming After the Civil War

Key Terms

dry farming A method of farming that leaves loose soil on top of the ground after plowing, keeping water in *(page 425)*

tenant farmer A farmer who works land owned by someone else and pays rent for it with part of the crop *(page 426)*

sharecropper A tenant farmer who is provided with tools and supplies and receives a share of the value of the crop *(page 426)*

★DRAWING FROM EXPERIENCE

Have you ever visited a farm in Texas? What was grown there? Who worked on the farm? Who owned it? In this section, you will learn about how farming expanded in Texas after the Civil War and why. You will also discover who worked on the farms and the problems they faced.

★ORGANIZING YOUR THOUGHTS

Use the diagram below to help you take notes as you read the summaries that follow. List problems farmers in Texas faced in the late 1800s.

Problems Farmers Faced

1.
2.
3.
4.

(continued)

Name ______________________ Date ______________ Class ______________

Chapter 18-3

★ **READ TO LEARN** *Write in complete sentences to answer the following questions. Use correct spelling, punctuation, and grammar.*

Farming on the Rise *(pages 424–425)*

After the Civil War, many new settlers came to Texas. They were looking for more and cheaper land. Settlers in the drier parts of Texas learned that they could still grow profitable crops. Windmills pumped water from underground sources. They used a method known as **dry farming.** In dry farming, loose soil is left on top of the ground after plowing. The layer of loose soil helps keep water in the ground by slowing the rate of evaporation.

The railroads also contributed to the settlement of West Texas and the Panhandle by farmers. Many towns grew up around the railroads. Farmers settled around these towns.

5. How did farmers raise profitable crops in the driest parts of Texas?

____

____

____

____

____

Texans Rely on King Cotton *(pages 425–426)*

Cotton was the most important crop in Texas. It was grown throughout the state. In the late 1800s, most Texans were cotton farmers. In most years, the value of the cotton crop in Texas was more than the combined value of all other crops grown. In 1900, Texas cotton farms produced more than 3.5 million bales from nearly 7,200,000 acres.

As with ranching, the railroads were important to cotton farming. The railroads provided a cheap and easy way for the farmers to get their cotton to market, where it could be sold.

Other crops were important in Texas, too. Before the end of the 1800s, Texas produced more honey than any other state. Farmers grew sugarcane and rice along the Gulf coast. Farmers grew wheat, corn, and oats in other parts of Texas.

(continued)

Some of the farmers who settled in Texas did not do well. This was usually because the Texas land was different from the land where these farmers used to live. They did not know how to use the land properly, or what crops would grow in Texas. In some years, large swarms of grasshoppers attacked and ate the plants. In the late 1800s, there was a long drought. This drought destroyed many farmers' hopes of making a living. Cotton farming in India and Egypt added to the world supply of cotton. A surplus of a crop often meant lower prices. Even though many farmers did not succeed, those who came after them learned from their experiences.

6. How did the spread of railroads help new farmers in Texas?

____

____

____

____

____

The Tenant System Replaces Slavery *(pages 426–427)*

A new system of farm labor developed after the Civil War. Before the war, slaves produced many of the cash crops in East Texas. These slaves worked on large plantations. After the war, the plantations were split into many small farms. Some of these farms were sold to new owners. Others were rented to **tenant farmers.** The tenant farmer gave part of the crop to the landowner as rent. Some landowners gave tenant farmers the tools, seeds, and supplies they needed to grow the crop. In return, these landowners would get a bigger share of the crop. Tenant farmers who did not supply their own tools and supplies were called **sharecroppers.** Sharecroppers got a share (usually one-half) of the value of the crop.

(continued)

The tenant system developed because there was a shortage of capital after the war. Since there was little money, labor was swapped, or traded, for part of the crop. Tenant farming also put an end to forced gang labor. Under slavery, men and women had often been forced to work in large gangs. Cotton farming still required a lot of workers. Children of the tenants and sharecroppers were often put to work.

Some African Americans owned their own land, but most were sharecroppers. Most had once worked as slaves on the plantations.

Life was difficult for tenant farmers, and especially for sharecroppers. Droughts, overproduction of crops, and high charges left many tenants with no money. Many found it difficult to get out of debt. In spite of this, tenant farming expanded. In 1870 about one-third of the farmers in Texas were tenant farmers.

Farming brought large numbers of people to the West. It required many more workers than ranching. Towns started up everywhere. Just like towns and cities today, these towns had schools, churches, roads, and businesses.

7. How were sharecroppers paid?

____

____

____

____

____

Name ______________________ Date ______________ Class ______________

Reading Essentials and Study Guide

Chapter 19-1

For use with textbook pages 432–436

Reconstruction Ends

Key Terms

suffrage The right to vote *(page 433)*

pensions Wages paid after retirement *(page 434)*

vigilante A member of a volunteer committee formed to punish suspected criminals *(page 435)*

★ DRAWING FROM EXPERIENCE

Have you ever seen the state capitol building? Have you seen the statues of Stephen F. Austin and Sam Houston? Did you know that the building in Austin today is not the original capitol?

In this section, you will learn about the Constitution of 1876 and the changes it brought to Texas in the late 1800s. You will discover that a new capitol was one of the changes outlined in the new constitution. You will also learn about how African Americans, Mexican Americans, and women became more involved in Texas politics during this period.

★ ORGANIZING YOUR THOUGHTS

Use the diagram below to help you take notes as you read the summaries that follow. Plot important events in the women's movement.

1868–1869	1888	1918	1920
1.	2.	3.	4.

(continued)

Name ______________________ Date ______________ Class ______________

Reading Essentials and Study Guide

Chapter 19-1

★ **READ TO LEARN** *Write in complete sentences to answer the following questions. Use correct spelling, punctuation, and grammar.*

A New Era Brings New Concerns *(pages 432–433)*

The late 1800s were a time of growth and expansion in Texas. Railroads spread throughout the state. Farming boomed. Industries expanded, and new industries started. The growth of the population and economy meant more money for the state. It also meant new problems and concerns. Many political and social issues left over from the Reconstruction Era still had to be resolved.

5. What issues did Texas need to resolve in the new era?

____

____

____

____

____

Democrats Rewrite the Constitution *(page 433)*

In 1874 the Democrats regained the governorship. Their goal was to write a new constitution. Democrats met in Austin in 1875. Many believed the old constitution gave too much power to a few officials.

The new Constitution of 1876 limited the powers of the government. The governor had less power. The legislature could meet only once every two years. Legislators' terms were limited. The constitution also lowered taxes and the pay of state employees. Convention delegates ignored requests to grant **suffrage,** or the right to vote, to women.

The constitution was approved in 1876. The Constitution of 1876 is still the constitution used in Texas today. It is long and has over 400 amendments, or changes.

6. What were two ways the new constitution affected the state's finances?

____

____

____

____

(continued)

Reading Essentials and Study Guide

Democrats Control State Politics *(page 434)*

Most leaders at the end of Reconstruction were Democrats. They were conservative. They cut public services to schools and hospitals for the mentally ill. They did this to reduce spending and taxes. They also passed laws limiting the rights of African Americans in Texas. Some African Americans went to federal courts for protection.

The Republican Party still put up candidates, but it had little power. Many African Americans supported the Texas Republican Party. Between 1868 and 1898, about 60 African Americans served in the state legislature or took part in important political conventions. Sometimes, African Americans were prevented from voting. They were often threatened, denied jobs, or harmed if they tried to take part in politics or vote.

Mexican Americans were also active in politics. Many officeholders in South Texas were Mexican Americans.

7. How were African Americans prevented from voting?

____

____

____

____

Spending Cuts Reduce State Debt *(page 434)*

At the end of Reconstruction, Texas was $3 million in debt. Governor Richard Coke cut government spending. Richard Hubbard, the next governor, also tried to save money. However, by 1879, the public debt had grown to $5.5 million.

Governor Oran M. Roberts took office in 1879. He balanced the budget during his term. He cut **pensions** for veterans. Pensions are wages paid after military service. He also cut funds for schools. He left the finances of Texas in good condition.

8. How did Governor Roberts balance the state budget?

____

____

____

____

(continued)

Reading Essentials and Study Guide

Lawmen Keep Order *(pages 434–435)*

Crime was a major problem in Texas after the Civil War. Restoring law and order was a major accomplishment for the state government and other groups. Communities formed **vigilante** committees. These vigilantes were volunteers who punished suspected criminals harshly, but not legally. Meanwhile, sheriffs and other local officers worked hard to enforce laws.

The Texas Rangers joined local officers in fighting crime. The Rangers pursued train bandits, bank robbers, and cattle thieves.

9. Who assisted local police in enforcing law and order?

____

____

____

____

____

Texas Needs a Capitol *(page 435)*

The Constitution of 1876 included a plan for a new capitol. A new capitol was needed after the old building and many state records burned in 1881. The new Capitol, modeled after the U.S. Capitol, opened in 1888.

10. After what building was Texas's new Capitol modeled?

____

____

____

____

____

Women Fight for Their Rights *(pages 435–436)*

By 1900, women made up about half the population in Texas. However, they did not have the same legal rights as men. Women's rights to own property or conduct business were limited, and they did not have the right to vote.

(continued)

Name ______________________ Date ______________ Class ______________

Reading Essentials and Study Guide

It took women in Texas 50 years of hard work and three different organizations to win the vote. The fight began after the Civil War during the Constitutional Convention of 1868–1869. It ended when women won the right to vote in Democratic Party primaries in 1918 and in federal elections in 1920.

The Women's Christian Temperance Union was the first group to support woman suffrage. Other groups also supported suffrage, but they were not successful. Women of Texas would not gain the right to vote until after World War I.

11. In what three ways were women's rights limited?

____

____

____

____

____

Women at Work *(page 436)*

Around 1900, most Texas women worked in their homes as wives, mothers, and homemakers. About half the women in the state worked on family farms or ranches. Many entered the paid work force as farm workers, laundresses, and maids. Teaching was the most important profession open to women at this time. Some women even founded schools.

Other women worked as journalists, artists, and merchants. In 1872 a woman became the state government's first female worker. Women made important contributions in the arts. Elisabet Ney was a noted sculptor. Ney became known for her statues of Stephen F. Austin and Sam Houston. Both of these are on display on the Capitol grounds.

12. What was the most important profession open to women around 1900?

____

____

____

____

Name ______________________ Date ______________ Class ______________

Reading Essentials and Study Guide

Chapter 19-2

For use with textbook pages 437–441

Transportation and Industry

Key Terms

refinery A factory where crude oil is processed *(page 441)*

★ DRAWING FROM EXPERIENCE

How far do your parents travel to get to work? How long does it take them to get there? How far is your school from your home? How long does it take you to get there?

The last section discussed the Constitution of 1876 and changes in Texas government. In this section, you will learn about improvements in transportation and the growth of industries in Texas during the late 1800s.

★ ORGANIZING YOUR THOUGHTS

Use the diagram below to help you take notes as you read the summaries that follow. Identify industries that became important in Texas in the late 1800s.

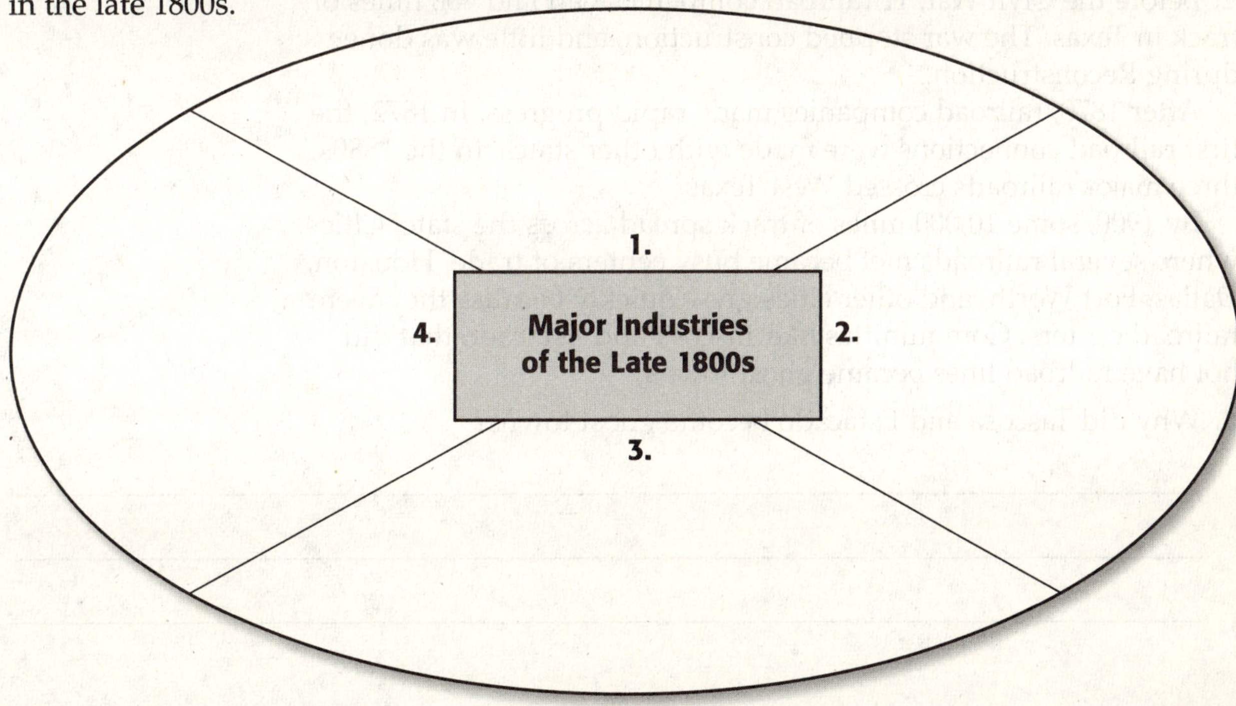

(continued)

Name ____________ Date ____________ Class ____________

Reading Essentials and Study Guide

Chapter 19-2

★ **READ TO LEARN** *Write in complete sentences to answer the following questions. Use correct spelling, punctuation, and grammar.*

Texans Demand Railroad Service *(pages 437–438)*

Before 1900, most families traveled by wagons and buggies. A 20-mile trip into town took most of a day. It usually meant an overnight stay and added expense.

Poor transportation slowed the growth of Texas. Farmers and merchants in many areas could not sell their products easily.

Railroads could move people and goods quickly and cheaply. People believed that railroads would help farms, ranches, and businesses.

Many towns paid railroad companies to build lines through their communities. To encourage the building of railroads, the state gave more than 32 million acres of land to railroad companies.

5. Why did people believe railroads would help farms and ranches?

____

____

____

A Network of Steel Connects Texas *(pages 438–439)*

Before the Civil War, 11 railroad companies had laid 400 miles of track in Texas. The war stopped construction, and little was done during Reconstruction.

After 1870, railroad companies made rapid progress. In 1872, the first railroad connections were made with other states. In the 1880s, three major railroads crossed West Texas.

By 1900, some 10,000 miles of track spread across the state. Cities where several railroads met became busy centers of trade. Houston, Dallas, Fort Worth, and other cities grew quickly because they were railroad centers. Communities like Tascosa and Estacado that did not have railroad lines became ghost towns.

6. Why did Tascosa and Estacado become ghost towns?

____

____

____

(continued)

Transportation Improves *(pages 439–440)*

In the late 1800s, Texas had no state road system supported by taxes. Each county built and took care of its own roads and bridges. Rain turned the unpaved roads into ruts and mud holes. Dust and dirt in dry weather also made travel unpleasant. However, some cities did make improvements.

By 1887, San Antonio had 40 miles of sidewalks and eight miles of paved streets. In 1903, Houston had 26 miles of pavement. Brick was the most common paving material. San Antonio paved some streets with mesquite wood.

Streetcars appeared in the 1870s. Mules and horses pulled the first street cars. Electric-powered trolleys were running by the 1890s. Ten years later, an occasional automobile could be seen.

7. Why were unpaved roads a problem for travelers?

____

____

____

____

Telephones in Texas *(page 440)*

Rapid communication helped industry grow. In the cotton industry, for example, prices were set in the cotton markets in Memphis and New Orleans. Traders who could quickly find out the price of cotton had an advantage over other traders.

The publisher of the *Galveston News*, A. H. Belo, saw a telephone at an exposition in Philadelphia in 1876. In 1878 he installed the first telephone in Texas between his home and office. Within a year hundreds of others in Galveston had telephones. By 1883 long distance service was set up between Galveston and Houston. Telephone calls had to be connected by employees called operators. The first operators were men, but by 1884 women were hired.

8. Who brought the telephone to Texas?

____

____

____

(continued)

Name ______________________ Date ______________ Class ______________

Reading Essentials and Study Guide

Chapter 19-2

Industries Begin and Grow *(pages 440–441)*

In 1870 Texas industry was just beginning. Less than one percent of the population worked in industrial jobs. The shops were small and supplied the needs of the local community. Gristmills ground corn and wheat. They made up the largest industry. Other products included lumber, buggies, wagons, plows, boots, harnesses, saddles, textiles, bricks, furniture, fishnets, glue, and soap.

In the late 1800s, new industries emerged. In 1868, the meat-packing industry began in Victoria. In the next 30 years, several packing plants were built in Fort Worth. Refrigerated railroad cars moved the meat to the customers.

9. Why were railroads important to the meat-packing industry?

____

____

____

Lumber and Minerals *(page 441)*

By 1900, lumbering was the most important industry in Texas. Timber companies harvested the pine forests of East Texas. They built towns along the Neches and Sabine Rivers. Orange and Beaumont became sawmill centers. Most of the lumber was used in construction.

Mining became important after railroads were built. The mining companies used the railroads to carry ore east. Coal mining began in Palo Pinto and Erath Counties. Salt came from mines at Grand Saline. Iron ore was produced at Rusk and Jefferson.

Oilmen drilled the first Texas wells at this time. They also built one **refinery** after another for crude oil processing. A hand-dug oil well in Central Texas produced oil used as a medicine and a lubricant. An oil field in East Texas produced oil for use as a train fuel and to be applied to dusty streets. Oil did not become a major industry until the twentieth century.

10. What three minerals were mined in Texas?

____

____

____

Name ________________ Date ________________ Class ________________

Reading Essentials and Study Guide

Chapter 19-3

For use with textbook pages 443–447

Demands for Reform

Key Terms

trust An arrangement among several companies to reduce or eliminate competition and free trade *(page 444)*
monopoly Exclusive control *(page 444)*
free enterprise The freedom of businesses to operate without government interference *(page 445)*
antitrust law A law prohibiting companies from joining together to fix prices or limit production *(page 446)*
interstate Between two or more states *(page 446)*
intrastate Within one state *(page 446)*

★ DRAWING FROM EXPERIENCE

Have you ever gone shopping and tried to find the lowest price for an item you wanted? Have you ever noticed that prices often differ from place to place?

The last section discussed the growth of transportation and industry in Texas. In this section, you will read about unfair prices and other problems that developed in transportation and business. You will learn how the state government tried to solve these problems.

★ ORGANIZING YOUR THOUGHTS

Use the diagram below to help you take notes as you read the summaries that follow. Explain the cycle of debt started by the drop in the prices of farm goods.

Cotton Prices Go Down

1.	3.
2.	4.

(continued)

Name ____________________ Date ____________________ Class ____________________

Reading Essentials and Study Guide

Chapter 19-3

★ **READ TO LEARN** *Write in complete sentences to answer the following questions. Use correct spelling, punctuation, and grammar.*

Monopolies Use Unfair Tactics *(pages 443–444)*

By the turn of the century, many large companies in Texas were helpful to the growth of the state. They provided new services, products, and jobs. As the companies became more powerful, problems arose.

Some companies formed organizations called **trusts.** A trust is an arrangement among several companies to reduce or eliminate competition and free trade. A trust was powerful enough to stop other companies from selling the same product or service. A trust held a **monopoly,** or exclusive control, of a business. This meant that trusts could pay low prices for the materials they bought. They could charge high prices for the goods they sold. Farmers, consumers, and some merchants could not protect themselves against such unfair practices.

5. Why was a trust able to charge high prices for goods?

____

____

____

____

Farmers Become Trapped in Debt *(pages 444–445)*

Railroad trusts also caused problems. The railroads charged higher rates to farmers and merchants who had no choice but to use the local railroad to ship their products. Large businesses that shipped their products to other states could choose from several competing railroads.

Farmers also worried about the profits they received for their crops. The prices of cotton and other farm products went down between 1875 and 1900. During this period, farmers plowed more land and needed more equipment. They borrowed money to buy more land and equipment. It was hard to repay these debts.

6. Why did railroads charge less to ship goods out of state than locally?

____

____

____

(continued)

Name ______________________ Date ______________ Class ______________

Reading Essentials and Study Guide

Chapter 19-3

Texans Call for Reforms *(pages 445–446)*

Some Texas farmers believed that the state officials were too cautious and afraid to fight monopolies. They felt the state was helping the monopolies and railroads and not the average Texan. However, others argued that the **free enterprise** system allowed businesses to operate without government interference.

Farmers organized to get help for their problems. The Patrons of Husbandry, also called the Grange, was an early farmers' group that called for economic change. It set up stores where farmers could buy supplies at cheaper prices. It also pressured the state to deal with the railroads' unfair shipping prices.

Another organization, the Farmers' Alliance, tried to get rid of the middleman's profits by arranging sales between producers and sellers. Some Alliance members believed that government reforms were necessary. They founded a new political party called the People's, or Populist Party. Most Texas populists were poor farmers. Sometimes African American farmers also joined the party.

The People's Party never won control of the state government, yet some populist candidates were elected to important offices. Populists led other politicians to help the passage of laws that aided farmers and workers.

7. What reforms did Texas farmers want?

____

____

____

____

____

New Law Prohibits Trusts *(page 446)*

In 1889, the legislature responded to public concerns. It passed an **antitrust law.** That law prevents companies from joining together to fix prices or limit production. Although changed many times, the law is still in effect. It has been used to stop unfair practices. Some companies have been forced to stop doing business in Texas or to pay large fines for breaking this law.

(continued)

Name ______________________ Date ______________ Class ______________

8. What does the antitrust law do?

____

____

____

____

____

Governor Hogg Regulates the Railroads *(pages 446–447)*

The regulation of railroads was an important reform of the period. In 1887, the U.S. Congress created the Interstate Commerce Commission (ICC). The ICC makes rules for **interstate** railroads that connect two or more states. Control over **intrastate** (within one state) railroads was also needed.

As attorney general, James S. Hogg helped pass the antitrust law. Hogg became governor in 1891. He asked the legislature to create a state agency to regulate, or control, railroads in Texas. The legislature set up the Texas Railroad Commission. The commission set rates and watched over the practices of railroads. Within a few years, many of the railroads' unfair practices were stopped.

James Hogg is remembered as one of the most important and popular governors of Texas. Reform-minded Texans liked Hogg because he would not back down from a fight with big business. Small-town and rural Texans considered Hogg one of their own. His personality and reforms made him a favorite of the "common" Texan.

9. Why was James Hogg a favorite of the "common" Texan?

____

____

____

____

____

Name ______________________ Date ______________ Class ______________

Chapter 20-1

For use with textbook pages 458–463

The Modern Era Begins

Key Terms

derrick A high tower that holds oil drilling equipment *(page 462)*

scrip Paper that takes the place of currency and can be spent only at company-run stores *(page 462)*

conservationist A person who wants to save natural resources *(page 462)*

retail Sold directly to the consumer in small quantities *(page 463)*

white-collar Jobs not requiring physical labor, professional workers such as lawyers, bankers, accountants, and business executives *(page 463)*

★ DRAWING FROM EXPERIENCE

Have you ever seen an oil derrick on land? Have you ever seen the oil platforms that are in the water? Have you seen other ways of drilling oil? Why do you think oil is so important to people?

In this section, you will learn about the discovery of oil in Texas. You will learn about the towns and cities that sprang up or grew because of oil. You will also learn about other industries and businesses that developed to meet the needs of the oil industry.

★ ORGANIZING YOUR THOUGHTS

Use the diagram below to help you take notes as you read the summaries that follow. Tell how oil helped economic growth in Texas.

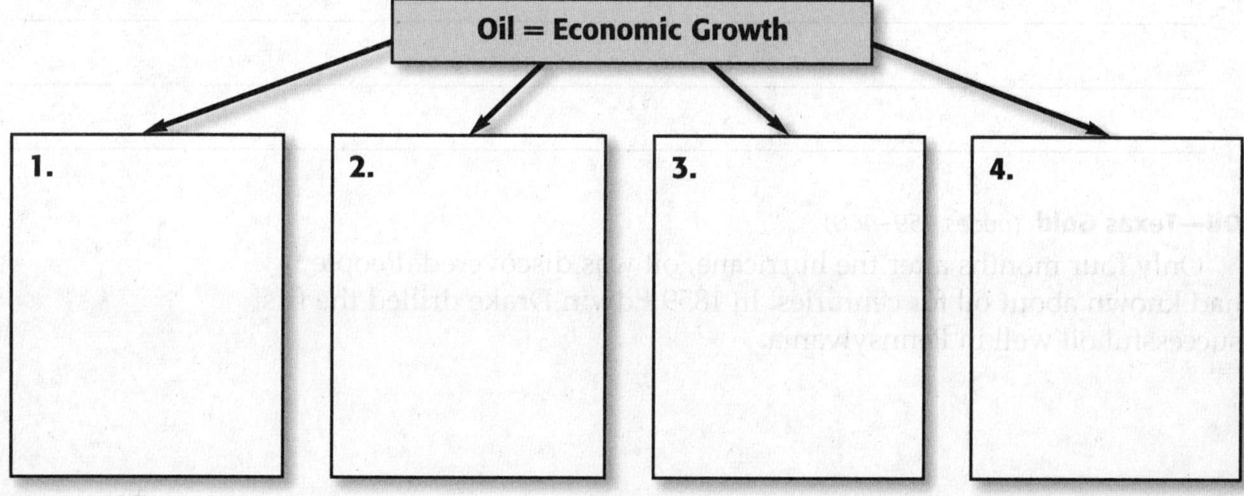

(continued)

Name ____________ Date ____________ Class ____________

Reading Essentials and Study Guide

Chapter 20-1

★ **READ TO LEARN** *Write in complete sentences to answer the following questions. Use correct spelling, punctuation, and grammar.*

Into the New Century *(page 458)*

Two events happened in Southeast Texas in 1900 and 1901. One involved water. The other involved oil.

5. What two things were involved in the events of 1900 and 1901?

____

____

____

Disaster Strikes Galveston *(page 459)*

Galveston was the most modern Texas city. It was the first city in Texas to have electric lights and telephones.

On September 8, 1900, a hurricane struck Galveston. Winds up to 120 miles per hour battered the city for 12 hours. Tidal waves completely covered the island. Half of the city was destroyed and 6,000 people died. Thousands more were left homeless. The Galveston storm took more lives than any other natural disaster in American history.

A seawall was built to protect Galveston from future hurricanes. The buildings behind the seawall had to be raised. Some were raised as much as 10 feet. Once the town was rebuilt, immigrants began to arrive again.

6. When Galveston was rebuilt, what helped protect the city and the homes there?

____

____

____

Oil—Texas Gold *(pages 459–460)*

Only four months after the hurricane, oil was discovered. People had known about oil for centuries. In 1859 Edwin Drake drilled the first successful oil well in Pennsylvania.

(continued)

Name ______________________ Date ______________ Class ______________

Reading Essentials and Study Guide **Chapter 20-1**

Lyne T. Barret drilled the first oil well in Texas near Nacogdoches in 1866. Then, other oil wells were drilled. Joseph S. Cullinan built a refinery at Corsicana to process crude oil. Cullinan pioneered using natural gas for home heating and lighting, and oil to power locomotives.

7. Who drilled the first oil well in Texas?

____

____

____

Spindletop—the First Gusher *(page 460)*

South of Beaumont, on the coastal prairie, is a hill named Spindletop. On January 10, 1901, a drill dug 1,139 feet into the ground of Spindletop. It caused mud, gas, and oil to shoot into the air as high as 100 feet. The well flowed nonstop for nine days. In its first year Spindletop produced more than four times what all the other oil wells in Texas had produced the year before. In 1902 its production was four times what it was in 1901.

Beaumont changed overnight. Oil prospectors and oil companies came. Within a few months the population increased from 9,000 to 50,000 people. Spindletop boosted the economy of Texas and other states. Oil refineries, pipelines, ocean tankers, and storage facilities were built. The success of Spindletop encouraged oil drilling in other locations.

8. Why do you think Spindletop was called a gusher?

____

____

____

Boomtowns in Southeast Texas *(page 461)*

Oil operators began drilling all around Beaumont. Many oil fields opened within the next two years. By 1904, oil was found in Humble, just north of Houston. The Humble Oil Company became what is now the Exxon-Mobil Corporation.

The early boomtowns were noisy, dirty, and crowded. Oil production moved near the Texas coast. Wells were even drilled in the waters off Galveston. The location was convenient because ships could easily go to the refinery built nearby.

(continued)

Name ______________________ Date ______________ Class ______________

9. What were the early boomtowns like?

____

____

____

____

Houston Benefits from Oil Discoveries *(pages 461–462)*

Houston became the center of the oil business because of all the oil discoveries around it. By 1900, it had many railway links. It also had the banking, insurance, transportation, and legal services the petroleum companies needed. Construction on the Houston Ship Channel began, and in 1914 it was officially opened.

10. What was built to help shipping into Houston?

____

____

____

____

Lumber Booms in East Texas *(pages 462–463)*

The oil boom created a demand for products needed by the oil industry. Lumber was needed to build **derricks,** the high towers that hold oil-drilling equipment. The lumber industry in the Piney Woods of East Texas expanded in the early 1900s. The lumber was carried by rail to market.

Workers often lived in towns built by the lumber companies. A lumber worker's life was difficult and dangerous. Many injuries could happen while cutting and sawing. In 1913 the Texas legislature created a system to pay for job-related injuries. The system is known today as workers' compensation.

Lumber workers often rented their houses from the lumber company. They were paid in scrip. The **scrip,** or paper that takes the place of currency, could be spent only at company-run stores. Many workers stayed in debt to the company store. Lumber workers tried to organize labor unions but were unsuccessful.

Lumbering caused deforestation. Since the trees were gone, some people thought the land should be turned into farmland. **Conservationists**

(continued)

thought trees should be replanted. Conservationists are people who want to save natural resources. Today, many lumber companies plant more trees than they cut.

Many leaders wanted Texas and the rest of the South to develop a variety of industries, like the North. A plow factory existed in Longview, and a steel industry was started near Rusk. Brickmakers took advantage of the excellent clay deposits in Henderson and Harrison Counties to produce high quality bricks.

11. Why were lumber workers often in debt to their companies?

____

____

____

____

____

Dallas Dominates Central Texas *(page 463)*

By 1900, Dallas was the major city of central Texas. Manufactured goods from the North came into Dallas by rail, and cotton was shipped out. Northern companies located branches in Dallas because it had good rail connections.

Dallas also became a center for banking, insurance, legal services, and retail. **Retail** stores sell directly to the consumer in small quantities. Neiman-Marcus department store was established in Dallas in 1907. Sears Roebuck, a Chicago mailorder company, chose Dallas for its southwestern distribution.

Dallas's rail connections helped make it a **white-collar** city, because its jobs did not require physical labor. Its work force included lawyers, bankers, accountants, and business executives. These community leaders supported the arts and cultural activities. Soon Dallas had a symphony orchestra, an art museum, many bookstores, and other attractions.

12. Why was Dallas an important city?

____

____

____

____

Name ______________________ Date ______________ Class ______________

Chapter 20-2

For use with textbook pages 465–468

The Progressive Movement

Key Terms

progressivism A movement involving people who worked for political and social change through the government *(page 465)*

commission A form of city government in which citizens elect officers to head departments; the mayor has little power *(page 466)*

primary election An election held by a political party before the general election to select that party's official candidate for office from a field of nominees *(page 466)*

★ DRAWING FROM EXPERIENCE

Have you ever voted in a school or club election? If so, did you keep your choice a secret? Have you ever heard an adult talk about voting for president? Have you ever seen the inside of a voting booth?

In this section, you will learn about political and social changes people worked for in Texas and in the United States. You will learn about the laws that were passed to support these changes.

★ ORGANIZING YOUR THOUGHTS

Use the diagram below to help you take notes as you read the summaries that follow. Identify and describe political and social changes of the progressive period in Texas.

Progressive Reforms

Government

1.

2.

3.

Society

4.

(continued)

Name ______________________ Date ______________ Class ______________

Reading Essentials and Study Guide

Chapter 20-2

★ **READ TO LEARN** *Write in complete sentences to answer the following questions. Use correct spelling, punctuation, and grammar.*

Galveston Reforms City Government *(pages 465–466)*

As more Texans moved to the cities, they found new problems and became more aware of existing problems. Reformers wanted to solve these problems. Their actions became known as the Progressive Movement. **Progressivism** involved people who worked for political and social change through the government.

After the storm of 1900, Galveston had the opportunity to make changes in its city government. The people of Galveston replaced their mayor and city council with a **commission** form of government. The five-member commission made the laws for the city. Each commissioner was in charge of one city department, such as fire, police, or water services. The new type of government worked so well that it became a model for government in other cities in Texas. Soon, 400 cities across the United States used the commission form of government.

5. Why do you think the five-member commission was more successful than the mayor/city council form of government?

____

____

____

____

____

____

The Terrell Election Law *(page 466)*

The Progressives believed that voting was the cornerstone of democracy. In 1903, the Texas state legislature passed the Terrell Election Law to make sure elections were held fairly. The law provided for secret balloting and limited campaigning near polling booths. It also required political parties to hold **primary elections.** A primary election is held

(continued)

Name ______________________ Date ______________ Class ______________

before the general election. It allows voters to select a political party's official candidate from a field of nominees. Although it has been amended since 1903, the Terrell Election Law is still the basic election law in Texas.

6. What did the Terrell Election Law ensure?

____

____

____

____

____

____

Votes for Women *(pages 466–468)*

Although election reforms had been made, women still could not vote. Many women organized to fight for suffrage, or the right to vote.

Some people strongly opposed woman suffrage. Some said women did not need to vote because men would protect their rights. They also said women would neglect their homes and children if they got involved in politics.

Suffragists—people who supported women's right to vote—argued that since women had some legal duties, such as paying taxes, they should be able to vote. From 1915 to 1918 suffragists wrote letters, signed petitions, and lobbied state legislatures to let women vote. Texas governor James Ferguson opposed woman suffrage. Ferguson had to resign from office for other reasons, and William P. Hobby became the new governor. He promised to sign a bill to let women vote in primary elections if they would support him in the upcoming election against Ferguson. Women in Texas got the right to vote in primary elections in 1918. They helped elect Hobby. In 1920 the Nineteenth Amendment to the U.S. Constitution gave women full voting rights.

(continued)

Name ______________________ Date ______________ Class ______________

Reading Essentials and Study Guide

Chapter 20-2

7. Why did some people think women should not vote?

____

____

____

____

____

____

Prohibition *(page 468)*

Some Texas Progressive reformers wanted to end the sale and use of alcoholic beverages. They felt that alcohol was at the center of social problems, such as gambling, selling stolen goods, and planning crimes. They also believed that men who spent their money in saloons forced their families to rely on charity.

Organizations such as the Woman's Christian Temperance Union and the Texas Anti-Saloon League worked for a law prohibiting alcoholic beverages. Certain church groups also supported the effort.

The brewing industry opposed prohibition of alcoholic beverages. Also against Prohibition were German and Italian immigrants and conservatives. Conservatives did not want a strong federal government. Texas passed a prohibition law in 1918. Ratified in 1919, the Eighteenth Amendment to the U.S. Constitution prohibited alcohol throughout the United States.

8. Why did some groups want to prohibit alcohol use?

____

____

____

____

____

____

Name ______________________ Date ______________ Class ______________

Reading Essentials and Study Guide

Chapter 20-3

For use with textbook pages 469–473

Discrimination

Key Terms

Jim Crow laws Laws discriminating against African Americans *(page 470)*

segregation Separation based on race or ethnicity *(page 470)*

lynched Put to death (as by hanging) without a legal trial *(page 470)*

poll tax A fee for voting *(page 470)*

★ DRAWING FROM EXPERIENCE

Are you a member of a minority? Have you ever been treated differently from other people because of your race or ethnic group? If you are not a member of a minority, how do you think people feel when they are discriminated against?

In this section, you will learn about discrimination against African Americans and Mexican Americans in Texas. You will also find out what these groups did to fight discrimination.

★ ORGANIZING YOUR THOUGHTS

Use the diagram below to help you take notes as you read the summaries that follow. Think of examples of discrimination faced by African Americans and Mexican Americans.

Discrimination

Public Facilities	Politics	Education	Housing
1.	2.	3.	4.

(continued)

Name _______________ Date _______________ Class _______________

Reading Essentials and Study Guide

Chapter 20-3

★ **READ TO LEARN** *Write in complete sentences to answer the following questions. Use correct spelling, punctuation, and grammar.*

African Americans Fight Discrimination *(pages 469–472)*

Reforms during the Progressive Era did not benefit African Americans. In fact, African Americans lost rights in the early twentieth century.

From Reconstruction to the 1890s, the Republican Party had strongly supported African American rights. However, the Republican Party was the minority party in the South. The Republicans had trouble building their party in the region because they supported African American rights. This led them to change their attitude toward African Americans.

The Democratic Party was more popular in the South. All across the South, Democrats had been working to pass **Jim Crow laws.** These laws discriminated against African Americans. One Jim Crow law required the segregation of public facilities. **Segregation** is separation by race or ethnic group. Under this law, hotels, restaurants, and entertainment events were closed to African Americans. African Americans had to use separate water fountains, restrooms, railway cars, and waiting rooms. Discrimination was also present in housing and schools.

Sometimes racial tensions led to violence. Riots in Brownsville and Houston resulted in the loss of life and property. African Americans accused of crimes were sometimes **lynched,** or hanged by white mobs.

African American participation in politics declined after 1900. In 1902, Texas adopted a constitutional amendment that established a **poll tax,** or a fee for voting. This meant that poorer citizens, particularly minorities, could not afford to vote. African Americans were also prohibited from running in Democratic Party primary elections.

During the first decades of the 1900s, many African Americans moved from farms to the cities. Although living in segregated neighborhoods, African Americans became active in business, education, religion, and cultural affairs. Some started their own businesses. Many businesses served the black community. African Americans such as

(continued)

Reading Essentials and Study Guide

Charles N. Love and W. E. King started newspapers. Love's paper, the *Texas Freeman,* joined with the Houston *Informer.* It is still published today. It is the oldest African American newspaper west of the Mississippi River. Both it and King's paper fought segregation and lynching.

African Americans also created organizations to work for racial equality. Chapters of the National Association for the Advancement of Colored People (NAACP) were organized in Houston, El Paso, and other places in Texas.

The church was an important African American institution. Churches worked for political equality for African Americans. They tried to find solutions to racial problems. Some churches established colleges. Black doctors, dentists, and lawyers went to other states for training. Texas universities admitted only whites.

Some African Americans moved North to escape discrimination in Texas and the rest of the South. In the early 1900s many African Americans migrated to Northern industrial cities where they found jobs.

5. What did churches do to help promote education for African Americans?

____

____

____

____

____

____

Cultures Clash in South Texas *(pages 472–473)*

South Texas also experienced dramatic changes in the early 1900s. Completion of the St. Louis, Brownsville, and Mexico Railway in 1904 brought many immigrants to the area.

(continued)

Reading Essentials and Study Guide

Two groups of immigrants moved to the Lower Rio Grande Valley. Midwestern farmers came to grow fruits, vegetables, cotton, and sugarcane. Immigrants from Mexico came to escape the Mexican Revolution of 1910–1920. People of Mexican background made up the majority of the population in South Texas. Anglo farmers often had anti-Mexican feelings. Discrimination and ethnic conflicts became common.

The problems were worse during the years of the Mexican Revolution. Bandits attacked Mexicans, Mexican Americans, and Anglos. Some of the violence was the work of Mexican revolutionaries seeking support or supplies. Some was the result of fear, hostility, distrust, and resentment between Anglo and Mexican groups. Citizens wanting revenge or protection formed vigilante groups. Texas Rangers, the state militia, and Mexican patrols all tried to protect the area. Some accused the Rangers of cruelty and the murder of innocent Mexicans. Most of the the victims of violence in the area were Mexican Americans or refugees from Mexico.

Mexican Americans experienced the same types of discrimination and segregation in Texas as African Americans. They had different neighborhoods and went to different schools from Anglos. They, too, organized to fight for better conditions. Mexican Americans joined labor unions and self-help groups. They took part in strikes.

6. Why did many Mexicans migrate to Texas in the early 1900s?

____

____

____

____

____

____

Name ______________________ Date ______________ Class ______________

Reading Essentials and Study Guide

Chapter 21-1

For use with textbook pages 478–482

International Affairs

Key Terms

recruit To enlist or join in the armed forces *(page 479)*

ration To limit or cut back on food or goods *(page 482)*

★DRAWING FROM EXPERIENCE

How far have you ever traveled from your home? Have you been outside of Texas? Have you traveled outside of the United States? What did you learn from your experiences away from home?

In this section you will learn how many Texans discovered a new world through their experiences as soldiers in World War I. You will also learn what Texans did to support the war effort.

★ORGANIZING YOUR THOUGHTS

Use the diagram below to help you take notes as you read the summaries that follow. Think about changes Texan soldiers and Texans at home experienced during World War I.

Changes			
Texas Soldiers	1.	4.	Texans at Home
	2.	5.	
	3.	6.	

(continued)

Name ______________________ Date ______________ Class ______________

Chapter 21-1

★ **READ TO LEARN** *Write in complete sentences to answer the following questions. Use correct spelling, punctuation, and grammar.*

United States Troops Enter Mexico *(pages 478–479)*

The outbreak of revolution in Mexico in 1910 soon became a concern for Texans. Pancho Villa **recruited,** or enlisted, thousands of men. Villa and his men were based at Ciudad Juárez, across the Rio Grande from El Paso. In 1916, 500 men under Pancho Villa raided Columbus, New Mexico, killing several Americans. President Woodrow Wilson ordered General John J. Pershing and 6,000 troops from San Antonio to chase Villa across northern Mexico. Pershing and his men could not capture Villa, but they did keep him from coming back into the United States.

7. What did Pancho Villa do that angered Americans?

____

____

____

____

The U.S. Enters World War I *(page 479)*

At the same time President Wilson was preparing American forces to fight in the "Great War," later known as World War I. The war had started in Europe in 1914. Great Britain, France, and Russia were fighting against Germany and Austria–Hungary. The United States tried to remain neutral. But, in 1917, German submarines sank ships carrying Americans. In addition, Germany promised to help Mexico take back Texas, Arizona, and New Mexico from the U.S. In return, Mexico was supposed to fight with Germany. The United States entered World War I in April 1917.

8. What countries were fighting against Germany and Austria–Hungary before the United States entered the war?

____

____

____

____

(continued)

Name ______________________ Date ______________ Class ______________

Reading Essentials and Study Guide

Chapter 21-1

Texas Mobilizes for War *(page 480)*

The United States was not ready for war. New soldiers needed to be trained. Texas supplied almost 200,000 soldiers for these troops. Because of its wide open spaces and rail network, Texas was a good place to train soldiers. The army established training camps at Houston, Fort Worth, Waco, and San Antonio. Kelly Field, at San Antonio became the largest flight training school in the world.

Several thousand Texan soldiers were killed during the war. About one-fourth of the Texans who served in the war were African Americans. One group of African American soldiers was stationed at Camp Logan in Texas. Trouble developed between some of these soldiers and Texas police enforcing Jim Crow laws. In 1917, a riot broke out between some African American soldiers and the Houston police, killing 17 people.

Many Mexicans and Mexican Americans fought in World War I. Mexicans living in Texas were not citizens. They were not required to serve in the army. Thousands volunteered to become soldiers. Several were honored for their bravery. They received the Distinguished Service Cross and Purple Heart.

9. Why were there problems between some African American soldiers and the police in Texas?

____

____

____

____

____

The War Changes Soldiers *(pages 480–481)*

The war brought a number of changes. Many recruited soldiers who came from the farms and ranches of Texas had never traveled outside of their home county. Joining the army meant more education and training. Going to another country opened up a whole new world for them.

African Americans were changed by the war more than any other group. Europeans generally showed less racial prejudice toward African Americans than people in the United States did. Restaurants, theaters, and other places welcomed African Americans as equals.

(continued)

10. How did the war affect African American soldiers?

____

____

____

____

Women and the War *(page 481)*

Many Texas women helped the war effort as nurses, factory workers, and farmers. Katherine Stinson of San Antonio wanted to volunteer as a pilot. When the army told her that women could not be military pilots, she and her sister helped train male pilots. Later, Katherine drove ambulances in France.

11. How did women help during the war?

____

____

____

____

At Home in Wartime *(pages 481–482)*

The Texans who stayed at home did their part to help win the war. They took part in the Liberty Loan campaigns and bought Liberty Bonds, Victory Bonds, and stamps to raise money for the war effort. They gave to the Red Cross and other caregiving organizations. Texans voluntarily **rationed,** or cut back on, food so there would be more for the soldiers in Europe.

Anti-German feelings developed during the war. Some German Texans felt pressured to join the army to show their patriotism. Others were forced to show their loyalty in other ways. Many schools stopped teaching German.

12. Why did Texans voluntarily ration food items?

____

____

____

Name ______________________ Date ______________ Class ______________

Chapter 21-2

For use with textbook pages 483–486

A Return to Peace

Key Terms

tenant farmer Farmer who rented the land but provided his own equipment *(page 484)*

sharecropper Farmer who traded labor for a share of the crop *(page 484)*

rural Having to do with the country *(page 486)*

urban Having to do with the city *(page 486)*

★ DRAWING FROM EXPERIENCE

How has your community changed over the time you have been living there? How do you think Texas has changed over the last ten years? What is your reaction to these changes?

In this section, you will read about the 1920s in Texas. You will learn about the social, economic, and political changes that took place in the years following World War I. You will also learn how Texans reacted to these changes.

★ ORGANIZING YOUR THOUGHTS

Use the diagram below to help you take notes as you read the summaries that follow. List changes that took place in Texas following World War I, use a check mark to identify each as good or bad for Texans, and explain why.

Change	Good?	Bad?	Why?
1.			
2.			
3.			

(continued)

Name ______________________ Date ______________ Class ______________

Chapter 21-2

★ **READ TO LEARN** *Write in complete sentences to answer the following questions. Use correct spelling, punctuation, and grammar.*

Wartime Prosperity *(pages 483–484)*

When soldiers came back to Texas after the war, the state was much different than when they left. Farmers and ranchers had grown rich producing things soldiers needed. Texas had cotton, wool, leather, meat, and grain. High wartime prices encouraged many farmers to buy more land and go into debt buying new machinery.

The petroleum industry expanded to meet the needs of war. Texas supplied large quantities of gasoline and lubricants, which the military needed.

4. Why had the Texas farmers done well during World War I?

____

____

____

____

____

____

Cotton Prices Fall *(pages 484–485)*

The high prices of cotton during the war did not last. After the war, prices dropped. As a result, more farmers rented their land instead of owning farms. By 1930 about 40 percent of farmers were **tenant farmers.** They rented the land, but provided their own equipment. About 20 percent were **sharecroppers.** They traded their labor for a share of the crops. Most farmers were poor, but the sharecroppers suffered the most.

When the farmers saw the price of cotton going down, they started growing more cotton. With more cotton than people needed, the price dropped even more. Tenant farmers and sharecroppers could not

(continued)

choose to grow a different crop. They had to grow what the landowners wanted. Landlords usually wanted cotton grown on the land because banks and merchants would not give credit to farmers who grew other crops.

5. What happened to the price of cotton following World War I?

____

____

____

____

____

____

The Ku Klux Klan *(pages 485–486)*

The Ku Klux Klan was started during Reconstruction by Confederate veterans. They terrorized African Americans. Their main goal was to keep African Americans from being active in politics. The Klan was a secret group. Members wore white robes and hoods and took part in rituals. The Reconstruction Klan died out in the 1870s, but a new Klan was formed in 1915. After World War I, the Klan became very active in Texas. They attacked mainly African Americans, Jews, and Catholics. They would beat, tar-and-feather, and use other forms of violence against their victims.

The Klan was active in politics. It was able to elect government officials at many levels, including state representatives, judges, and sheriffs. It controlled local governments in Dallas, Fort Worth, Beaumont, Wichita Falls, and other cities. In 1922, the Klan elected Earle Mayfield to the United States Senate.

In 1924, however, Miriam Ferguson was elected governor. She was against the Klan. The next governor, Dan Moody, was also against the Klan and put Klan members in jail for violent crimes. Moody's election was a sign that most Texans were tired of Klan violence.

(continued)

6. How did members of the Ku Klux Klan affect politics?

____

____

____

____

____

____

Texans Face Rapid Changes *(page 486)*

Soldiers returning from World War I found that Texas was changing in many ways. It was becoming an **urban,** or city, state. Most people were leaving **rural,** or country, areas and moving to towns and cities. The urban population increased by more than 50 percent. Families were getting smaller. Fewer children were working outside the home, thanks to school attendance laws. There was also better enforcement of child labor laws.

Many houses in Texas cities were wired for electricity. Texans had refrigerators, electric irons, vacuum cleaners, and washing machines. These machines changed household routines and made housework easier. Many consumer items were available on credit by mail order or in department stores in the cities.

7. How did electricity change the lives of Texan city dwellers?

____

____

____

____

____

____

Name ______________________ Date ______________ Class ______________

Chapter 21-3

For use with textbook pages 488–491

Progress in the 1920s

Key Terms

appropriated Set aside for a specific use *(page 490)*

★DRAWING FROM EXPERIENCE

What do you enjoy doing in your spare time? Do you like watching movies or listening to music on the radio? What kinds of music do you like?

In this section, you will read about changes that gave Texans more leisure time. You will learn about new technologies that created new forms of entertainment as leisure activities. You will also learn about improvements in education and transportation and other progress made in Texas in the 1920s.

★ORGANIZING YOUR THOUGHTS

Use the diagram below to help you take notes as you read the summaries that follow. Give an example of the progress made in each area of life in Texas.

Progress in . . .

Education	Women's Equality	Transportation	Leisure Activities
1.	2.	3.	4.

(continued)

Name ______________________ Date ________________ Class ________________

Reading Essentials and Study Guide

Chapter 21-3

★ **READ TO LEARN** *Write in complete sentences to answer the following questions. Use correct spelling, punctuation, and grammar.*

Blanton Fights for Better Schools *(pages 488–489)*

Education was one of the most important areas of change in Texas in the 1920s. In 1918, Annie Webb Blanton was elected superintendent of public instruction in Texas. Blanton worked hard to improve schools. Under her administration the state raised school taxes and began to give children free textbooks. Blanton worked to influence voters to give schools more money. Texas passed a constitutional amendment allowing local school districts to collect property taxes. Blanton later started an organization that worked to encourage women to become leaders in education.

5. How did Texas get the additional money needed to pay for better schools?

____

____

____

____

____

Women and Equality *(page 489)*

During the 1920s, women worked hard to be treated the same as men. More women were working in business and the professions. More married women were working outside the home.

Women became more active in politics. The election of women as governor and superintendent of public instruction were important victories. Women also won seats in the state legislature. Women were elected to other state and local offices.

Several women's groups joined together to form the Women's Joint Legislative Council. Also known as the Petticoat Lobby, this group supported the passage of laws that helped women and children. The Council was extremely successful. The entire legislative program of this organization was adopted.

(continued)

The struggle for equality, however, was only partly successful. Few women were physicians, attorneys, accountants, engineers, or ministers. Women still earned less than men for doing the same job. African American and Hispanic women were still limited to certain kinds of low-paying jobs. Women still did not have the same legal rights as men, especially with respect to selling and owning property.

6. How did women's work change during the 1920s?

____

____

____

____

____

Improvements in Transportation *(page 490)*

The "horse and buggy" era in Texas ended in the 1920s. The number of cars and trucks increased. Laws were needed to control vehicles and their drivers. City governments passed laws stating speed limits. Often the speed limits were 5 or 10 miles an hour. Police officers were hired to make sure drivers followed the new laws. Better roads were needed. Each county built its own roads. The quality of roads varied from place to place. The U.S. Congress **appropriated,** or set aside, money to build new highways. The Texas Highway Department was created. Texas used federal money to build new and better roads. Texas highways are among the best in the United States.

7. Why were more police officers needed during the 1920s?

____

____

____

____

____

(continued)

Name ______________________ Date ______________ Class ______________

Reading Essentials and Study Guide

Chapter 21-3

Texans Enjoy Leisure Activities *(pages 490–491)*

Texas was changing from a rural, agricultural state to an urban, diversified state. In an urban state, more people live in cities and towns than on ranches and farms. This shift led to an increase in the amount of time people spent on recreation and leisure. New technologies, such as motion pictures and radio, provided entertainment.

Radio stations started all over Texas. They broadcast many kinds of programs. There were news shows, sporting events, and political speeches. Many radio stations often had live music. Many musicians who later became famous started their careers with Texas radio stations.

Texas music reflected its diverse population. African American jazz was popular. Cowboy songs found a wide audience. Several recording companies set up studios in Texas. These companies included Columbia and RCA. They helped Mexican American musicians become stars in Texas and throughout the United States and Mexico in the late 1920s and 1930s.

The motion picture industry in Texas grew. Movies were often made in the San Antonio area.

Sports, including hunting and fishing, were very popular in the 1920s. A new sport, football, became an important part of Texas recreation during this period. Huge crowds went to high school football games. University football teams were also very popular.

8. What does it mean to say that Texas was becoming an urban state?

____

____

____

____

____

Name ______________________ Date ______________ Class ______________

Chapter 22-1

For use with textbook pages 498–502

Depression Hits Texas

Key Terms

stock Shares of ownership in a company *(page 498)*

unemployment Loss of jobs *(page 499)*

wildcatter A person who drills for oil in an area not known to contain oil *(page 499)*

law of supply and demand An economic principle that expresses the relationship between the supply of a product and its price *(page 500)*

martial law Law and order enforced by government military forces in an emergency *(page 500)*

economies of scale The cost of the operation decreases as the size of the operation increases *(page 501)*

Dust Bowl The area, including the Texas Panhandle, hardest hit by the drought in the 1930s, during which the soil was so dry it blew away in clouds of dust *(page 502)*

★DRAWING FROM EXPERIENCE

Have you ever known anyone who lost a job because a factory closed or a business shut down? Have you ever known someone who wanted a job but could not find one?

In this section, you will learn about the Great Depression and how it affected Texans. You will also learn how Texans and the government struggled to resolve the problems caused by the Great Depression.

★ORGANIZING YOUR THOUGHTS

Use the diagram below to help you take notes as you read the summaries that follow. Identify products and crops whose surplus caused a drop in prices in the 1930s.

Surplus Products
1.
2.
3.

(continued)

Name ______________________ Date ______________ Class ______________

Chapter 22-1

★ **READ TO LEARN** *Write in complete sentences to answer the following questions. Use correct spelling, punctuation, and grammar.*

The Great Depression Begins *(pages 498–499)*

Seven months after Herbert Hoover became president, Wall Street stock market prices fell. **Stock** is shares of ownership in companies. During the 1920s, people hoped to make quick money in the stock market. This drove up the price of the stock of many companies. Some people had borrowed money to buy stock. Often they paid only a small part of what they owed. When stock prices fell, they and the banks that had loaned the money were wiped out.

Many factories closed, causing **unemployment,** or loss of jobs. Unemployed people could not buy products, so even more factories closed. People could not afford new houses. As a result, East Texas timber workers were laid off from their jobs.

President Hoover misjudged the seriousness of the Great Depression, as the economic crisis came to be called. He asked churches and charities to increase help to the poor. He asked people to hire their unemployed neighbors to do odd jobs around the house.

4. What solutions did President Hoover offer to relieve the problems of the Great Depression?

____

____

____

____

Too Much Oil *(pages 499–500)*

In October 1930, Columbus Marion "Dad" Joiner drilled the first well, named the Daisy Bradford No. 3, of the East Texas Field. He was a **wildcatter,** a person who drills an oil well in an area not known to contain oil. The East Texas Field was the biggest oil field discovered in the United States at that time. Many small towns boomed as thousands of people came to East Texas.

Drilling on the new field created high-paying jobs for farmers and timber workers. Sawmills reopened to provide wood for houses and derricks. Automobile dealerships, pharmacies, and clothing stores all profited from the East Texas oil field boom. The Great Depression seemed far away.

(continued)

Name ______________________ Date ______________ Class ______________

Reading Essentials and Study Guide

Soon the East Texas Field was producing more oil than all the other fields in the rest of the state combined. As the **law of supply and demand** predicted, prices went down as supply increased and demand stayed the same. In the early 1930s, the price of a barrel of oil fell.

However, producers kept drilling, fearing that if they waited for prices to go up, someone drilling somewhere else would get the oil. In April 1931, the Texas Railroad Commission ordered drillers in the East Texas Field to limit production. Independent drillers believed this order favored large oil companies. There was widespread cheating.

Governor Sterling declared **martial law,** government military forces in an emergency, to enforce the order. He sent the National Guard to the East Texas Field. Eventually martial law ended, but overproduction continued. In 1935, state and federal laws successfully controlled production, and oil prices became more stable.

5. Why did the large production of oil in East Texas cause oil prices to drop?

____

____

____

Crisis for Cotton Farmers *(pages 500–501)*

The Great Depression forced cotton prices to decline. As with petroleum, production needed to be limited.

The Texas Department of Agriculture asked farmers to reduce cotton production. Louisiana Governor Huey Long pushed a law through the legislature stopping the planting of cotton in Louisiana. The law, known as "drop-a-crop," required that other cotton-growing states stop production for the law to go into effect.

Texas was the largest cotton-producing state, and did not agree to stop production. Eventually a law calling for partial reduction was passed. A state court declared it unconstitutional, and the whole plan collapsed.

6. Why did the law requiring a partial limit to cotton production fail?

____

____

____

(continued)

Name ______________________ Date ______________ Class ______________

Reading Essentials and Study Guide

Chapter 22-1

Dust Storms Blanket the High Plains *(pages 501–502)*

Wheat prices were high after World War I, and farmers bought tractors and expanded their production. As prices declined during the 1920s, farmers planted more crops to make more money. The Plains seemed perfect for the **economies of scale,** a reduction in unit costs, that came with farming with machines. As with oil and cotton, overproduction drove wheat prices down.

The decline in the price of wheat was only one problem for High Plains farmers. When farmers plowed grasses under, there was nothing left to hold the soil when strong winds blew. There was a severe drought in the 1930s. The soil blew away. The area became known as the **Dust Bowl.** Motorists in cities in the Plains often could not see 20 feet down the street. People became ill from lung diseases. Many families lost their farms because of the difficult economic times.

7. What caused the Dust Bowl?

____

____

____

Texans Look for Answers *(page 502)*

At first, Texans and other Americans turned to each other for answers. As banks failed, some merchant associations printed coupons that could be used as money. Universities that could not pay salaries allowed their professors and families to eat in their dining halls. Many churches paid their preachers with eggs, chickens, and vegetables.

Mexican Americans and African Americans in Texas were hit hard by the Great Depression. Between 1929 and 1931, many Mexicans and Mexican Americans moved to Mexico. The number of unemployed African Americans was twice that of the rest of the population.

8. How did the people of Texas and the United States try to solve the economic problems of the Great Depression?

____

____

____

Name ______________________ Date ______________ Class ______________

Chapter 22-2

For use with textbook pages 504–507

Texas and the New Deal

Key Terms

alphabet agencies Government organizations known by their initials *(page 505)*

mural A picture painted on a wall or ceiling *(page 506)*

cooperatives Organized groups that borrowed money from the government to pay for stringing electrical wires *(page 506)*

contour plowing Plowing around hills, rather than straight up and down, to conserve water *(page 507)*

★ DRAWING FROM EXPERIENCE

Have you ever been to a state park, like Garner, Bastrop, or Palo Duro? Have you ever seen the Hall of State in Dallas or the museum at the Alamo in San Antonio?

The last section discussed the causes of the Great Depression and how Texans dealt with the problems of unemployment and drought. In this section, you will learn about President Roosevelt's solution to the Great Depression and how it affected Texans. You will discover that Roosevelt's plan, called the New Deal, included many programs. As you will learn, some put Texans back to work in new ways, such as creating state parks and building museums.

★ ORGANIZING YOUR THOUGHTS

Use the diagram below to help you take notes as you read the summaries that follow. Think about how each measure helped Texan farmers.

The New Deal for Farmers	
Cooperatives	1.
Laws passed by Congress	2.
Dams	3.
Contour plowing	4.

(continued)

Name ______________________ Date ______________ Class ______________

Chapter 22-2

★ **READ TO LEARN** *Write in complete sentences to answer the following questions. Use correct spelling, punctuation, and grammar.*

The New Deal Begins *(pages 504–505)*

President Hoover did not win reelection in 1932. Voters blamed him for the Great Depression. Franklin D. Roosevelt was elected. Texans gave almost 90 percent of their votes to Roosevelt. He had promised "a new deal for the American people." His programs became part of what was called the New Deal.

President Roosevelt was very active during "the first hundred days." He ordered all banks to close. Examiners decided which ones were strong enough to stay in business. He also asked Congress to pass laws to help solve the financial problems.

Vice President John N. Garner had been a Texas congressman. He helped push New Deal programs in Congress. Texans had some of the most powerful positions in Congress. President Roosevelt needed their cooperation.

5. What was the first thing President Roosevelt ordered?

____

____

____

____

New Deal Programs in Texas *(pages 505–506)*

The New Deal increased the government's involvement in people's lives. Before the 1930s, the government's main economic activities were collecting taxes, minting a money supply, and setting up courts to decide financial disputes. The New Deal created agencies to deal with problems of the Depression. The new organizations were known as **alphabet agencies** because people called them by their initials.

Some agencies such as the Federal Emergency Relief Administration (FERA) gave money to unemployed people. Other agencies tried to solve the unemployment problem. They hired people for various projects. The Civilian Conservation Corps (CCC) employed young men and helped preserve the nation's resources. Nearly 50,000 Texans took part in the CCC. They lived in camps. They planted trees, built erosion control structures, and completed other similar projects. They were paid $30 per month. They developed many state parks, including Garner, Bastrop, and Palo Duro.

(continued)

Reading Essentials and Study Guide **Chapter 22-2**

The National Youth Administration (NYA) hired high school and college students. They performed clerical and maintenance jobs. The students often worked at schools and playgrounds. They also helped build roadside parks and spread gravel on highway shoulders. Lyndon Johnson was head of the NYA in Texas. He later became president of the United States. Many of Johnson's programs as president in the 1960s reminded people of the New Deal.

The Public Works Administration (PWA) built bridges, dams, schools, and other structures of permanent value to the state. In Fort Worth, the PWA built 13 schools and expanded 13 more. The Works Progress Administration (WPA) hired 600,000 Texans. They built swimming pools, recreation centers, stadiums, and parks. New Deal programs also involved the arts. The WPA hired artists to paint **murals** in post offices. Murals are paintings on walls or ceilings. Theater and musical groups were hired to entertain in Texas cities. Historians were hired to write community histories.

6. How did the alphabet agencies help solve the unemployment problem?

____

____

____

____

Rural Texans and the New Deal *(pages 506–507)*

Almost 60 percent of Texans lived in rural areas in 1930. The New Deal created programs for farmers, ranchers, and other rural residents. At that time, city residents enjoyed electric lights and appliances. However, farmers still relied on kerosene lamps and hand-powered machines. The New Deal helped rural people form **cooperatives.** Cooperatives were groups that borrowed money from the government to pay for stringing electrical wires. Electricity made house and farm work easier. Electric water pumps brought water into homes. Electricity allowed farm families to listen to the latest news broadcasts and radio programs.

Congress passed laws to help farmers. Farmers were paid to reduce production by plowing under their crops. They cut down peach trees and poured excess milk into streams. The government encouraged this in order to drive up prices.

(continued)

Name ____________ Date ____________ Class ____________

Reading Essentials and Study Guide

Chapter 22-2

Dams were constructed on the Colorado River to provide electricity. They also provided flood control and water for rice farmers. The lakes behind the dams were used for recreation.

New Deal programs tried to slow soil erosion. Farmers in the Dust Bowl planted strips of wheat and grain sorghum. The sorghum was taller and protected the topsoil from being blown away. Farmers also plowed at angles to the wind so ridges would collect the blowing soil. The federal government paid farmers to plant trees as windbreaks.

The federal government encouraged Texas farmers to fill up gullies in the cotton fields with brush. This would slow the water as it ran downhill. Farmers used **contour plowing,** plowing around the hills, rather than straight up and down plowing. This conserved water. Farmers were paid to plant crops that would enhance the soil.

7. Why were farmers paid to reduce production and destroy any surplus?

____

____

____

____

Texas Centennial *(page 507)*

Texas celebrated its 100th anniversary of independence in 1936. Some of the construction projects during the Great Depression celebrated this event. Dallas was chosen to host the celebration. The main celebration was held at the 185-acre Fair Park. The Hall of State and Hall of Negro Life were built. Exhibits highlighted Texas history. They also showed examples of Texas products and culture. The San Jacinto Monument was built on the battlefield to the east of Houston. Museums were built at the Alamo grounds in San Antonio; at the University of Texas; and at Canyon, Huntsville, Goliad, and Gonzales.

8. How did the New Deal contribute to the Texas Centennial?

____

____

____

____

Name ______________________ Date ______________ Class ______________

Chapter 22-3

For use with textbook pages 508–511

Politics in the 1930s

Key Terms

pardon Excuse from punishment *(page 509)*

strike A refusal to work *(page 511)*

arbitration The process of allowing an impartial observer to solve a dispute *(page 511)*

★ DRAWING FROM EXPERIENCE

How diverse is your school? What ethnic groups are represented in your school?

The last section discussed the New Deal and the relief it gave to many Texans suffering during the Depression. In this section, you will learn more about politics in Texas in the 1930s. You will also read about the continuing struggle of African Americans and Mexican Americans in Texas.

★ ORGANIZING YOUR THOUGHTS

Use the diagram below to help you take notes as you read the summaries that follow. Identify the cases, organizations, or events that helped African Americans and Mexican Americans to further their causes in the 1930s.

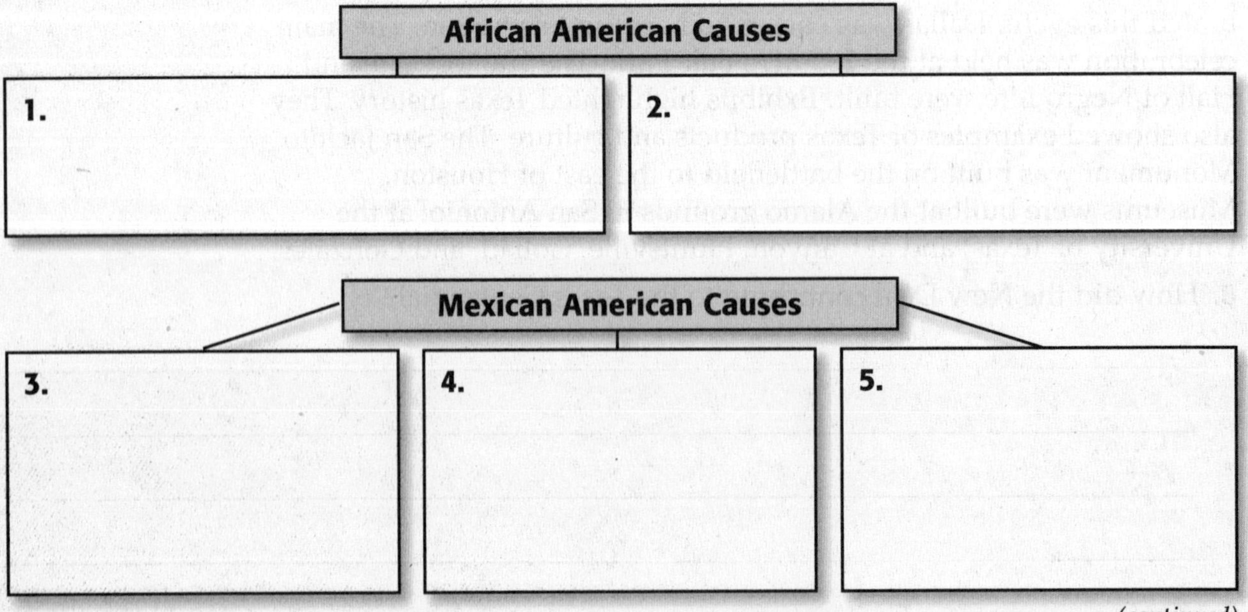

(continued)

Name ______________________ Date ______________ Class ______________

Chapter 22-3

★ **READ TO LEARN** *Write in complete sentences to answer the following questions. Use correct spelling, punctuation, and grammar.*

1930s Governors *(pages 508–509)*

Ross Sterling ran for reelection as governor in 1932. He ran against Miriam Ferguson. Ferguson had already served a term as governor. Ferguson won by fewer than 3,800 votes.

Ferguson asked President Roosevelt to lend farmers money for lost income on cotton. She amended the state constitution to allow $20 million in bread bonds to feed the poor. She proposed a tax on oil. Her administration was also affected by controversy. She fired several experienced Texas Rangers. She used her **pardon** power to release many criminals from prison. The governor and the legislature had trouble meeting the needs of the state. There was not enough money available.

James Allred became governor in 1935. He reorganized the Texas Rangers. They became part of the Department of Public Safety. They were known for their ability to solve hard cases. Allred created the Board of Pardons and Paroles. This was a system to control the release of prisoners. He also created retirement systems for teachers and state employees.

In 1938, W. Lee O'Daniel was elected governor. He had never been involved in politics. He promised to raise pensions, get rid of capital punishment, and veto any sales tax. His theme song "Beautiful, Beautiful Texas," became an unofficial state song. However, once he was in office, he could not keep his campaign promises.

6. What were two important accomplishments of Governor James Allred?

____

____

____

____

African American Voting Rights *(pages 509–510)*

Despite the poll tax and other actions to keep African Americans from voting, some African Americans continued to vote. In 1923, the legislature passed a law that only whites could vote in the Democratic Party's primary election. Since Texas was mostly Democratic, victory in

(continued)

Name ______________________ Date ______________________ Class ______________________

Reading Essentials and Study Guide

Chapter 22-3

the primary meant victory in the election. Dr. Lawrence Nixon was an African American physician and a member of the NAACP. He was turned away from voting in the primary. He then sued. He won *Nixon v. Herndon* in the U.S. Supreme Court. The justices said that his rights under the Fourteenth and Fifteenth Amendments had been violated.

The state continued to exclude African Americans from voting. The Democratic Party then drew up unfair rules. Dr. Nixon sued again and won the case of *Nixon* v. *Condon*. The fight for African Americans' right to vote did not end. The struggle for civil rights would continue until the 1950s and 1960s.

7. What two actions did the state legislature take to try to prevent African Americans from voting?

____

____

____

Mexican Americans Fight for Their Rights *(page 510)*

The League of United Latin American Citizens, or LULAC, was founded at Corpus Christi in 1929. Ben Garza was its first president. LULAC worked for Mexican American rights in the court system, in hiring, and in education.

Mexican American children had to attend segregated schools in Del Rio. In 1930, Jesús Salvatierra sued the schools. He was supported by LULAC. He lost his case, but LULAC had shown that it was a strong voice for Mexican Americans.

Education was also important to other groups. The School Improvement League was founded in 1934 in San Antonio. Eleuterio Escobar, Jr., and María L. de Hernández were the founders. They were upset about the poor schools for Mexican American children. The schools were too crowded and poorly maintained. The School Improvement League put on a rally attended by 10,000 people. The League also prepared documents that proved Mexican American students had been treated unequally.

8. What problems did the School Improvement League try to solve?

____

____

____

(continued)

The Pecan Shellers' Strike *(pages 510–511)*

San Antonio was also a place where people organized for better working conditions. More than 10,000 people, mostly Mexican Americans, worked in San Antonio picking the nut meats out of pecans. Working conditions were terrible. Pecan shellers worked in crowded, dirty rooms. They breathed pecan dust all day. In 1938, their wages were cut. Emma Tenayuca Brooks helped lead more than 10,000 workers on a **strike,** a refusal to work. The strike lasted three months. Police arrested more than 700 strikers. Finally, both sides agreed to **arbitration,** a process that allows an impartial observer to solve a dispute. The workers went back to work for higher pay.

9. Why did the pecan shellers strike?

____

____

____

____

Miners and Farmers *(page 511)*

Farmers and miners also saw their working conditions worsen during the Great Depression. Many New Deal farm programs paid farmers not to grow crops. However, payment went to the landowners. Many Texas farmers were tenants who did not own the land. Payments to the landowners meant eviction for the tenants because their work was no longer necessary. Coal miners also suffered. The productivity of the East Texas Field and low prices for petroleum caused demand for coal to decrease. Coal mines closed, and miners were laid off.

10. How were farmers hurt by some of the New Deal programs?

____

____

____

____

Name ______________________ Date ______________ Class ______________

Chapter 23-1

For use with textbook pages 516–519

Texans Support the War

Key Terms

dictator An absolute ruler *(page 516)*

Axis Powers The countries of Germany, Italy, and Japan, whose leaders believed the world would revolve around them *(page 517)*

neutral Not taking sides in a conflict *(page 517)*

Allies The countries of England, China, France, Russia, and later the United States, which joined together to fight the Axis Powers in World War II *(page 517)*

Lend-Lease Act A program in which the United States made military equipment available to the Allies *(page 517)*

★ DRAWING FROM EXPERIENCE

What reasons might a country have for going to war? Do you know anyone who is in the armed forces? Why do you think someone would join the armed forces?

In this section, you will learn how World War II started and why the United States entered the war. You will also learn about the role Texas and Texans played in the war.

★ ORGANIZING YOUR THOUGHTS

Use the diagram below to help you take notes as you read the summaries that follow. Identify Texans who contributed to the war effort.

Texans Support the War	
Who?	**How?**
1.	
2.	
3.	
4.	
5.	
6.	

(continued)

Name ______________________ Date ______________ Class ______________

Reading Essentials and Study Guide

Chapter 23-1

★ **READ TO LEARN** *Write in complete sentences to answer the following questions. Use correct spelling, punctuation, and grammar.*

Dictators Come to Power *(pages 516–517)*

The Great Depression affected nations all over the world. In some countries, **dictators,** or absolute rulers, came to power. Military leaders in Germany, Italy, and Japan took control. They began wars of expansion. Germany, Italy, and Japan signed a treaty and promised not to attack each other. They were called the **Axis Powers** because they thought the world would revolve around them.

In 1939, Germany invaded Poland. The democratic countries of England and France were forced into action. World War II had begun. It did not take long for Germany to conquer Belgium, Denmark, France, Holland, and Norway.

Although the United States was officially **neutral,** or not taking sides, it supported the **Allies.** The Allies were the nations at war with the Axis Powers. The Allies were England, China, France, and Russia. Americans debated whether the United States should become involved in the war. Meanwhile President Roosevelt made military equipment available to the Allies through the **Lend-Lease Act.** The debate about entering the war ended when Japan bombed Pearl Harbor, Hawaii, on December 7, 1941. The United States was officially at war.

7. What made the United States enter World War II?

____

____

____

____

____

Texans Respond *(pages 517–518)*

Texans were involved in the war from the beginning. Doris "Dorie" Miller, an African American from Waco, Texas, was a sailor on the U.S.S. *West Virginia* during the attack on Pearl Harbor. He fired at the Japanese airplanes. Miller was awarded the Navy Cross by Admiral Chester Nimitz of Fredericksburg, Texas.

(continued)

Name _______________ Date _______________ Class _______________

Reading Essentials and Study Guide

Chapter 23-1

Texans of all ethnic groups and regions enlisted in the armed forces. Texas had the highest percentage of its population of all the states in the nation enlist. About 750,000 Texans served.

Texans served in every branch of the armed forces. Many climbed to very high ranks. Admiral Nimitz was one of 12 admirals from Texas. William Simpson, Ira Eaker, and Lucian Truscott were 3 of 155 Texans who were generals. Dwight Eisenhower was commander of the Allied forces in Europe.

Many Texans in the military were decorated with medals for their bravery. They included Audie Murphy and from Dallas Samuel D. Dealey. Murphy received more medals than any other American. He was "the most decorated soldier" in U.S. history. Dealey was "the most decorated man" in the U.S. Navy. Hispanic Marcario García was one of 34 Texans to receive the Medal of Honor awarded by Congress.

Texan service personnel included 12,000 women. Many rose to high ranks. Colonel Oveta Culp Hobby of Houston was commander of the Women's Army Corps (WAC). She wrote policies, designed uniforms, and recruited women all over the country. Women's Airforce Service Pilots (WASPs) trained at Avenger Field at Sweetwater.

8. Who was the commander of the Allied forces in Europe?

____

____

____

____

____

The Armed Forces Train in Texas *(page 519)*

Because of its climate, location between the two coasts, and open spaces, Texas was a good place for military bases. More than 100 bases were built or enlarged. Soldiers, sailors, and airmen from all over the United States came to Texas to train. The Midland Army Air Field was the largest bombardier training base in the world. Though far from the sea, Dallas was a site for training naval pilots.

(continued)

9. Why was Texas a good place for military bases?

______

______

______

______

______

Prisoner of War Camps *(page 519)*

More than 20 camps in Texas housed thousands of German, Italian, and Japanese prisoners. Most were soldiers captured in battle, but many were civilians. The captured soldiers often were put to work on farms near the camps. They did agricultural work picking cotton and harvesting rice. Prisoners were treated well, and only a few tried to escape. When the war ended, almost all of the prisoners were returned to their native countries. Those who died of wounds or natural causes are buried in the Fort Sam Houston National Cemetery.

10. Why did only a few captured soldiers try to escape from Texas Prisoner of War camps?

______

______

______

______

______

Name ______________________ Date ______________ Class ______________

Chapter 23-2

For use with textbook pages 521–524

The Home Front

Key Terms

ration board A group of people (during wartime) who determine how goods should be distributed to the public after military needs are met *(page 522)*

smelter A place where metal is melted and separated *(page 522)*

concentration camp A place where Jews and other innocent people were imprisoned and killed during World War II to advance the Nazi government's idea of racial superiority *(page 524)*

Holocaust The name given to the mass murder of millions of Jews and other innocent people in Nazi Germany during World War II *(page 524)*

★DRAWING FROM EXPERIENCE

Have you ever recycled paper, metal, or glass? Do you know how these recycled goods are used? Why might recycling be important during wartime?

In this section, you will learn how the war led to the development of new industries and products. You will also learn about the contributions and sacrifices Texans at home made to help the war effort.

★ORGANIZING YOUR THOUGHTS

Use the diagram below to help you take notes as you read the summaries that follow. Think about how each event or development during the war affected Texans on the home front.

Event or Development	Effect on Texans
Scientists develop a way to make synthetic rubber.	1.
Workers are needed in factories.	2.
FEPC is created.	3.
Food is rationed.	4.
Millions of Jews and other innocent people are killed in concentration camps in Germany.	5.

(continued)

Name ______________________ Date ______________ Class ______________

Chapter 23-2

★**READ TO LEARN** *Write in complete sentences to answer the following questions. Use correct spelling, punctuation, and grammar.*

Industrial Production *(pages 521–522)*

The war effort required large amounts of oil. War planners expected Texas to supply 80 percent of this oil.

Besides oil, Texas had natural gas, timber, water, and sulphur. Wartime industrial expansion created boomtowns similar to those of the oil boom. When Texans registered with their county **ration boards** in 1943, it was obvious that the Texas population had changed dramatically since 1940.

The military needed airplanes and ships most of all. Aircraft factories were located in the Dallas-Fort Worth area. Shipyards were built along the coast at Houston and other locations. They employed tens of thousands of workers.

Steel was produced at Daingerfield and Houston. The coastal region between the Brazos and Sabine Rivers became one of the most heavily industrialized areas of the world. Texas produced large amounts of gasoline, aviation fuel, and petrochemicals.

6. What were the two most important needs of the military?

____

____

____

New Methods of Production *(pages 522–523)*

Wartime needs encouraged the development of new products and better methods of production. The Japanese had cut off the supply of rubber. Scientists discovered a way to make synthetic rubber from petroleum. Plants for manufacturing rubber were built in Texas.

Before 1941, there was no tin **smelter,** or place for producing tin, in the entire United States. After the Japanese conquered Southeast Asia, the United States had no supply of tin. The problem was solved by building the world's largest tin smelter in Texas City.

It was dangerous to ship gasoline and aviation fuel by tanker from refineries to the East Coast ports. German submarines were known to attack tankers in the Gulf of Mexico. Engineers planned and constructed underground pipelines for carrying fuel.

(continued)

Name ______________________ Date ______________ Class ______________

Reading Essentials and Study Guide

Chapter 23-2

7. How did engineers solve the problem of transporting fuel during the war?

____

____

____

____

Home Front Workers *(page 523)*

Wartime construction required many workers. Between 1940 and 1943 at least 450,000 rural Texans moved to cities to work in factories. They earned high wages there and worked many hours per week.

There were new opportunities for women, African Americans, and Mexican Americans. War, however, did not end discrimination and prejudice. Many African Americans found work in refineries and construction that had been closed to them before the war. However, they earned lower wages and were not promoted. Restaurants and hotels still denied service to African American soldiers and sailors as well as Mexican Americans. The federal government created the Fair Employment Practices Committee to reduce discrimination.

8. What kind of discrimination did minorities experience at work during the war?

____

____

____

____

Lives Touched by War *(pages 523–524)*

Texans at home had to make sacrifices, too. Sugar, meat, gasoline, and tires were rationed, or distributed, according to each item's value to the war effort and a family's needs. Texans added to their food supplies by planting "victory gardens." They also helped the war effort by collecting scrap iron for use in manufacturing. They contributed to the Red Cross and other agencies that served people in the armed forces. Cities conducted blackouts at night to protect against possible enemy air attacks.

(continued)

War brought death and hardship, but it also brought jobs and rising production. Farmers plowed more land, planted more acreage, and harvested more crops. More factories were built to supply the military. Because many Americans were in the armed forces, there was a great demand for workers. Many new Mexican immigrants came to Texas to work in agriculture and industry. In the early 1940s, 12 percent of Texas's total population was of Mexican ancestry.

9. Why do you think food had to be rationed?

____

____

____

____

____

An Allied Victory *(page 524)*

The war came to an end in 1945 with an Allied victory. When the Allies entered Germany, they discovered that millions of Jews and other innocent civilians had been killed in **concentration camps.** The Nazi government set up the camps to carry out their idea of a superior race. The Nazi destruction of millions of Jews and other people is known as the **Holocaust.** Many Texas Jews lost relatives during this time.

10. What did Allied troops discover when they entered Germany at the end of the war?

____

____

____

____

____

Name ________________ Date ________________ Class ________________

Reading Essentials and Study Guide

Chapter 23-3

For use with textbook pages 526–529

After the War

Key Terms

consumer goods Products such as refrigerators and cars used by the general public *(page 527)*

mechanized Equipped with machinery *(page 527)*

civil rights Rights guaranteed by the U.S. Constitution *(page 527)*

GI Bill of Rights A law passed by the U.S. Congress in 1944 that helped veterans pay for a college education *(page 528)*

baby boom A sudden large increase in the number of babies born *(page 528)*

army of occupation Foreign troops that remain in a conquered nation to ensure an orderly change to peacetime *(page 529)*

Communist A person who believes in communism, an economic system in which property and goods are owned by the government and are to be shared in equal portions by all the people *(page 529)*

Cold War A time of smaller, localized hostilities between the United States and the Soviet Union *(page 529)*

★DRAWING FROM EXPERIENCE

Have you ever heard the term "baby boomer"? Do you know someone who is a baby boomer? When was he or she born?

In this section, you will learn about the years following World War II. You will learn about the changes that took place in Texas in the workplace, civil rights, education, and population.

★ORGANIZING YOUR THOUGHTS

Use the diagram below to help you take notes as you read the summaries that follow. Identify the cause of each event following World War II.

Cause	Effect
1.	Some wartime factories start to produce consumer goods.
2.	Fewer farm workers are needed.
3.	Mexican American veterans form the American GI Forum.
4.	The nation experiences a baby boom.

(continued)

★ **READ TO LEARN** *Write in complete sentences to answer the following questions. Use correct spelling, punctuation, and grammar.*

Demobilization *(pages 526–527)*

After the war, the United States began to shift from a wartime economy to a peacetime economy. Many wartime factories that produced gasoline, rubber, and metals remained open because these products were still needed. Other factories, such as those producing airplanes and ships, either closed or began producing **consumer goods.** Consumer goods are products such as refrigerators and automobiles that the general public uses.

Women working in factories were forced out of their jobs so returning servicemen could have them. Few tenant farmers who had left for war or factory work returned to the farm. Texas agriculture had become more **mechanized,** equipped with machines, and needed fewer farm workers.

5. How were many factories able to stay open after the war?

____

____

____

____

____

New Attitudes *(pages 527–528)*

World War II made many African Americans and Mexican Americans think about the discrimination they experienced. They realized that although they fought and died for democracy, they were denied many of their **civil rights** at home. These are rights guaranteed by the U.S. Constitution.

Many Mexican American veterans joined LULAC to work to end discrimination. Others, under the leadership of Hector P. García, formed the American GI Forum of Texas to fight for equal treatment. The National Association for the Advancement of Colored People (NAACP) became more active during the war. In the late 1940s and the early 1950s the NAACP was successful in several U.S. Supreme Court cases that guaranteed various constitutional rights to African Americans. More African Americans in Texas became members of the NAACP.

(continued)

Name ______________________ Date ______________ Class ______________

6. How did the war make African Americans and Mexican Americans more aware of how unfairly they were treated?

____

____

____

____

____

GIs Return to Civilian Life *(page 528)*

Various economic problems developed after the war. Factories were closing down just when returning servicemen needed jobs. People had money for extras, but there was a shortage of consumer goods. Labor unions had promised not to strike during the war. Now they wanted to solve problems that had been ignored.

In 1944, the U.S. Congress passed a law known as the **GI Bill of Rights.** This law helped returning servicemen in many ways. One provision of the law paid veterans to attend college. The education they received helped the United States enjoy economic prosperity for many years after the war.

7. How did the GI Bill of Rights contribute to economic prosperity in the United States?

____

____

____

____

____

Population Increases *(page 528)*

With the increase in the number of students, Texas universities had to provide more classrooms, libraries, and laboratories. There was also a need for housing for married students. The number of marriages had declined during the Great Depression and part of World War II. After

(continued)

the war, many people were eager to get married and start families. The increase in marriages led to a **baby boom,** or a sudden large increase in the number of babies born. People born in this period are often called baby boomers.

8. Why do you think the number of marriages declined during the Great Depression and part of World War II?

____

____

____

____

____

Foreign Affairs *(page 529)*

The United States did not bring all of its troops home after the war. **Armies of occupation,** foreign troops that stay in a conquered nation, stayed in Germany and Japan. They made sure there was an orderly change to peacetime in those countries. New threats also emerged. The Soviet Union, an ally of the United States during the war, set up **Communist** dictatorships in several Eastern European countries and in northern Korea. The United States was determined to stop the spread of communism, an economic system in which the government owns property and goods. A new kind of conflict, called the **Cold War,** developed. The Cold War was a time of smaller, local conflict between the United States and the Soviet Union. In 1950, the Cold War heated up. When North Korean soldiers invaded South Korea, the United States found itself at war again.

9. Why did U.S. troops stay in Germany and Japan after World War II?

____

____

____

____

____

Name ______________________ Date ______________ Class ______________

Reading Essentials and Study Guide

Chapter 24-1

For use with textbook pages 540–547

Politics and New Problems

Key Terms

liberal A person who believes the government should help ensure equal rights and opportunities for minorities *(page 541)*

conservative A person who believes that government assistance weakens the ability of people to do things for themselves *(page 541)*

moderate A person who is neither conservative nor liberal *(page 541)*

sovereignty The right to rule *(page 542)*

redistricting The process of changing, or redrawing, legislative district lines to reflect changes in population *(page 543)*

unconstitutional Not legal *(page 544)*

McCarthyism The act of making unfounded, sensational charges against a person *(page 547)*

libel The act of printing statements known to be false and intentionally spreading them to do damage *(page 547)*

★ DRAWING FROM EXPERIENCE

What are civil rights? What do you know about the civil rights movement? Are there groups in Texas or the United States as a whole for whom civil rights are an issue today? What are these groups? What are their concerns?

In this section, you will learn about many political issues Texans faced after the war. You will learn how developments in civil rights made Texans think about the issues of freedom and democracy.

★ ORGANIZING YOUR THOUGHTS

Use the diagram below to help you take notes as you read the summaries that follow. Identify the different groups within the Texas Democratic Party and describe each.

Texas Democratic Party	
1.	4.
2.	5.
3.	6.

(continued)

Name ______________________ Date ______________ Class ______________

Reading Essentials and Study Guide

Chapter 24-1

★ **READ TO LEARN** *Write in complete sentences to answer the following questions. Use correct spelling, punctuation, and grammar.*

Political Parties *(pages 540–541)*

Vice President Truman became the new president after Roosevelt died. During his years in office both Democrats and Republicans were divided about the new, post-war conditions. Some Republicans wanted to be involved in world affairs. Others did not. Many favored civil rights for African Americans, while others supported segregation.

Democrats were also divided. The party had a strong civil rights program. Still many favored segregation.

Texas Democrats were divided after World War II. The **liberals** backed Roosevelt's New Deal programs. They wanted to do more to make sure minorities had equal rights and opportunities. They also supported labor unions. **Conservative** Democrats believed that government help weakened people's ability to do things for themselves. They believed that helping people by giving them money did not teach them to be responsible. Many Democrats considered themselves **moderates.** They were neither liberal nor conservative. Most of the government officials in Texas were either moderates or conservatives.

7. Why were Texas Democrats divided?

____

____

____

____

Texans Support Republican Eisenhower *(pages 541–542)*

Large oil and gas deposits were discovered in the waters near the Texas coast, or tidelands. There was a dispute over who owned these lands. The United States government said that Texas's **sovereignty,** or right to rule, stopped 3 miles from shore. Texas claimed its sovereignty extended 10.5 miles from shore.

The Republican nominee for president was Dwight Eisenhower. Eisenhower said Texas should have the tidelands. Because of this, Governor Shivers supported Eisenhower for president. Even though Eisenhower was a Republican, Governor Shivers encouraged other Democrats to vote for Eisenhower. With the help of these Texans, Eisenhower was elected the new president.

(continued)

8. Why did many Texas Democrats vote for Eisenhower?

____

____

____

____

____

Shivers Helps Modernize Government *(page 542)*

Governor Shivers served as governor or lieutenant governor from 1947 to 1957. He helped make Texas government more modern. He got money for state hospitals, retired teachers and state employees, and roads and bridges. He encouraged the legislature to allow women to serve on juries. In 1954 women finally gained that right.

9. How did Governor Shivers modernize Texas government?

____

____

____

____

____

"One-Man, One-Vote" *(pages 542–543)*

For most of Texas history, voting districts were based on land area, not population. It could take fewer votes to win in a rural district than a city district. For a long time, this didn't seem important because there were not many big cities. By the 1960s, as the number and size of cities grew, this became an issue of concern.

In 1962, the U.S. Supreme Court ruled that each state senator or representative must represent about the same number of voters. This was based on the idea that everyone's vote should be of equal value. This idea is sometimes known as "one-man, one-vote."

This ruling required major changes in Texas. Legislative district lines had to be redrawn, or changed, to reflect changes in population. This process is called **redistricting.**

(continued)

10. What does "one-man, one-vote" mean?

______

______

______

______

National Politics *(pages 543–544)*

The population and wealth of Texas grew. This increased the state's influence in the federal government. Texans held important positions in committees in the U.S. House of Representatives. Sam Rayburn was speaker of the House. Texan Lyndon Johnson was majority leader of the Senate. In 1960, Lyndon Johnson became vice president.

The Democratic victory helped the Texas Republican Party indirectly. When Johnson became vice president, he had to give up his Senate seat. A special election was held to pick a new senator. A Republican, John Tower, was elected to the Senate. A split between liberal and conservative Democrats helped him win. The Republicans continued to gain power in Texas.

11. How did the Democratic victory in the presidential election of 1960 help the Republican Party in Texas?

______

______

______

______

______

A National Tragedy *(page 544)*

President Kennedy asked Lyndon Johnson to become involved with the space program. Johnson served as the chairman of the National Aeronautics and Space Council.

In November 1963, President Kennedy was on a political trip to Texas. While riding in an open car in a parade in Dallas, he was shot and killed by Lee Harvey Oswald. Johnson became president of the United States.

(continued)

Name ______________________ Date ______________ Class ______________

12. Who became president when Kennedy was shot?

____

____

____

____

The Warren Court *(page 544)*

President Eisenhower appointed Earl Warren to be chief justice of the U.S. Supreme Court. In the American political system, the final decision about questions of rights, liberties, and justice is made by the Supreme Court. Under Chief Justice Warren's leadership, the Supreme Court decided case after case in favor of people and groups seeking to end discrimination.

13. What government body in the United States has the final say about questions of civil rights, liberties, and justice?

____

____

____

____

____

School Desegregation *(pages 544–545)*

Civil rights lawyers argued that segregation was **unconstitutional,** or not legal. In a court case named *Brown* v. *Board of Education of Topeka, Kansas,* the Supreme Court ruled that segregation in public schools was unconstitutional. Schools separated by race could never be equal. The Supreme Court ordered schools to desegregate as quickly as possible.

Many Texas officials were against this court ruling and decided to delay and resist desegregation. In some school districts, schools were desegregated one grade a year. Other districts created schools with African American and Mexican American but no Anglo American students. Sometimes African American students were allowed to attend white schools but were placed in separate classrooms and assigned separate lunch periods.

(continued)

14. What were two ways that some Texas officials interfered with desegregation of schools?

____

____

____

____

____

Desegregation of Public Facilities *(pages 545–546)*

Desegregating schools was very important to African Americans. However, they also wanted public places like parks, libraries, and swimming pools to be desegregated. Tax money had been used to build these facilities. People who supported civil rights thought everyone should be able to use them. Some groups went to court to force the government to let them use these facilities. Facilities in some places were desegregated. Other local officials resisted desegregation.

15. What places besides schools did African Americans want desegregated?

____

____

____

____

____

Individual Rights Versus National Security *(pages 546–547)*

Fears about the rise of communism also affected Americans' lives. The U.S. Congress reacted by making it a crime to belong to the Communist Party. Many people were willing to restrict rights such as freedom of speech, press, assembly, and association to protect national security.

People were accused of having Communist ties. In 1953 the legislature passed a law requiring all state employees to sign a loyalty oath before they could be paid.

(continued)

16. Why were some people willing to give up rights such as freedom of speech and freedom of the press?

____

____

____

____

____

The Red Scare *(page 547)*

The most famous anti-Communist was Senator Joseph McCarthy. McCarthy accused leaders in the U.S. Army of being Communists. He led televised hearings to investigate charges. His behavior was seen by many to be cruel. Soon afterwards, McCarthy lost his influence. Because of his activities, the word **McCarthyism** was used. It means the act of making unfounded charges against persons.

The "red scare" was seen in schools, libraries, and churches. Textbooks and library books were closely examined for content. People who belonged to certain organizations were closely watched. John Henry Faulk, an Austin radio star, was fired because a group claimed he was a member of the Communist Party. He sued and won $3.5 million. This was the largest **libel** ruling at the time. Libel is the act of printing statements known to be false to hurt someone's reputation.

17. Who was John Henry Faulk?

____

____

____

____

____

Name ______________________ Date ______________ Class ______________

Reading Essentials and Study Guide

Chapter 24-2

For use with textbook pages 549–553

Foundations for Growth

Key Terms

convoy A group of vehicles that travel together *(page 550)*

suburb A residential area at the outskirts of a city or large town *(page 550)*

reservoir An open water storage area *(page 551)*

synthetic Human-made *(page 552)*

vacuum tube An electron tube containing little air that was used to control the flow of electricity in televisions and radios before the invention of the transistor *(page 552)*

transistor A very small electronic device used to control the flow of electricity in electronic equipment such as televisions and computers *(page 552)*

integrated silicon circuit A tiny group of electronic devices, along with their connections, placed on a small slice of material made of silicon (sand); today known as a chip *(page 552)*

★DRAWING FROM EXPERIENCE

Have you ever traveled on an interstate highway? Where did it take you? Do you live in the suburbs, or do you know someone who does? How do you think life in the suburbs differs from life in the city? From life in a rural area? What kinds of electronic devices do you use? What do you think has been the most important technological advance during your lifetime?

In this section, you will read about construction, movement, and technological developments that changed Texas in the 1950s and 1960s. You will discover how these changes laid the foundations for growth.

★ORGANIZING YOUR THOUGHTS

Use the diagram below to help you take notes as you read the summaries that follow. Tell how each development or device changed how Texans lived or worked.

Development or Device	Change in Life or Work
Highway construction	**1.**
Growth of suburbs	**2.**
Transistor	**3.**
Integrated silicon circuit	**4.**

(continued)

Name _______________ Date _______________ Class _______________

Chapter 24-2

★ **READ TO LEARN** *Write in complete sentences to answer the following questions. Use correct spelling, punctuation, and grammar.*

Highway Construction *(pages 549–550)*

While people in the 1950s were focused on politics, international affairs, and civil rights, other changes were taking place. When President Eisenhower was a young man, he led a military **convoy** (group of vehicles) across the country. The trip took months. Eisenhower realized then that the United States needed a better system of highways. He supported building an interstate highway system. The new highway system would connect the states with well-built roads. People could drive faster on the new highways. The military could use the highway system to move troops and equipment quickly in times of crisis.

Interstate highways were built with both federal and state money. The highway system consisted of east-west highways, north-south highways, and loops around cities. The first interstate highway in Texas was the Gulf Freeway in Houston, Interstate 45.

Building highways caused some problems. Some people had to move to make room for the highways. Sometimes businesses had to close. However, the new highways brought more people to Texas. This resulted in new businesses such as gas stations and motels. Truck drivers could deliver products more quickly and efficiently than ever.

5. What made up the interstate highway system?

____

____

____

____

____

Texans Move to the Suburbs *(pages 550–551)*

Improved highways made it possible to live farther away from the central city and still work in the downtown area. Developers began building **suburbs,** or residential areas at the outskirts of cities or large towns. Many Texans moved to the suburbs in the 1950s and 1960s. Shopping centers, schools, and recreational facilities were built in the suburbs.

(continued)

The growth of the suburbs had a negative effect on downtown areas of cities. Many suburban Texans no longer had a reason to go downtown. Movie theaters and stores downtown closed. As more wealthy people moved to the suburbs, lower income people took their place in the downtown, or inner city. City governments directed their resources at suburbs rather than at the needy people in the inner city.

6. How did highways change where many people lived?

____

____

____

____

____

Drought Puts a Strain on Water Resources *(pages 551–552)*

Suburban, urban, and rural Texans all faced the problem of drought in the 1950s. Rainfall amounts had been less than normal since 1949. In 1956, there was a severe drought. Towns depended on human-made **reservoirs,** or open water storage areas, for their water supply. These reservoirs began drying up. Rivers and wells began to run dry. Cattle went thirsty. Thousands of acres of grass dried up and died. The drought was finally ended by rains in 1957.

Texans knew they had to be prepared for the next drought. Cities built new reservoirs. Ranchers built more ponds to store water. Farmers turned more to irrigation. More dams were built across Texas rivers. The whole state became aware of the need for water conservation.

7. How did the 1956 drought affect ranchers?

____

____

____

____

____

(continued)

Name ______________________ Date ______________ Class ______________

Reading Essentials and Study Guide

Chapter 24-2

Science and Technology *(pages 552–553)*

In the 1950s and 1960s, there was much interest in science and technology. Tax money, federal grants, churches, and wealthy donors helped build advanced hospitals in many cities. Besides treating patients, hospitals trained doctors and were places for important research. In Houston, for instance, Doctor Michael DeBakey discovered a way to use **synthetic,** or human-made, materials to replace damaged blood vessels.

In Dallas, engineers and scientists were making advances in electronics. Radio had become widespread in the 1920s. In the 1950s, television was becoming popular. Both radios and television sets used **vacuum tubes,** electronic tubes used to control the flow of electricity. These tubes, however, were heavy and slow and broke easily. In the early 1950s, a device called the **transistor,** a solid state electronic device, was invented. The transistor did the same work as a vacuum tube, but it was much smaller and less likely to break. A Dallas company called Texas Instruments made the first transistor radio. It could be carried around easily and was battery operated.

In 1958, an engineer at Texas Instruments invented the **integrated silicon circuit,** or what we call a "chip" today. Its invention made it possible to build even smaller and faster electronic devices. Integrated circuits are still used today. We use them in computers, calculators, watches, and many other devices.

Chips were part of many devices used in space exploration. The Soviet Union launched the first artificial satellite, *Sputnik,* in 1957. A short time later, the Soviets sent the first man into space. President Kennedy then announced that the United States would land a man on the moon before 1970. NASA worked on this project. In 1962 John Glenn traveled around the earth three times. In July 1969, Americans walked on the moon.

8. What are some devices that use integrated silicon circuits, or chips?

____

____

____

____

____

Name ______________________ Date ______________ Class ______________

Chapter 25-1

For use with textbook pages 560–563

The Politics of Protest

Key Terms

prosperous Wealthy, successful *(page 561)*

refugee A person who flees from place to place to find safety *(page 563)*

★DRAWING FROM EXPERIENCE

What images come to mind when you think about the Vietnam War? Are you or is anyone you know of Vietnamese descent?

In this section, you will learn about Lyndon Johnson's "Great Society," the scandalous administration of Richard Nixon, and important political events of the 1960s, including the Vietnam War. You will find out how Texans and their fellow Americans reacted to this time of change.

★ORGANIZING YOUR THOUGHTS

Use the diagram below to help you take notes as you read the summaries that follow. Identify and order the crises that led to the election of Richard Nixon in November 1968.

1.

2.

3.

4.

Richard Nixon is elected president.

(continued)

Name ______________________ Date ______________ Class ______________

Reading Essentials and Study Guide

Chapter 25-1

★ **READ TO LEARN** *Write in complete sentences to answer the following questions. Use correct spelling, punctuation, and grammar.*

A Texan in the White House *(pages 560–561)*

Judge Sarah T. Hughes gave the oath of office to Lyndon Johnson hours after John Kennedy died. A Texan was now president. The nation grieved over the loss of Kennedy. Johnson challenged the nation to honor President Kennedy by supporting the programs he had favored. In 1964, Johnson was reelected.

5. What did Johnson encourage Americans to do in honor of John Kennedy?

____

____

____

The Great Society *(page 561)*

President Johnson believed in a government that was involved in its citizens' lives. Congress passed so many laws during the Johnson administration that his presidency has been compared to Franklin Roosevelt's New Deal. Johnson declared a "war on poverty." The nation as a whole was **prosperous,** or wealthy. Some regions and groups of people, however, were not. President Johnson believed that education was the best way to solve problems of poverty. The Elementary and Secondary Education Act was passed during Johnson's term of office. Johnson also supported laws that created Head Start, Job Corps, and federal aid for college students.

Johnson supported civil rights. As president, he helped push the Civil Rights Act of 1964 through Congress. He also supported the Voting Rights Act. This law protected the rights of all people, no matter what their race, to vote.

6. How did Johnson hope to fight the "war on poverty"?

____

____

____

____

(continued)

Reading Essentials and Study Guide

Foreign Affairs *(page 562)*

Foreign affairs became very important during Johnson's time in office. Since the end of World War II, the country of Vietnam had been divided into two parts. North Vietnam had a Communist government. The United States supported South Vietnam against communism. In the mid-1960s, President Johnson ordered combat troops to the country.

As more and more Americans were killed and wounded in Vietnam, more and more Americans opposed the war. Many Americans believed the war was necessary to stop communism. A large number of Americans, however, felt the war was immoral and unnecessary.

Opposition to the war in Vietnam grew stronger. Also, conflict over civil rights sometimes turned violent. There were riots in cities like Los Angeles, Detroit, and Washington, D.C.

7. Why did foreign affairs become central to President Johnson's administration?

____

____

____

A Critical Year *(page 562)*

On March 31, 1968, President Johnson announced he would not run for a second term. Less than a week later, on April 4, Dr. Martin Luther King, Jr., was killed in Memphis, Tennessee. Dr. King was the country's African American leader in the struggle for civil rights. His message of nonviolence brought many people together. Only two months later, on June 5, Robert Kennedy, John Kennedy's brother, was killed in Los Angeles.

These and other events produced a sense of crisis by the election in 1968. Many Americans wanted an end to the disorder. They turned to Richard Nixon, the Republican candidate for president.

8. Why was Dr. Martin Luther King, Jr.'s message of nonviolence important?

____

____

____

____

(continued)

Name ____________________ Date ____________________ Class ____________________

Reading Essentials and Study Guide

Chapter 25-1

Nixon as President *(page 563)*

Richard Nixon was elected president in 1968 and was reelected in 1972. A majority of Texans supported him. Shortly after reelection, he was involved in a scandal, now known as "Watergate." The Democratic Party's headquarters in the Watergate Hotel had been burglarized. Taped conversations and other evidence showed that President Nixon had helped cover up the burglary. Two Texans, Jack Brooks and Barbara Jordan, served on the committee investigating Nixon. Nixon resigned from office on August 8, 1974.

9. Why did President Nixon resign?

____

____

____

____

____

Refugees Seek Homes in Texas *(page 563)*

Everyone was relieved when the last U.S. troops left Vietnam in 1973. After the war, thousands of Vietnamese came to the United States. Many **refugees** came to Texas. Refugees are people who flee from place to place to find safety. Some Vietnamese found work in the shrimping industry on the Texas coast. They lived in cities like Rockport, Port Aransas, and Kemah. Most Vietnamese immigrants, however, lived in cities like Houston, Beaumont, Port Arthur, and Galveston. By the 1980s, several schools in western and southwestern Houston were more than 10 percent Vietnamese.

10. Where in Texas did most refugees from Vietnam settle?

____

____

____

____

____

Name ______________________ Date ______________ Class ______________

Reading Essentials and Study Guide

Chapter 25-2

For use with textbook pages 565–568

Civil Rights and Politics

Key Terms

boycott Refuse to buy goods as a protest *(page 566)*

sit-in The act of taking seats in a racially segregated facility to protest discrimination *(page 566)*

freedom ride A ride made by civil rights workers through Southern states to find out whether public facilities, such as bus terminals and lunch counters, were desegregated *(page 566)*

keynote address The speech at an event that focuses on the event's main issues *(page 568)*

★ DRAWING FROM EXPERIENCE

Have you ever run for student council? Have you ever wanted to change anything about your school or community? Have you ever thought of starting your own club or group at your school?

The last section discussed important political events of the 1960s and 1970s. In this section, you will learn about how African Americans, Mexican Americans, and women became active in politics and worked for civil rights.

★ ORGANIZING YOUR THOUGHTS

Use the diagram below to help you take notes as you read the summaries that follow. Identify and describe the organizations African Americans and Mexican Americans formed in the 1960s and 1970s to fight for racial equality.

Group	Full Name	Purpose
CORE	1.	2.
MAYO	3.	4.
RUP	5.	6.
MALDEF	7.	8.

(continued)

Name ______________ Date ______________ Class ______________

Chapter 25-2

★ **READ TO LEARN** *Write in complete sentences to answer the following questions. Use correct spelling, punctuation, and grammar.*

Growing Involvement of African Americans *(pages 565–566)*

During the televised Congressional hearings in the Watergate scandal, America became aware of Representative Barbara Jordan of Houston. In 1966, Jordan became the first African American elected to the state Senate since the end of Reconstruction. In 1972, she was elected to the U.S. House of Representatives. Jordan's statements while on the Watergate committee were so impressive. The Democratic Party invited Jordan to give a major speech at its 1976 convention.

James Farmer was another leader in the struggle for equal rights. He studied the teachings of Mohandas Gandhi, leader of a nonviolent movement for the independence of India. Farmer founded the Congress of Racial Equality (CORE). It believed in peaceful change. Farmer was its director during the 1960s, when the group organized **boycotts, sit-ins,** and **freedom rides.** These are nonviolent ways to fight segregation. Farmer received the Presidential Medal of Freedom in 1998.

9. How did Mohandas Gandhi influence the work of James Farmer?

____

____

____

____

____

Mexican Americans and Politics *(page 566)*

During the same period, Mexican Americans also worked for fair treatment from school officials, employers, and state and local government. In 1956, Henry B. González was elected to the state Senate. He was the first Mexican American to serve in modern times. In 1958, he ran for governor. Two years later, Hector García helped form "Viva Kennedy" clubs to support John Kennedy. People who supported González and Kennedy later formed the Political Association of Spanish-Speaking Organizations (PASSO). In 1960, García was elected to the U.S. House of Representatives. Many Mexican Americans were elected to school boards and city councils.

(continued)

10. What were two important accomplishments of Hector García?

Forming New Groups *(page 567)*

In 1966, an event caused many Mexican Americans to become more politically active. Farm workers in the Rio Grande Valley worked under harsh conditions. They had to use dangerous chemicals without proper safety equipment. To protest this, they went on strike. They asked for a minimum wage, decent housing, toilets and drinking water, and the banning of the short-handled hoe. Some farmers marched from the Rio Grande Valley to Austin. Governor John Connally met with them in New Braunfels. His actions did not satisfy the farmers. Many became more active in politics.

New groups developed as a result of this event. The Mexican American Youth Organization (MAYO) was founded, with education as its main concern. It wanted more Mexican American teachers, Mexican American studies in schools, and an end to discriminatory school policies. MAYO members led walkouts in several high schools.

MAYO members felt that neither Republicans nor Democrats represented their interests. They and others founded a new party, *La Raza Unida Party* (RUP). It successfully placed a candidate for governor on the ballot in 1972. It also won city offices in Crystal City and Cottula. Another group, the Mexican American Legal Defense and Education Fund (MALDEF), organized and worked to end discrimination through lawsuits. This activity resulted in more Mexican Americans being elected to local and state offices.

11. In what way was the farmer's strike of 1966 a success for Mexican Americans?

(continued)

Mexican American Heritage *(page 568)*

Many Mexican Americans in the 1960s and 1970s took pride in their Mexican roots. Diego Rivera and José Clemente Orozco inspired Mexican American artists. These artists created murals that told stories and themes. Writers such as Rolando Hinojosa-Smith and Tomás Rivera wrote works reflecting the Mexican American experience. During this period, many younger Mexican Americans began calling themselves *Chicanos* or *Chicanas* as a way of showing their pride in their roots.

12. How did Mexican Americans show pride in their heritage?

____

____

____

____

____

Women and Politics *(page 568)*

In 1958, Hattie Mae White became the first African American to serve on the Houston School Board. When Barbara Jordan was in the state Senate and Frances "Sissy" Farenthold was in the state House, they were the only women in the state legislature. The Texas Women's Political Caucus, the National Organization for Women (NOW), and the *Mujeres por la Raza* urged women to run for office.

Women's political power kept growing. Anne Armstrong became the first woman to give a **keynote address** at a national political party convention. A keynote address is a speech at an event that focuses on the event's main issues.

13. What groups encouraged women to become more involved in politics?

____

____

____

____

____

Name ______________________ Date ______________ Class ______________

Reading Essentials and Study Guide **Chapter 25-3**

For use with textbook pages 569–573

Growth and Development

Key Terms

productivity Rate of production *(page 570)*

feedlot A large outdoor facility where cattle are fed grain until they are large enough to be processed into meat *(page 570)*

boom and bust cycle An economic cycle in which high demand and production are followed by oversupply and falling prices *(page 570)*

cartel An association of commercial or industrial producers formed to limit competition *(page 571)*

interdependence The act of two or more groups relying on each other for support *(page 573)*

★ DRAWING FROM EXPERIENCE

Are you concerned about the environment? What kinds of pollution are you aware of, if any? What can people do to take care of the environment?

In this section, you will learn about the environmental concerns of Texans in the 1960s and 1970s. You will also learn about changes in the agricultural and oil industries and growth in construction in Texas in this period.

★ ORGANIZING YOUR THOUGHTS

Use the diagram below to help you take notes as you read the summaries that follow. Describe growth in these areas of the Texas economy in the 1960s and 1970s.

Agriculture	Oil	Construction
1.	2.	3.
Growth		

(continued)

Name ______________________ Date ______________ Class ______________

Chapter 25-3

★ **READ TO LEARN** *Write in complete sentences to answer the following questions. Use correct spelling, punctuation, and grammar.*

Agriculture *(pages 569–570)*

During the 1960s and 1970s, Texas experienced increased economic growth. Although oil and agriculture remained important to Texas, other industries also became important.

Fewer Texans worked in agriculture than ever before. However, they continued to produce large quantities of food and cotton. The state's greater **productivity** (rate of production) was based on several factors. First, mechanization, the expansion of irrigation, and increased use of fertilizers and insecticides, played a role. These methods increased harvests.

Second, agriculture became more productive as cotton production moved westward. After World War II, land that was not good for growing cotton was changed to cattle pastures and pine plantations. Cotton was grown in the High Plains, the Rio Grande Valley, and the Blackland Prairie. The soils in these places were better for growing cotton.

A third reason for increased productivity was that farmers and ranchers used economies of scale. Factory methods were used for raising cattle and poultry. Cattle were placed in **feedlots,** large outdoor facilities. The High Plains had a boom in cattle feeding. However, President Nixon ordered a price freeze on beef. Ranchers withheld their cattle from the market. When they finally tried to sell their cattle, the oversupply made prices drop. The result was a "bust" after the "boom." Feedlots went out of business. This was a **boom and bust cycle,** or economic cycle. These cycles would happen in other industries too.

4. How did cotton farming change after World War II?

____

____

____

____

Environmental Concerns *(pages 570–571)*

The use of feedlots and changes in the chicken industry increased productivity and lowered costs. However, new techniques raised new issues. Many animals in one place caused offensive odors and waste products. Other Texas industries also polluted the air. Cotton gins,

(continued)

smelters, foundries, paper mills, steel plants, petroleum refineries, and petrochemical plants were also at fault. The air quality was worst in the regions of Texas where those activities were heaviest, such as El Paso and Houston. Pollution in the Houston Ship Channel was also very bad. Tests showed no oxygen in the water. Without oxygen, fish and plants could not survive.

Both the state and federal government took steps to clean up Texas's air and water. Many young people became involved. In 1965, the state created an Air Control Board. In 1968, the state stopped cities from burning garbage. Industries along the Houston Ship Channel worked to reduce pollutants. By 1980, scientists found that fish, shrimp, and crabs had returned to those waters.

5. What steps were taken to clean up the environment in Texas?

____

____

____

____

____

Oil Economics *(pages 571–572)*

Events in the 1960s and 1970s connected the Texas oil industry to world affairs. A group of foreign nations created a **cartel,** or association to limit competition. It was called the Organization of Petroleum Exporting Countries (OPEC). The cartel drove up the price of oil. In 1973, Arab nations in OPEC stopped shipping oil to the United States. They did this because the United States supported Israel. The result was an "energy crisis." The price of oil and gasoline rose very high.

Higher oil prices caused problems for many Texans. However, the high prices led to the drilling of more oil wells and more activity in other areas of the oil industry. Texas oil companies hired more people and paid high wages. Also, other businesses thrived, including real estate and banking. Oil prices were high until the 1980s. When prices came down, they brought down other parts of the economy as well.

The oil industry made Texas more global in its outlook. Texans traveled throughout the world. Their skills and knowledge were in demand in "oil patches" everywhere. They went to places like Indonesia, Nigeria, Saudi Arabia, Scotland, and Venezuela. Some Texans were geologists and geophysicists who looked for oil. Others

(continued)

drilled and built pipelines. Some were engineers who built refineries and petrochemical plants. Also, Texas companies were called to put out raging oil well fires if disaster struck in oilfields.

6. How did Texas benefit from the energy crisis?

____

____

____

____

____

New Construction for a Modern State *(pages 572–573)*

Construction projects increased during the 1960s and 1970s. Construction of the Harris County Domed Stadium (Astrodome) in 1963–1964 was very important. It was the first baseball stadium with a roof. Texas had a growing **interdependence** with the rest of the world. This encouraged Dallas and Houston to build new airports. Housing developments were built near both airports. Suburbs such as Arlington, Grapevine, Grand Prairie, and Irving developed near the Dallas/Fort Worth Airport.

In downtown San Antonio contruction began on HemisFair '68. This was the first international exposition in the southwestern United States. It marked the 250th anniversary of the founding of San Antonio. More than 6 million visitors came to San Antonio between April and October 1968. The most important building was the Institute of Texan Cultures. World visitors could see and appreciate the rich ethnic diversity of Texas.

7. How did the construction of new airports lead to more growth for Texas?

____

____

____

____

____

Name ______________________ Date ______________ Class ______________

Reading Essentials and Study Guide **Chapter 26-1**

For use with textbook pages 578–581

Political Events

Key Terms

urban dweller A person who lives in a city *(page 579)*

cabinet A group of advisers to the president of the United States *(page 580)*

third-party Having to do with an organized political group that is neither Republican nor Democrat *(page 581)*

bill A proposed law presented to a legislature for consideration *(page 581)*

★DRAWING FROM EXPERIENCE

Have you ever visited Washington, D.C.? Have you ever visited the Texas capital of Austin? Can you name an elected official who is Republican? An elected official who is a Democrat? Whom do you know who is a Republican? Who is a Democrat?

In this section, you will learn about some of the differences between the Republican and Democratic Parties. You will also learn about important government positions women, Mexican Americans, and African Americans have held.

★ORGANIZING YOUR THOUGHTS

Use the diagram below to help you take notes as you read the summaries that follow. List two Texans who made important contributions for each level of government and identify their positions.

Level	
Federal	1.
	2.
State	3.
	4.
Local	5.
	6.

(continued)

Name ______________________ Date ______________ Class ______________

Reading Essentials and Study Guide

Chapter 26-1

★ **READ TO LEARN** *Write in complete sentences to answer the following questions. Use correct spelling, punctuation, and grammar.*

A Broader Political Base *(pages 578–579)*

Politics in Texas continue to change. The events of the 1960s and the 1970s affected the politics of the 1980s and the 1990s. Many groups that had not been included in politics before were now included. The political power of minorities, women, and **urban dwellers** grew. Urban dwellers are people who live in cities.

7. What groups of people gained political power in Texas in the 1980s and 1990s?

____

____

____

____

Republicans *(page 579)*

By the year 2000, all major statewide elected officials were Republicans. People moving into Texas included rich Northerners who often voted Republican. The Republican Party became identified with oil producers, and the Democratic Party became identified with oil consumers and environmentalists. The Republican Party also supported less government regulations. They also fought for free enterprise.

For many years, Senator John Tower was the best-known Texas Republican. Then, in 1978, William Clements became the first Republican governor of Texas since Reconstruction. He was an oil man with no political experience. Many Texas voters had lost faith in politicians. They found Clements' lack of political experience appealing.

8. What groups in Texas did the Republican and Democratic Parties represent?

____

____

____

____

(continued)

Reading Essentials and Study Guide

Women *(page 579)*

Women have become involved in both political parties. Democrats elected Ann Richards to be state treasurer in 1982. Richards was elected governor of Texas in 1991. African American women Sheila Jackson Lee and Eddie Bernice Johnson represented Texas as Democrats in the U.S. House of Representatives. Republican Kay Bailey Hutchison was elected to the U.S. Senate in 1993 and reelected in 1994 and 2000. In 1996 Kay Granger became the first Texan Republican woman elected to the U.S. House of Representatives.

At the end of the 1990s, 32 members of the state legislature were women. Texas women from both parties have also served as mayors of the cities of Dallas, Houston, and El Paso. Women have also become judges, city council members, county commissioners, and school board members.

9. In what major Texas cities have women been elected mayor?

____

____

____

____

____

Mexican Americans *(page 580)*

Mexican American Texans became involved in politics during the civil rights struggles of the 1960s. Some rejected the Republican and Democratic Parties and formed another party, *La Raza Unida*, in 1970. This third party did not last long. By 1978 Mexican Americans were active again in the two major political parties.

Gains in education helped many Mexican Americans become well-educated professionals who are active in politics. After receiving nearly 60 percent of the vote, Gus Garcia became the first Hispanic mayor of Austin. Many Mexican Americans represented their fellow Texans in both the U.S. Congress and the Texas legislature. Mexican Americans also held local positions such as sheriff, judge, commissioner, and mayor. The former mayor of San Antonio, Henry Cisneros, served in President Clinton's **cabinet,** or group of advisers. He was secretary of housing and urban development.

(continued)

Name ______________________ Date ______________ Class ______________

10. What new party did Mexican Americans form?

____

____

____

____

____

African Americans *(page 580)*

African Americans also increased their political involvement in the 1980s and 1990s. Barbara Jordan was a member of the U.S. Congress. When she retired, another African American, Mickey Leland, was elected to her seat in Congress. Representative Leland worked hard to fight world hunger. He died in a plane crash while delivering food to starving people. African Americans have also been active in state and local governments. They have represented Texans in the state legislature and have served as mayors and members of city councils.

11. What African American was elected to the U.S. Congress after Barbara Jordan retired?

____

____

____

____

____

Influential Texans in Washington, D.C. *(page 581)*

Many Texans from both major political parties have exercised great power in the federal government. George H. W. Bush, a Republican, served as vice president and president of the United States. Bush was defeated in his second run for the presidency. Some people think another Texan, H. Ross Perot, helped cause Bush's defeat. Perot was a **third-party** candidate, not a Democrat or a Republican. Bush's son, George W. Bush, became president in 2001. George W. Bush is a Republican.

(continued)

When Democrats were in the majority in the U.S. Congress, Jim Wright of Fort Worth was speaker of the House of Representatives. Texan Democrats Henry B. González of San Antonio and Eligio de la Garza of Mission headed powerful committees in Congress. When Republicans replaced Democrats as the majority party in the House in 1995, Richard Armey of Irving, Tom DeLay of Sugar Land, and Bill Archer of Houston became leaders in Congress.

Texans made important contributions to the nation's financial policy in the 1980s and 1990s. Phil Gramm was a Democratic member of the U.S. House of Representatives. Because of his role as co-author of President Reagan's economic program, Democratic leaders tried to remove Gramm from his seat on the House Budget Committee. He resigned. Later, he was elected to the U.S. Senate. Senator Gramm wrote important **bills** dealing with taxation, spending, and banking. Bills are proposed laws presented to a legislature for consideration. Former U.S. Senator Lloyd Bentsen served as secretary of the Treasury Department.

12. How did third-party candidate Perot affect George H. W. Bush's run for a second term as president?

____

____

____

____

____

Name ______________________ Date ______________ Class ______________

Chapter 26-2

For use with textbook pages 583–586

International Events

Key Terms

deactivation The act of taking apart or dismantling *(page 584)*

appropriate Set aside, usually money, by a formal action *(page 584)*

mortgage A loan to pay for property *(page 585)*

National Guard A reserve military force organized by states, available for national defense in a time of crisis *(page 585)*

★DRAWING FROM EXPERIENCE

Have you ever traveled to Mexico? Did you have any problems crossing the border? Do you speak or know someone who speaks Spanish?

In this section, you will learn about some of Texas's connections with the rest of the world. You will also learn about the special relationship between Texas and Mexico.

★ORGANIZING YOUR THOUGHTS

Use the diagram below to help you take notes as you read the summaries that follow. Think about positive and negative aspects of the Mexico-Texas trade relationship.

Mexico-Texas Trade Relationship	
Positive	**Negative**
1.	4.
2.	5.
3.	6.

(continued)

Reading Essentials and Study Guide

★**READ TO LEARN** *Write in complete sentences to answer the following questions. Use correct spelling, punctuation, and grammar.*

The End of the Cold War Affects Texas *(pages 583–584)*

After World War II, U.S. foreign policy focused on limiting expansion of the Soviet Union. The threat of Soviet expansion basically disappeared while George H. W. Bush was president. The destruction of the Berlin Wall on November 9, 1989, ended the Cold War.

Foreign policy changed, and the changes affected Texas. The United States and the Soviet Union signed a series of treaties to reduce the number of missiles and nuclear weapons each owned. Pershing missiles that had been built during the Cold War were destroyed at Karnack, Texas. The Pantex Plant near Amarillo, where many U.S. nuclear weapons were constructed, was the site that began their **deactivation.** Deactivation is the act of taking apart or dismantling. The nuclear material from the weapons was removed. Many military bases in Texas were closed or converted to nonmilitary use. Bergstrom Air Force Base in Austin, for example, became a city airport.

New opportunities in the petroleum industry arose with the collapse of the Soviet Union. The former Soviet Union has large reserves of oil, natural gas, and minerals. Many Texas companies have provided technology and engineers and other experts to help develop these reserves.

7. How did the end of the Cold War affect Texas?

____

____

____

____

____

The Expansion of Trade *(pages 584–585)*

Texas and Mexico share a long, common border. Halfway between the two coasts of the United States, Texas is well located to serve as Mexico's gateway to the markets of the United States.

(continued)

Reading Essentials and Study Guide

The Texas-Mexico border trade has always been important. Many Mexican citizens cross the border to shop in Texas. Stores along the border on the Texas side depend on these shoppers for most of their business. Some accept Mexican *pesos*. Some Mexican businesses accept dollars.

Maquiladoras are a recent development in trade with Mexico. These factories near the border use Mexican labor and U.S. materials. The goods they make are then shipped to the United States. Many companies, attracted by low labor costs and tax breaks from both nations, have set up such factories. There are thousands of plants with hundreds of thousands of workers along the border. El Paso is closely linked with this industry. As many as 100,000 jobs in El Paso and Ciudad Juárez, just across the border, depend on *maquiladoras*.

Serious problems are connected with *maquiladoras*. Wages are very low by U.S. standards. Many workers live in *colonias* (neighborhoods) on both sides of the border. These areas lack proper streets and water and sewer services. The Texas legislature has **appropriated,** or set aside, funds to help provide basic services to the *colonias*. Pollution is another problem. The factories and cars cause air and water pollution in cities in Texas and Mexico. Both the United States and Mexico will need to work together to solve these problems.

Political leaders in Mexico, Canada, and the United States realized that increased cooperation could bring many benefits. As a result, the three nations signed the North American Free Trade Agreement (NAFTA). NAFTA removed many barriers to the shipment of goods among the three nations. NAFTA went into effect at the beginning of 1994.

Because of its location, Texas was affect by NAFTA more than any other state. Companies that wanted to do business under NAFTA set up offices in Dallas, San Antonio, and Houston. Trucking and warehouse businesses in Texas boomed. Laredo and El Paso received most of the traffic. New bridges had to be built. Plans were made to widen Highway 59 and connect it to the Port of Houston. The highway would be an important route between Mexico and Canada.

8. What three countries signed the North American Free Trade Agreement?

____

____

____

____

(continued)

Name _______________ Date _______________ Class _______________

Reading Essentials and Study Guide

Boom and Bust Oil Cycle *(page 585)*

Texans had seen oil prices go up and down. The Organization of Petroleum Exporting Countries (OPEC) had driven up prices in the 1970s. Oil companies and related industries prospered. Tax revenues and government income increased. Banks issued **mortgages,** loans to purchase property. Some loans were for the construction of office buildings or shopping centers. People moved to Texas in large numbers to find jobs. They found it easy to get loans for homes and businesses.

The weakening of OPEC and overproduction of oil made oil prices drop. Texas felt the effects of lower prices immediately. Companies cut back on drilling and fired workers. Borrowers could not pay their loans to banks and mortgage companies. With so much money that could not be repaid, some lending institutions had to close or were bought by banks in other states.

9. What happened to businesses in Texas when oil prices dropped?

____

____

____

____

____

The Persian Gulf War *(page 585)*

In August 1990, Iraq invaded its oil-rich neighbor, Kuwait. President George H. W. Bush met with many nations to decide how to drive Iraq out and protect the oil resources of the region. The military action was called Operation Desert Storm.

Many Texans were involved in Desert Storm. Some of the preparations for this conflict took place at Fort Hood in central Texas. Many of the **National Guard** troops that took part were from Texas. The National Guard is a reserve military force organized by states, available for national defense in a time of crisis. Members of the Texas Guard had the skills needed for fighting a war in the desert. One Guard unit from Texas laid pipelines to supply water to the troops. Other units supervised the loading of ships at Texas ports. The Gulf War was short but reemphasized the connection of Texas to the rest of the world.

(continued)

10. How did Texas troops help in Operation Desert Storm?

____

____

____

____

____

Texans Respond to Terrorism *(page 586)*

The terrible events of September 11, 2001, showed that there still were threats to world peace. Four airplanes were hijacked. Two planes crashed into the World Trade Center in New York City. The third plane hit the Pentagon building in Washington, D.C. The fourth plane crashed in a field in rural Pennsylvania. In all, several thousand people were killed.

Texans, like other Americans, were angry and grief-stricken. Generous people donated cash, relief supplies, and blood donations. Houses of worship were crowded with people who wanted to pray. President George W. Bush explained that terrorists had committed acts of war against the United States.

In the following weeks, letters containing deadly anthrax bacteria arrived at some government and media offices. Several people died as a result. Security was increased at airports and along the Texas coast.

In October 2001, the United States attacked Afghanistan. The Taliban government refused to surrender Osama bin Laden, the accused terrorist. By the end of the year, the Taliban government was forced out of power. The United States and its allies had won a victory against terrorism, but they were still acting to stop it elsewhere.

11. How did Texans help after the September 11 attacks?

____

____

____

____

____

Name ______________________ Date ______________ Class ______________

Chapter 26-3

For use with textbook pages 588–591

Reforms Come to Texas Schools

Key Terms

extracurricular Relating to school activities but not part of the course of study *(page 590)*

bilingual education A program that serves students whose native language is not English *(page 590)*

★DRAWING FROM EXPERIENCE

Have you ever taken a test in which you had to fill in a circle or bubble to show the correct answer? What was the subject of the test? How did the test differ from other tests your teachers give?

In this section, you will learn how changes in the economy of the United States and Texas brought about changes in Texas schools. You will discover that some familiar parts of your school experience are a result of these changes.

★ORGANIZING YOUR THOUGHTS

Use the diagram below to help you take notes as you read the summaries that follow. Show the chain of causes and effects that resulted in educational reforms in Texas.

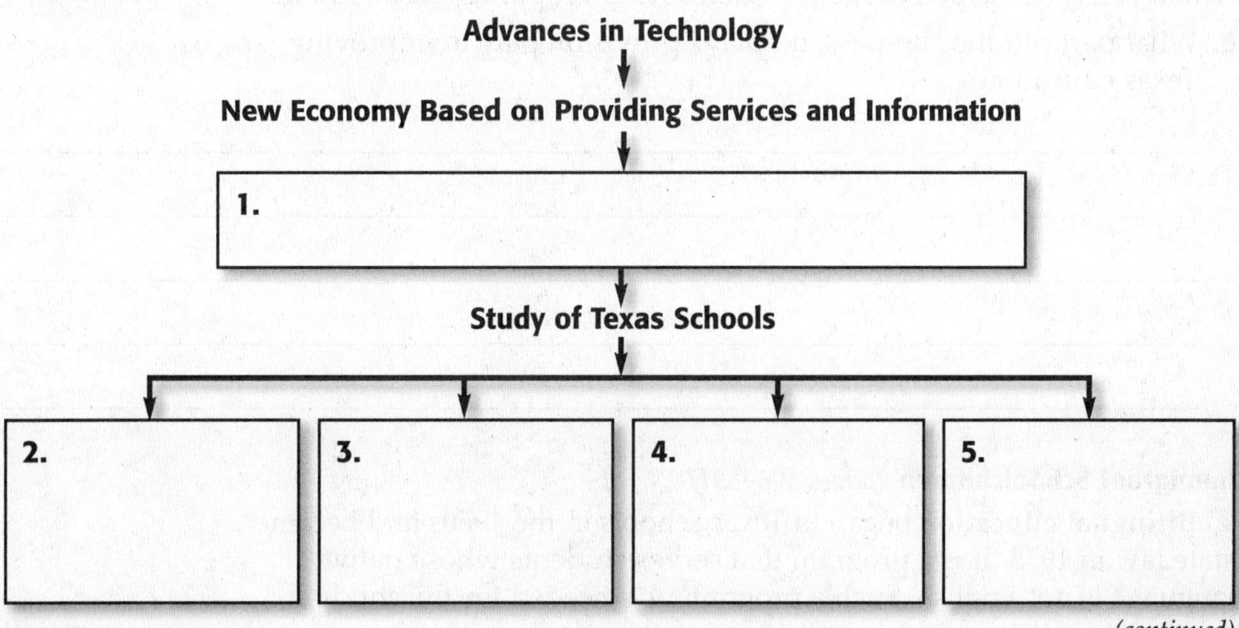

(continued)

Name ______________________ Date ______________ Class ______________

Reading Essentials and Study Guide

Chapter 26-3

★ **READ TO LEARN** *Write in complete sentences to answer the following questions. Use correct spelling, punctuation, and grammar.*

The Reforms of 1984 *(pages 588–590)*

The United States moved away from an economy based on manufacturing. The "new economy" focused on providing services and information. New industries were driven by technology. These new technologies included personal computers, fiber optics, cellular telephones, and satellite communications.

Texas needed more highly skilled and better-educated workers to work in the new industries. Even the traditional industries, such as ranching, farming, saw mills, and oil drilling, needed workers with new skills. Governor Mark White appointed a commission headed by businessman H. Ross Perot to study the Texas schools. The state legislature acted on many of the commission's recommendations. It increased the amount of money for poorer school districts and for teacher pay. It reduced class sizes and created free summer classes for students learning English.

Two parts of the new education laws caused debate. First, teachers had to pass a test to stay employed. The other part was the "no-pass, no-play" provision for school sports. To participate in **extracurricular** activities, or activities that are not part of the course of study, such as sports or band, students could not have even one failing grade. A minimum grade of 70 was considered passing. Some coaches and teachers thought the new sports rule was too strict. They argued that extracurricular activities helped prevent students from dropping out of school.

6. What part did the "no-pass, no-play" provision play in improving Texas education?

____

____

____

____

____

Immigrant Schoolchildren *(pages 590–591)*

Bilingual education began in Texas schools in the 1960s and became state law in 1973. It is a program that serves students whose native language is not English. Such a program was needed for the children

(continued)

of immigrants from Mexico, Central America, India, and Southeast Asia. Some people did not agree with bilingual education. They thought that only English should be used in schools. A law was passed in Texas forbidding children of undocumented aliens from attending public school. A Houston judge ruled that the law was unconstitutional. The U.S. Supreme Court supported his ruling.

7. What does a bilingual education program do?

____

____

____

____

____

Educational Testing *(page 591)*

The Texas legislature has made reforms in education. Students had to take more tests, like the Texas Assessment of Academic Skills (TAAS), now called the Texas Assessment of Knowledge and Skills (TAKS). High schools were encouraged to offer more Advanced Placement courses so students could earn college credit. Other programs such as Gifted and Talented Education and School-to-Work instruction received more state money. Students were encouraged to take more challenging courses. There has been an increase in the number of students attending community college. The state legislature passed a law ensuring that high school graduates can go to a state university if they are in the top 10 percent of their class.

8. How can high school students get admitted to state universities?

____

____

____

____

____

Name ______________________ Date ______________ Class ______________

Chapter 27-1

For use with textbook pages 596–599

Turn-of-the-Century Texas

Key Terms

census An official count of the people living in a country *(page 596)*

growth rate The percentage increase in population *(page 597)*

ethnicity National or cultural heritage *(page 597)*

★ DRAWING FROM EXPERIENCE

How many people live in your city or town? How is the number of people living in a place determined? What are some uses of population information?

In this chapter, you will learn how the United States gathers information about its population. You will also learn what this information shows and how it is used.

★ ORGANIZING YOUR THOUGHTS

Use the diagram below to help you take notes as you read the summaries that follow. Answer each question about the population of Texas based on the 2000 census.

Texas Population	
What is the population of Texas?	**1.**
How does Texas rank in terms of population growth?	**2.**
What percentage of the Texas population claims mixed heritage?	**3.**
Where do most Texans live?	**4.**
How old are Texans?	**5.**

(continued)

Name ______________________ Date ______________ Class ______________

Chapter 27-1

★ **READ TO LEARN** *Write in complete sentences to answer the following questions. Use correct spelling, punctuation, and grammar.*

The Census *(pages 596–597)*

The Constitution requires the United States to count its people every 10 years. This official count of the people living in the nation is called a **census.** The first census was taken in 1790. Texas was first included in the census in 1850. The main reason for the census is to determine how many people each state can send to the U.S. House of Representatives. States with large populations can send more members than states with smaller populations. The census also provides information about how Texas and other states change. By comparing census data from various years, historians can note trends.

6. How often is the census taken in the United States?

____

____

____

____

____

Population *(page 597)*

The 22nd U.S. census was taken in April 2000. The census showed that Texas was similar in some ways to the rest of the United States. It also showed that Texas was different in some ways. According to the 2000 census, the population of the United States was 281,421,906. Texas's population was 20,851,820, about 7 percent of the total U.S. population. Texas has the second largest population in the country. Only California has more people.

Texas grew by 3.8 million people in the 1990s. The percentage increase in population is called the **growth rate.** If more people are born or move to a state than die or leave the state, the state has a positive growth rate. Texas had the seventh highest growth rate in the nation. As a result of its increase in population, Texas gained two members in the House of Representatives. Because the number of representatives in the House stays at 435, this means other states lost members.

(continued)

Name ______________________ Date ______________ Class ______________

Chapter 27-1

7. How would you describe the growth rate of Texas in relation to that of other states?

____

____

____

____

____

Ethnicity *(page 597)*

The census asked people to identify their race and ethnicity. **Ethnicity** is national or cultural heritage. The 2000 census allowed people for the first time to mark more than one ethnic group. This helps to show a multicultural heritage. Eighteen percent of Texans said they belonged to more than one ethnic group. Nationally, about 4 percent of the population claimed a multicultural heritage. To find out how many people there are per square mile, divide the population by the land area. There are 79.6 people per square mile in Texas. This figure is the same for the United States.

8. What did the 2000 census allow people to do for the first time?

____

____

____

____

____

Where Do Texans Live? *(pages 597–598)*

The population of Texas is not evenly distributed. Forty percent of Texans live in only four counties. Harris, Dallas, Tarrant, and Bexar Counties have populations of more than 1 million. More than half the population of Texas lives in only 8 of the state's 254 counties. Fifty-one of Texas's counties have fewer than 5,000 people. The least populated county is Loving County. It also is the least populated in the entire United States. Its population is 67.

(continued)

9. Where do 40 percent of Texans live?

____

____

____

____

____

The Growth Rate *(page 598)*

Population growth is one of the most important statistics learned from the census. Some areas of the state are growing very rapidly. The number of people living in suburbs around the cities of Dallas, Fort Worth, Austin, San Antonio, and Houston increased. Collin County in the eastern part of the state was the fastest growing. It grew by 86 percent. The U.S.–Mexico border area also experienced significant growth, with increases in population and business activity in the lower Rio Grande Valley and El Paso. Other parts of the state had declines in population or stayed the same.

10. What two areas of Texas experienced rapid population growth?

____

____

____

____

____

How Old Are Texans? *(pages 598–599)*

People in Texas are younger than people in the United States as a whole. In the year 2000, nearly 28.2 percent of Texans were under 18 years of age.

It is important for business, education, and government planners to know the age distribution of the population because older people and younger people have different needs. For example, if an area has many young children, more elementary schools will be needed. If there are more older people, communities usually need more retirement homes.

(continued)

11. How does the age distribution of Texas's population compare with that of the U.S. population as a whole?

Looking Ahead *(page 599)*

An increase in the population of Texas and an increase in the diversity of Texas's population seem likely in the future for many reasons. Population growth is often related to economic conditions. Texas's economy is varied enough that economic downturns in one area can be balanced by growth in other areas. In addition, increases in international trade can lead to increases in diversity. Texas has strong historical and cultural ties with Mexico. The ability to speak Spanish allows Texans to do business in Mexico and other Latin American countries. Texas's petroleum industry has linked it with the Middle East, Indonesia, and Africa. As trade increases to those places, Texans are likely to be involved. Texans have learned that their state works best when people of diverse backgrounds share their skills and work together.

12. What can lead to increases in diversity?

Name ______________________ Date ______________ Class ______________

Reading Essentials and Study Guide

Chapter 27-2

For use with textbook pages 600–606

Texas and the Arts

Key Terms

folklore Stories passed down orally from generation to generation *(page 600)*

los corridos Mexican American folk ballads *(page 601)*

pictograph An ancient drawing or painting on rock walls *(page 605)*

petroglyph A carving or inscription on rocks *(page 605)*

★DRAWING FROM EXPERIENCE

Have you ever heard a folktale? Do you know any legends? Would you like to read a book that takes place in Texas? Have you ever been to a play or concert? What is your favorite kind of music? Have you ever been to an art museum?

In the last section, you learned that Texas is home to people of many backgrounds. In this section you will discover how the diversity of Texas's population is reflected in the arts.

★ORGANIZING YOUR THOUGHTS

Use the diagram below to help you take notes as you read the summaries that follow. Describe one person's contribution to each art form.

Texas and the Arts	
Folklore	1.
Literature	2.
Theater	3.
Music	4.
Art	5.

(continued)

Name ______________________ Date ______________ Class ______________

Chapter 27-2

★ **READ TO LEARN** *Write in complete sentences to answer the following questions. Use correct spelling, punctuation, and grammar.*

Folklore *(pages 600–601)*

Texas's ethnic diversity has created a rich literary and artistic heritage. **Folklore** is especially valuable in telling the history of Texas. Folklore stories are told orally and passed down from generation to generation. Some of these stories are true. Others are fiction. Many are legends, which blend fact and fiction. These stories might be told in verse, song, and ballad.

J. Frank Dobie is one of the best known Texas folklorists. Dobie once noted that J. Mason Brewer was the "best storyteller of [African American] folklore."

Américo Paredes preserved much Mexican American folkore. He is well-known for his work on ***los corridos,*** or Mexican American folk ballads. Jovita González de Mireles also collected and published many stories about Mexican Americans.

6. How is folklore preserved?

____

____

____

____

____

Historical Literature *(pages 601–602)*

The Spanish explorer Cabeza de Vaca was the first outsider to write about his travels in Texas. Members of the de Soto and Coronado expeditions also wrote about their travels.

Many other travelers wrote about their experiences in Texas when it was part of Mexico, during the time of the Republic, and during the Civil War. Mary Austin Holley, cousin of Stephen F. Austin, wrote the first books in English about Texas. George W. Kendall wrote colorful descriptions during the time of the republic.

Historians have told the story of Texas many times and in many ways. One of the best early histories was written by Henderson Yoakum in 1855. Anna Pennybacker wrote a history of Texas for use in schools. Other historians have written about particular regions, periods, and topics.

(continued)

Name ______________________ Date ______________ Class ______________

Reading Essentials and Study Guide

Chapter 27-2

7. Who were the first outsiders to write about Texas?

____

____

____

____

____

Fiction and Poetry *(page 602)*

Texans have written memoirs, novels, short stories, and poems. Good writers often use their personal experiences. The Texas experience has been portrayed in many novels. Katherine Anne Porter set some of her important short works of fiction in Central Texas. Larry McMurtry wrote novels set in both the 1800s and modern times. His novels such as *Lonesome Dove, Terms of Endearment,* and *The Last Picture Show* have been made into successful motion pictures.

The Texas heritage is also important in the works of many short-story writers. William Sydney Porter used the name O. Henry on his books. "The Ransom of Red Chief" and "The Gift of the Magi" are some of his widely read short stories.

Every two years, the Texas Poetry Society picks a poet laureate. This is the most outsanding or representative poet. Many Texans have received this honor.

Another important area is children's literature. Pat Mora, a popular children's author from El Paso, was one of the 1998 Texas Institute of Letters Award winners.

8. What kinds of literature have Texas authors written?

____

____

____

____

____

(continued)

Theater, Film, and Television *(page 603)*

Since the days of the Texas Republic, Texans have been interested in the theater. Many Texas cities had opera or theater houses by the late 1800s. Universities have continued the theater tradition. Lon Morris College in Jacksonville specializes in theater training. Both amateur and professional theater groups have performed scripts by Texas playwrights. Texas has produced many television and film celebrities. These famous Texans donate their time to support benefits for Texas causes.

9. Where in Texas might a person study to be an actor?

____

____

____

____

____

Music *(pages 603–605)*

Many cultures have helped shape the music of Texas. African Americans contributed spirituals, work songs, and blues. Blues is an expressive and emotional African American folk music. Jazz is an American music form that blends African rhythms and scales with European harmony and instruments. Scott Joplin, born the son of a former slave, was known as the "father of ragtime."

Country western is the most popular radio format in America today. Willie Nelson developed his talent while working at a Fort Worth radio station. Due to his popularity, interest in country music exploded in the 1970s and 1980s.

Some of Texas's best-known ballads came from well-known Mexican tunes. Today, Tejano music, a sound that varies from country to pop, is very popular. Performers such as Freddie Fender, Tish Hinojosa, and more recently Selena, have attracted the attention of the nation.

Texas has also contributed to rock and roll music. Stars such as Buddy Holly, Janis Joplin, and Roy Orbison are just some of the well-known Texans. Elvis Presley, the "King of Rock and Roll," got his start singing in Gladewater, Texas.

(continued)

Name ______________________ Date ______________ Class ______________

10. What kinds of music have African Americans contributed to the Texas music experience?

____

____

____

____

____

Artists of Texas *(pages 605–606)*

The first Texas artists were prehistoric people. They created **pictographs** (ancient drawings and paintings) and **petroglyphs** (carvings or inscriptions on rocks). These can be found on rock ledges and cave walls in far west Texas and other locations.

Europeans contributed their artistry in the days of the Spanish Colonial era. Mission artists blended Spanish and Native American patterns in their works. The Rose Window of Mission San José in San Antonio is an outstanding example of mission artistry. It is considered one of the finest works of its kind in the United States.

Throughout history, artists have painted Texas scenes and people. Artists from Mexico, Germany, and France have painted landscapes, city scenes, and portraits of Native Americans and Mexicans. Some artists, such as H. A. McArdle, have painted historical scenes. William Huddle also painted historical scenes. His *Surrender of Santa Anna* hangs in the entrance of the Capitol in Austin. Other artists have illustrated cowboy life.

11. What scenes from Texas history do you think artists may have painted?

____

____

____

____

____

(continued)

Name ______________________ Date ______________ Class ______________

Reading Essentials and Study Guide

Chapter 27-2

Landscape Painters *(page 606)*

Robert J. Onderdonk and his son Julian are known for their paintings of Texas landscapes. Frank Reaugh painted mostly ranch and cattle scenes. Porfirio Salinas's paintings of the Texas Hill country and bluebonnets are popular. Works by African Americans such as John Thomas Bigger and Carroll Simms are in major galleries.

Georgia O'Keeffe was the first American woman painter to receive recognition from art critics. While living in Canyon, Texas, she painted over 50 watercolors. These watercolors were in her first show in 1917.

12. Why do you think artists like to paint the Texas landscape?

____

____

____

____

____

Sculpture *(page 606)*

Well-known sculptors such as Elisabet Ney and Charles Umlauf have ties to Texas. Two Italian sculptors, Pompeo Coppini and Enrico Cerracchio, have also contributed sculptures to Texas. Coppini created the Littlefield Memorial in Austin and the Alamo Cenotaph in San Antonio's Alamo Plaza.

13. Where can you see a sculpture connected with Texas history?

____

____

____

____

____

Name ______________________ Date ______________ Class ______________

Reading Essentials and Study Guide

Chapter 27-3

For use with textbook pages 608–611

Texans Create a Unique Culture

Key Terms

reenactment An event in which people dress in historical costumes and act as if they are actually living in a particular historical period or taking part in a historic event *(page 611)*

★ DRAWING FROM EXPERIENCE

Have you ever been to a festival? What did it celebrate? What did you do there? What did you like best about it?

In this section, you will read about the many celebrations that are part of Texas life. You will learn why they are held. You will also learn why such celebrations are important.

★ ORGANIZING YOUR THOUGHTS

Use the diagram below to help you take notes as you read the summaries that follow. Identify a festival or celebration you have enjoyed and four things that made it special.

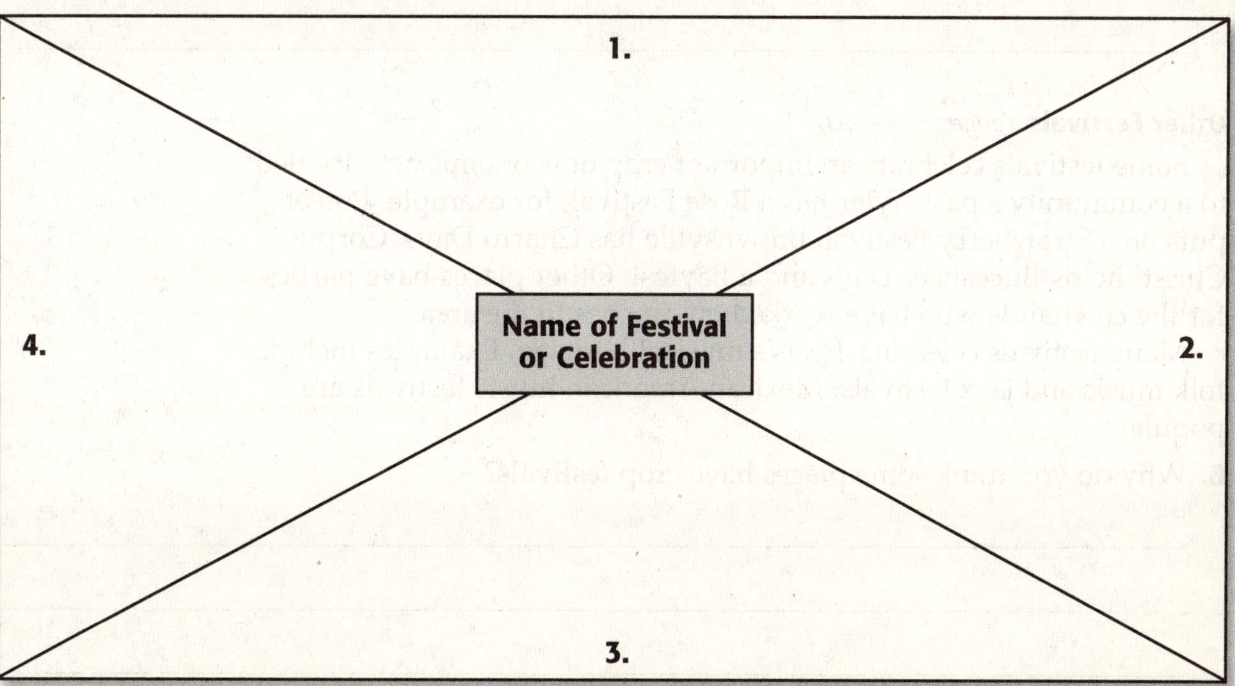

(continued)

Name ______________________ Date ______________ Class ______________

Reading Essentials and Study Guide

Chapter 27-3

★ **READ TO LEARN** *Write in complete sentences to answer the following questions. Use correct spelling, punctuation, and grammar.*

Ethnic Celebrations *(pages 608–609)*

Throughout Texas history, people from different cultures have celebrated together. Spanish explorers and Native Americans often had feasts together. Later, Texans celebrated religious holidays, events connected with cattle roundups, and the crop harvest. Rodeos and county fairs honor these traditions today.

During the 1960s African Americans and Mexican Americans took a renewed interest in their ethnic heritage. People of other ethnic groups also began to celebrate their ethnic roots. Many groups celebrated with festivals that featured music, food, crafts, dance, art, games, and other forms of entertainment. These celebrations reflect Texans' rich heritage. These celebrations include the Vietnamese holiday Tet, the Hispanic holiday *Cinco de Mayo,* July 4, Juneteenth, a German event known as Oktoberfest, the Irish holiday St. Patrick's Day, and various Cajun festivals. Cajuns have a French heritage.

5. What traditions do rodeos and county fairs honor?

____

____

____

Other Festivals *(pages 609–610)*

Some festivals celebrate an important crop or economic activity tied to a community's past. Tyler has a Rose Festival, for example. Poteet puts on a Strawberry Festival. Brownsville has Charro Days. Corpus Christi holds Buccaneer Days and a Bayfest. Other places have parties for the cowhands who have worked on ranches in the area.

Many festivals celebrate Texas's musical heritage. Examples include folk music and jazz festivals. Mexican American music festivals are popular.

6. Why do you think some places have crop festivals?

____

____

____

(continued)

Historical Festivals and Celebrations *(page 610)*

Texas celebrates state holidays such as Independence Day (March 2), San Jacinto Day (April 21), and Emancipation Day (June 19). In addition, many Texas cities hold celebrations around historic events or buildings. Events of the Texas Revolution, for instance, are remembered with the "Come and Take It" Festival at Gonzales. There is a celebration at the Alamo in San Antonio and on the San Jacinto battleground in Houston.

7. What do historical festivals celebrate?

____

____

____

____

The Importance of Celebrations *(pages 610–611)*

We can draw two conclusions from the many celebrations held each year in Texas. First, ethnic diversity is one of Texas's most important strengths. The number of celebrations in Texas show that Texans take pride in their own heritage and can also appreciate other people's cultures. Texans enjoy the music, food, and dance of many traditions at these celebrations. They also share in things that other groups value. The result of these experiences is a stronger society and a better world for people to live in. We can also conclude that history is important.

Many of the events held in Texas include living histories and **reenactments.** In reenactments people dress in historical costumes. They act as if they are actually living in a particular historical period or taking part in a historic event. Reenactments help us understand who we are. To understand Texas today, we must look back and learn more about our heritage.

8. What two conclusions can be drawn from all the festivals held each year in Texas?

____

____

____

Name ______________________ Date ______________ Class ______________

Reading Essentials and Study Guide

Chapter 28-1

For use with textbook pages 622–625

Texas Constitutions

Key Terms

constitution A document that outlines fundamental laws and principles of law *(page 622)*

amendment A change made to a constitution *(page 623)*

bill of rights A series of laws in a constitution that protects specific individual freedoms *(page 623)*

federalism The sharing of powers and duties between the states and the national government *(page 624)*

separation of powers The powers of government are divided into three separate branches: legislative, executive, and judicial *(page 624)*

legislature The branch of the government that makes the laws *(page 624)*

executive Relating to the branch of government that carries out the laws *(page 624)*

judiciary The branch of government that interprets the laws and decides how they should be applied *(page 624)*

checks and balances A system whereby each branch of government has the ability to limit the actions of the other branches *(page 624)*

bond A certificate issued by a government or company promising to pay back money borrowed, with interest *(page 625)*

★ DRAWING FROM EXPERIENCE

What is the purpose of a constitution? What rights does a bill of rights protect? What do you consider the most important right of a U.S. citizen?

In this section, you will read about Texas's seven constitutions. You will also learn about the individual freedoms protected by the Texas bill of rights.

★ ORGANIZING YOUR THOUGHTS

Use the diagram below to help you take notes as you read the summaries that follow. Identify the branch of government with each power.

Checks and Balances	
makes the laws	**1.**
can veto a law	**2.**
can override veto with 2/3 vote	**3.**
can rule a law unconstitutional	**4.**

(continued)

Name ______________________ Date ______________ Class ______________

Chapter 28-1

★ **READ TO LEARN** *Write in complete sentences to answer the following questions. Use correct spelling, punctuation, and grammar.*

The Texas Constitution in Early Government *(pages 622–623)*

A **constitution** is a document that outlines fundamental laws and principles of law. It describes the nature, functions, and limits of government. We live under both the U.S. and the Texas constitutions.

In 1827, the legislature of Coahuila y Tejas wrote the first of seven Texas constitutions. It strictly controlled regional and individual rights. Texas became an independent nation in 1836 and wrote another constitution. Texas became part of the United States in 1845 and a third constitution was written. During the Civil War and Reconstruction, three more constitutions were written. The present constitution was written at the end of Reconstruction. It was adopted in 1876.

5. When was the current constitution of Texas adopted?

____

____

____

The Role of Constitutions *(page 623)*

Each Texas constitution has had four important features. Each has outlined parts of the government and described the duties of each part. Each constitution gave officials and governmental bodies certain powers. Each described the rights of citizens. Finally, each provided a way for making changes, or **amendments.**

Constitutions reflect the ideals and values of citizens. Later Texas constitutions were modeled after the U.S. Constitution. Defining citizen rights and powers became important. Most constitutions stress that political power belongs to the people and that they should be heard at all levels of government. Sometimes a constitution includes a **bill of rights.** A bill of rights specifically lists individual freedoms.

6. What part of a constitution protects individual rights?

____

____

____

(continued)

Name ____________ Date ____________ Class ____________

Federalism *(pages 623–624)*

Texas is part of a federal system of government. In such a system, some powers belong to the federal government and others belong to state governments. The state and national governments share powers and duties. This sharing of powers is called **federalism.** Powers given to the states are reserved powers. Examples of reserved powers are a state's right to regulate commerce within its borders and provide for a state militia. However, Texas does not have the power to create its own money or declare war, which are federal powers.

7. What are reserved powers?

____

____

____

____

____

Three Branches of Government *(page 624)*

The Texas Constitution of 1876 states that "the powers of the government of the State of Texas shall be divided into three distinct departments." This **separation of powers** means that powers of the government are divided into the three branches of government. The branches of state government are the legislative, executive, and judicial.

The **legislature** consists of the Senate and House of Representatives. The legislature makes the laws of the state. It also approves the state's budget. The Constitution of 1876 limited the Senate to 31 members. It gave the House of Representatives one representative for every 15,000 people in the state, not to exceed 150 members. Today, the House has reached that limit. Texas has 20.8 million people, so a House member represents many more than 15,000 people.

The **executive** branch sees that laws of the state are carried out. It is made up of a chief executive (the governor), lieutenant governor, secretary of state, comptroller of public accounts, commissioner of the General Land Office, commissioner of agriculture, and attorney general.

The judicial branch—or the **judiciary**—interprets the laws of the state and decides how they should be used. The judicial branch also may try people accused of crimes and settle other disputes. It includes several courts, including the supreme court and courts of appeals.

(continued)

The writers of the Texas constitution wanted each branch of government to act as a check on the powers of the other two. This is called the principle of **checks and balances.** For example, the legislature makes the laws. The governor, who heads the executive branch, can check the legislature's power through the veto power. With a two-thirds vote, the legislature can pass a law over a veto. Additionally, the Texas Supreme Court and the Texas Court of Criminal Appeals both can rule that state laws are unconstitutional.

8. Why was the principle of checks and balances used when writing the Texas constitution?

____

____

____

____

____

The Bill of Rights Protects Citizens *(page 625)*

Protecting the rights of citizens is important to Texans. The Texas constitution begins with a bill of rights protecting freedom of speech, religion, and the press. It guarantees the right to bear arms. It forbids unreasonable searches and seizures. It assures accused people a speedy trial. Finally, it lists special rights for crime victims. These freedoms are needed for a free, democratic society.

9. What are three freedoms promised by the Texas Bill of Rights?

____

____

____

____

The Constitution of 1876 *(page 625)*

Governor Edmund Davis took more power than other governors had because he wanted to enforce Reconstruction laws. The Constitution of 1876 was designed to keep a strong governor from controlling all branches of government.

(continued)

The current constitution set up a public school system. It separated government into three branches and strengthened the system of checks and balances. It guaranteed that men could not be prevented from voting because of their race. It did not mention women. The Constitution of 1876 took much of the governor's powers away. It cut salaries for state officials. Additionally the legislative sessions were scheduled to meet once every two years instead of every year.

Many feel the constitution is outdated. Several tries to adopt a new constitution have failed. Texans prefer to update the constitution with amendments.

10. Why was it important to people in 1876 to limit the governor's power?

____

____

____

____

____

Amending the Constitution *(page 625)*

Amendments are formal additions to the constitution. During every legislative session, amendments are considered to keep up with changing times. Amendments have been passed to authorize the issuing of **bonds.** A bond is a certificate issued by a government or company promising to pay back money borrowed, with interest. Amendments have also been issued to get rid of political offices, excuse school districts from taxes, and to deal with other issues.

The House and Senate must approve all amendments by a two-thirds vote. It then must get voter approval. The governor cannot veto amendments to the constitution.

11. What is necessary for an amendment to be added to the Texas constitution?

____

____

____

____

Name ______________________ Date ______________ Class ______________

Reading Essentials and Study Guide

Chapter 28-2

For use with textbook pages 627–631

The Texas System of Justice

Key Terms

civil law Laws that deal with disputes between private citizens, businesses, and governments *(page 628)*

criminal law Laws that describe what people can and cannot do and that deal with crime and punishment *(page 628)*

felony A serious crime, such as murder, arson, or kidnapping *(page 628)*

misdemeanor A crime less serious than a felony, such as disorderly conduct, gambling, or traffic violations *(page 628)*

grand jury A group of citizens who decide whether there is enough evidence to charge someone with a crime *(page 629)*

indictment A formal statement by a grand jury charging a party with a crime *(page 629)*

no bill A formal statement by a grand jury that there is not enough evidence to justify a trial *(page 629)*

petit jury A group of citizens who decide on a verdict of guilty or not guilty in a court case and who may also decide on a punishment *(page 629)*

plea bargain An agreement between a prosecutor and a defendant whereby the defendant pleads guilty to a lesser charge *(page 629)*

juror A member of a jury sworn to hear testimony, review facts, and hand down a verdict in a case *(page 629)*

mediate Solve a problem through discussion and compromise rather than through the court system *(page 631)*

★DRAWING FROM EXPERIENCE

Do you know any adults who have had to report for jury duty? Do you know anyone who has gotten a divorce? Do you know any police officers or sheriffs?

In this section, you will learn about the Texas judicial system and how it deals with civil disputes and criminal cases.

★ORGANIZING YOUR THOUGHTS

Use the diagram below to help you take notes as you read the summaries that follow. Think about the different levels of each kind of court.

The Texas Court System	
Trial Courts	**Appeals Courts**
1.	4.
2.	5.
3.	6.

(continued)

★ **READ TO LEARN** *Write in complete sentences to answer the following questions. Use correct spelling, punctuation, and grammar.*

The Judicial System *(pages 627–628)*

The judicial branch serves three purposes. It tries people accused of crimes and punishes them, settles disputes, and interprets the laws. Texas has two general areas of law—civil and criminal. Most Texas judges are elected by voters.

7. What three purposes does the judicial branch serve?

____

____

____

____

Texas Civil Law *(page 628)*

Civil law concerns disputes between private citizens, businesses, and governments. These lawsuits are known as civil suits. They are based on civil laws.

Most civil cases are about property, money, child custody, or insurance claims. Civil cases may be decided by a judge or by a judge and jury. Trials can be very expensive and take up a lot of time. People involved in a civil case are often encouraged to work out an agreement, or out-of-court settlement.

8. What are civil cases commonly about?

____

____

____

____

Criminal Law *(page 628)*

Criminal law is the set of laws that describes what people can and cannot do. It deals with crime and punishment. Criminal codes make it illegal for someone to break into your home and steal your property. Punishments for crimes are also part of the criminal codes.

(continued)

Name ______________________ Date ______________ Class ______________

Reading Essentials and Study Guide

Chapter 28-2

Two types of offenses recognized under criminal law are **misdemeanors** and **felonies.** A misdemeanor is a less serious crime, such as disorderly conduct, gambling, or traffic violations. A felony is a serious crime, such as murder, arson, or kidnapping.

If found guilty of a felony, the accused person usually goes to prison. Depending on the nature of the crime, the person might be given the death penalty. People found guilty of a misdemeanor may pay a fine, go to county jail, or both.

9. What is the difference between a felony and a misdemeanor?

____

____

____

____

____

Justice for Juveniles *(pages 628–629)*

The Texas Youth Commission (TYC) is the state's juvenile corrections agency. The TYC provides care, custody, and rehabilitation for Texas's most seriously troubled juvenile criminals. The TYC is responsible for young people between the ages of 10 and 17 who have committed serious crimes. The young people in this system receive a medical evaluation, educational testing, and a psychological evaluation. Treatment for drug abuse and violent behavior is also provided. If a crime is serious enough, a youth may be transferred to the adult prison system (Texas Department of Criminal Justice) to complete a sentence.

10. How does the TYC evaluate juvenile criminals?

____

____

____

____

____

(continued)

Name ______________________ Date ______________ Class ______________

The Jury System *(page 629)*

Whenever a person is accused of a felony, a **grand jury** considers the case. A grand jury is a group of citizens who decides if there is enough evidence to charge someone with a crime. The grand jury has 12 members. If nine or more members believe there is enough evidence against the person, an **indictment**—a formal statement called a "true bill"—is issued. If the grand jury decides there is not enough evidence for a trial, it issues a **"no bill."** In most cases, grand juries agree with what the prosecuting attorney recommends.

A **petit jury** decides the cases once they go to court. Petit juries are citizens who decide guilt or innocence in a court case. The attorneys present the evidence. After that, all members of the jury must agree on a decision of "guilty" or "not guilty." If the person is found guilty, either the judge or the jury decides on a sentence.

Some cases are settled by **plea bargaining.** Usually, the accused agrees to plead guilty to a less serious charge. Plea bargaining is useful because the courts cannot handle all the cases that come up for trial. The government saves money and time with a plea bargain.

11. What is the difference between a grand jury and a petit jury?

____

____

____

____

____

Working for Justice *(page 629)*

State and local agencies work together to enforce the laws. The Texas Department of Public Safety (DPS) investigates crimes. It also supervises highway traffic and licenses drivers. County sheriffs and city police enforce laws at the local level. The Texas Department of Criminal Justice runs the adult state prisons. The TYC oversees juvenile correctional facilities.

The state attorney general is the state's lawyer. He or she gives advice to all parts of state government. If a case goes to court, the attorney general's office represents the state.

When a case comes to court, the attorneys argue the facts of the case before a jury. The **jurors,** or members of the jury, must determine the facts. They may also decide the punishment. To serve on a jury, a

(continued)

Name ______________________ Date ______________ Class ______________

Reading Essentials and Study Guide

Chapter 28-2

person must be a citizen of Texas, at least 18 years old, and able to read and write. Jurors must be of a sound mind. Those who have been convicted of a felony, or are under indictment for committing a felony, may not serve on a jury.

12. What three departments work together to enforce the laws of Texas?

____

____

____

____

The Court System of Texas *(page 630)*

There are two kinds of courts in Texas—trial courts and appeals courts. Trial courts hear cases and reach a decision. Their decision is called a verdict. Appeals courts decide if trials held in trial courts were fair. They can order a new trial if the first trial was not fair.

13. What is the purpose of an appeals court?

____

____

____

____

____

Trial Courts *(page 630)*

Trial courts deal with civil and criminal cases. Most civil cases are about divorce settlements, personal injuries, and uncollected taxes. Criminal cases include burglary, assault, driving while intoxicated (DWI), theft, and more serious offenses. Texas has three levels of trial courts: municipal and justice of the peace, county, and district courts. Municipal and justice of the peace courts deal with civil and less serious criminal cases.

County courts are the second level of trial courts. The Texas constitution requires each county to have at least one county court. These courts hear civil cases in which the amount of the dispute is between $500 and $5,000. They also hear criminal misdemeanor cases in which the fine is greater than $200.

(continued)

District courts are important trial courts in Texas. They hear criminal felony cases. District courts may also hear civil cases and those involving juveniles or disputes of over $500.

14. What are the highest level of trial courts in Texas?

Appeals Courts *(page 631)*

In almost every court case, one party wins and one party loses. The loser has to pay attorneys' fees and court costs.

The losing party in a trial can file an appeal, or a request to have the court's decision set aside. Except for divorce cases, lower court decisions can be appealed in Texas. Appeals usually begin in the district court of appeals. The two highest appeals courts are the Court of Criminal Appeals (for criminal cases) and the Supreme Court of Texas (for civil cases).

Divorce cases cannot be appealed. However, many counties require that people going through divorce first **mediate.** This means they meet with unbiased professionals to solve a problem through discussion and compromise. They try to negotiate a preliminary settlement. This frees the courts from having to divide the property, listen to arguments, and decide child custody.

15. What is the only kind of decision that cannot be appealed?

Name ______________________ Date ______________ Class ______________

Reading Essentials and Study Guide

Chapter 29-1

For use with textbook pages 636–640

The Texas Legislature

Key Terms

bicameral Having two chambers or houses, such as a Senate and a House of Representatives *(page 636)*

oversight The power of the legislature to review the actions of other branches of government *(page 637)*

redistricting Redrawing legislative and congressional districts to reflect population changes *(page 638)*

resolution The legislature's opinion about a subject *(page 639)*

★DRAWING FROM EXPERIENCE

Have you ever been a member of your school's student council? How does someone become a member of the student council? How many people make up the student council? What does the student council do?

In this section, you will learn about the legislative branch of Texas government. You will also learn how bills, or proposed laws, are passed.

★ORGANIZING YOUR THOUGHTS

Use the diagram below to help you take notes as you read the summaries that follow. Think about how committees in the state legislature handle bills.

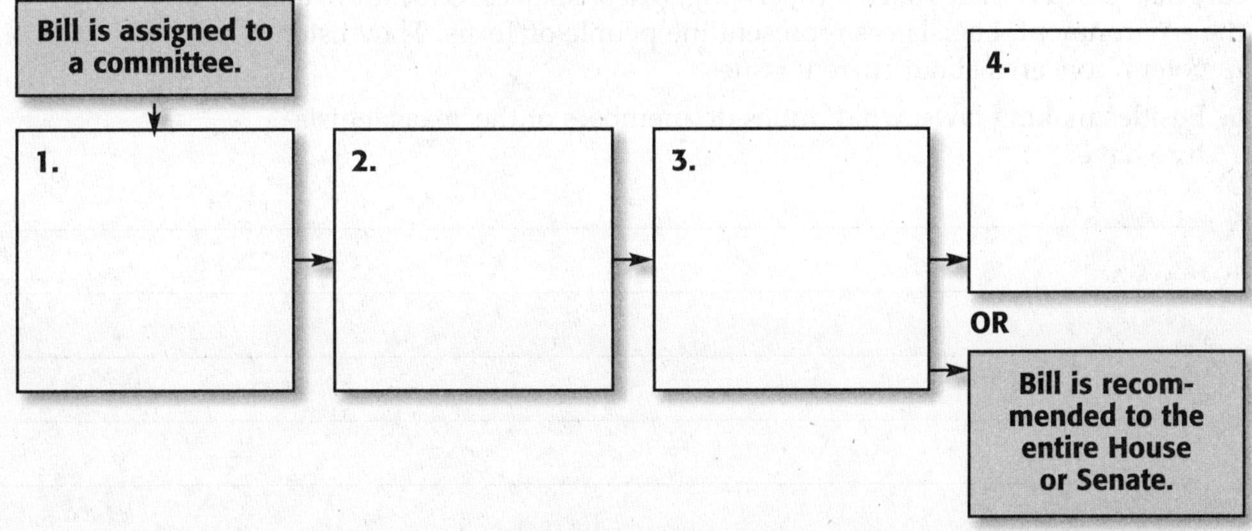

(continued)

Name ______________________ Date ______________ Class ______________

Chapter 29-1

★**READ TO LEARN** *Write in complete sentences to answer the following questions. Use correct spelling, punctuation, and grammar.*

The Function of the Legislative Branch *(pages 636–637)*

Like the federal government, Texas has a **bicameral** legislature. This means the legislature has two chambers, a Senate and a House of Representatives. Both the Senate and the House have committees that oversee state matters, including education, public health, agriculture and livestock, and natural resources. The members of the legislature also debate issues such as how much should be spent on education, whether taxes should be raised or lowered, and how to help the economy.

5. What are the two chambers of the Texas legislature?

____

____

____

____

____

Duties *(page 637)*

The Texas legislature makes the laws that govern Texas. Besides making laws, it also approves or rejects the people the governor appoints to office. The legislature has the power of **oversight.** That means it reviews the actions of the other branches of government. Members of the legislature also discuss issues such as spending, prisons, taxes, education, and the environment. Legislators represent the people of Texas. They listen to voters' concerns about current issues.

6. Besides making laws, what duties do members of the Texas legislature have?

____

____

____

____

____

(continued)

Name ______________________ Date ______________ Class ______________

Reading Essentials and Study Guide

Chapter 29-1

Running the State Government *(page 638)*

The Senate has 31 members. The House of Representatives has 150 members.

Unlike legislatures in other states, the Texas legislature meets every two years. The governor may call special sessions to handle problems.

Both the Senate and the House have leaders. The lieutenant governor, who is elected by voters, is the president of the Senate. House members elect their leader, called the Speaker of the House. These leaders have a great deal of power.

Committees help legislators study problems and draft bills. The appointment of legislators to committees is an important responsibility for the speaker and lieutenant governor. Committee chairpeople are powerful. They have the power to "kill" a bill they do not like by not scheduling it for discussion. Until a committee recommends a bill, the whole House or Senate cannot vote on it.

One important duty of the legislature is redrawing legislative and congressional districts as the population changes. This is known as **redistricting.** Sometimes redistricting causes a change in who controls the legislature, Republicans or Democrats. Because it changes the distribution of political power, redistricting causes many arguments.

7. If a chairperson does not agree with a bill, what can he or she do?

____

____

____

____

____

How a Bill Becomes a Law *(pages 639–640)*

Any state law considered by the legislature must be presented as a bill or a resolution. A bill is a proposed new law. A **resolution** expresses the legislature's opinion about a subject. For example, a resolution might set aside a certain day to honor a group or individual.

(continued)

Name ______________________ Date ______________ Class ______________

Reading Essentials and Study Guide

Chapter 29-1

The legislature considers thousands of bills each session. A bill that is approved by both the House and the Senate and signed by the governor becomes a law. A bill is first "read" before the entire House or Senate. Then it is assigned to a committee. The committee members consider the bill carefully. They listen to testimony from people who support it and from people who oppose it. Then the committee members decide whether the rest of the House or Senate should consider the bill. If the committee does not think the bill should be considered further, it "dies" in committee.

A bill that is recommended for consideration must be debated by the entire House or Senate. After a debate, the representatives or senators vote. If a majority votes in favor of the bill, then it must be considered by legislators in the other house. The bill must be approved in exactly the same form by a majority of members of the other chamber. If the House and Senate approve different forms of the same bill, the Speaker of the House and the lieutenant governor appoint a conference committee. This committee, which is made up of members from both houses, works out the differences. After the committee members agree on the bill, it must then be passed by both the House and the Senate another time.

Once it has been approved by both the House and the Senate, the bill goes to the governor. If the governor signs the bill, it becomes law. If the governor vetoes the bill, it does not become law unless two-thirds of the House and two-thirds of the Senate vote to override the veto.

8. What is the final step for a bill to become law?

____

____

____

____

____

Name ______________________ Date ______________ Class ______________

Reading Essentials and Study Guide

Chapter 29-2

For use with textbook pages 641–644

The Executive Branch

Key Terms

line-item veto The governor's ability to reject certain items in appropriations bills *(page 643)*

commander in chief The leader of the armed forces of a state or nation *(page 643)*

★ DRAWING FROM EXPERIENCE

Did you know the former governor of Texas became the president of the United States in 2000? Do you know his name? Would you like to be governor or president someday?

In this section, you will learn about the executive branch of the Texas government. You will learn about the powers of the governor and about other members of this branch of government.

★ ORGANIZING YOUR THOUGHTS

Use the diagram below to help you take notes as you read the summaries that follow. Categorize the governor's powers.

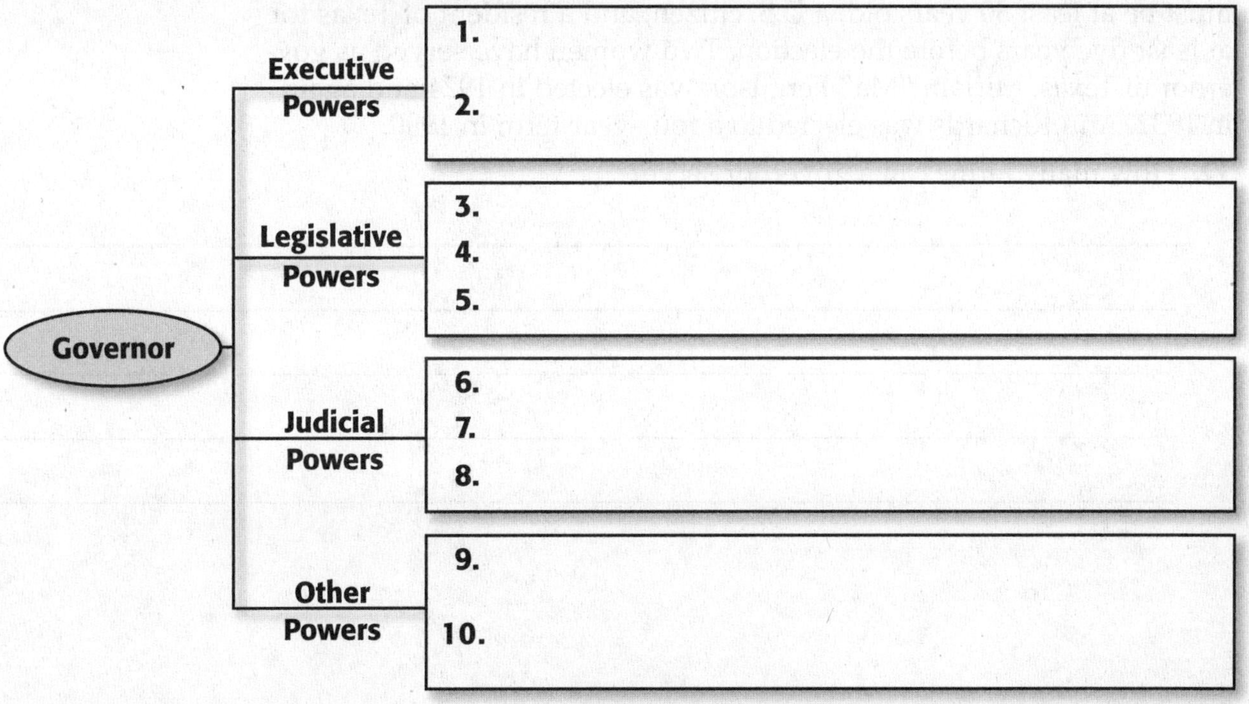

Governor

- Executive Powers
  1.
  2.
- Legislative Powers
  3.
  4.
  5.
- Judicial Powers
  6.
  7.
  8.
- Other Powers
  9.
  10.

(continued)

Name ______________________ Date ______________ Class ______________

Reading Essentials and Study Guide

Chapter 29-2

★ **READ TO LEARN** *Write in complete sentences to answer the following questions. Use correct spelling, punctuation, and grammar.*

The Function of the Executive Branch *(page 641)*

The executive branch of the state government carries out the laws passed by the legislature. It also conducts the business of the state. Executive power is shared by elected officials and those appointed by the governor.

11. What are two jobs of the executive branch?

The Governor of Texas *(page 642)*

The governor is the head of the executive branch of the Texas government. The governor's term of office is four years, but there is no limit to the amount of terms a person can serve. To qualify, a person must be at least 30 years old, a U.S. citizen, and a resident of Texas for at least five years before the election. Two women have served as governor of Texas. Miriam "Ma" Ferguson was elected in 1924 and again in 1932. Ann Richards was elected to a four-year term in 1990.

12. How many terms can a governor serve?

(continued)

Name ______________________ Date ______________ Class ______________

Chapter 29-2

Executive Powers of the Governor *(page 642)*

One of the governor's executive powers is to make appointments to boards and commissions. The appointments must be approved by two-thirds of the Senate. The governor can remove certain officials for serious misconduct. To remove appointees to boards or commissions, the governor must get the approval of the Senate.

13. Who chooses members of boards and commissions?

____

____

____

____

____

Legislative Powers of the Governor *(page 643)*

The governor also holds three important legislative powers. The governor has the power to send messages to the legislature. The governor gives a speech to the legislature at the beginning of each regular session. He or she also sends messages throughout the session. These messages usually explain the governor's policy goals. The legislature gives them careful consideration but does not have to act on them.

The governor has veto power. This power gives the governor an important check over legislation. By threatening a veto, the governor can get the legislature to change a bill so that it is more acceptable. The **line-item veto** is an important part of the governor's veto power. It gives the governor the power to reject parts of appropriations bills. These are bills that outline how the state's money will be spent.

The governor has the power to call special sessions of the legislature for emergency business. At these sessions the governor decides what business needs to be done. The legislature cannot consider any other topics unless the governor approves. Because regular sessions are short and happen only every two years, much important business is completed in special sessions. There is no limit to the number of special sessions the governor may call.

(continued)

14. If the governor does not agree with part of an appropriations bill, what can he or she do?

Other Powers of the Governor *(pages 643–644)*

The governor has certain judicial powers. The governor appoints the members of the Board of Pardons and Paroles, the Board of Criminal Justice, the Texas Youth Commission, and other commissions that deal with adults and juveniles who have violated the law. The governor can delay the execution date of prisoners and appoint judges to fill temporary vacancies.

The governor is the **commander in chief** of Texas. This means the governor is in charge of the Texas Guard. The Texas Guard includes the Army National Guard, the Texas Air National Guard, and the Texas State Guard.

The governor represents Texas at meetings, celebrations, and ceremonies.

15. What are the governor's judicial powers?

(continued)

Name ______________________ Date ______________ Class ______________

Reading Essentials and Study Guide

Other Elected Members *(page 644)*

Besides the governor, five other members of the executive branch are chosen in statewide elections. Because they are elected rather than appointed, they are not as dependent on the governor. This makes the office of governor of Texas weaker than the office of governor in other states. The elected members of the executive branch are the lieutenant governor, the attorney general, the comptroller of public accounts, the commissioner of the General Land Office, and the commissioner of agriculture.

16. What other members of the executive branch are elected?

____

____

____

____

____

Boards and Commissions *(page 644)*

The heads of boards and commissions are either appointed by the governor or elected by voters. Some of the larger agencies in the executive branch include the Texas Transportation Commission and the Railroad Commission. Another agency, the State Board of Education, manages and invests the $20 billion Permanent School Fund used to support public schools in Texas.

17. How are the heads of boards and commissions chosen?

____

____

____

____

____

Name ______________________ Date ______________ Class ______________

Reading Essentials and Study Guide

Chapter 29-3

For use with textbook pages 646–649

Financing State Government

Key Terms

budget A plan for how much one expects to earn and how one proposes to spend the money *(page 647)*

fiscal Relating to financial matters, taxes, revenues, and debts *(page 647)*

franchise tax A tax based on the value of machinery and equipment that businesses use to produce income *(page 648)*

windfall Money from an unexpected source *(page 648)*

★ DRAWING FROM EXPERIENCE

Have you ever paid sales tax on something you purchased? What do you think the state does with the money people pay in sales taxes? What programs at your school or in your community are paid for by the state of Texas?

In this section, you will learn about the Texas state budget. You will find out how Texas gets and spends money. You will also learn what influences the budget makers.

★ ORGANIZING YOUR THOUGHTS

Use the diagram below to help you take notes as you read the summaries that follow. List at least three sources and three uses of state money.

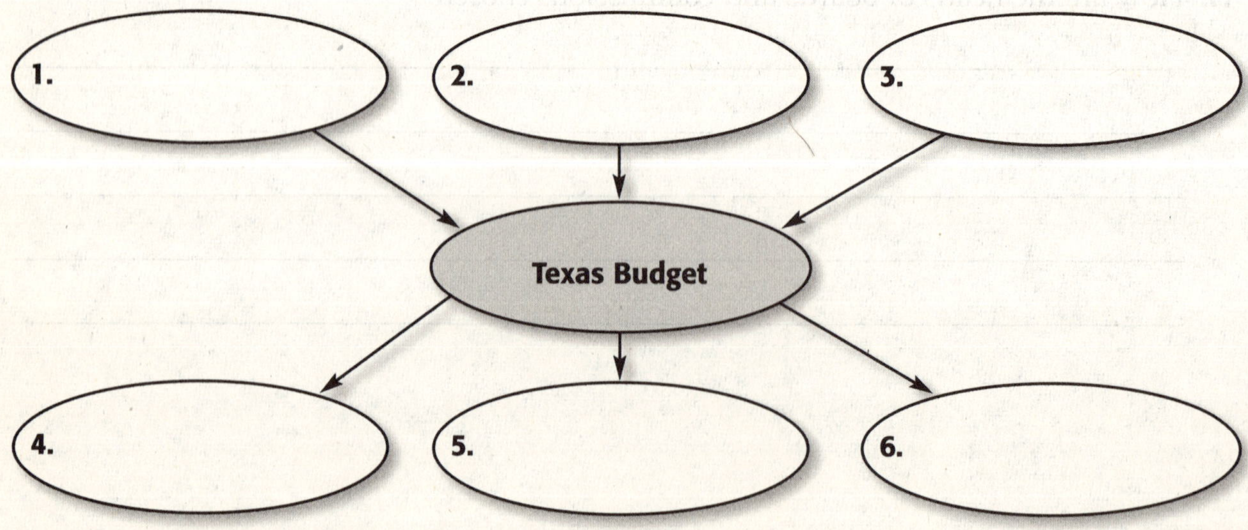

(continued)

Name ______________________ Date ______________ Class ______________

Reading Essentials and Study Guide

Chapter 29-3

★ **READ TO LEARN** *Write in complete sentences to answer the following questions. Use correct spelling, punctuation, and grammar.*

Setting the State Budget *(pages 646–647)*

Running a state government as large as that of Texas calls for careful planning and budgeting. The state budget identifies the most important economic and social needs of Texas. The budget also estimates how much money the state will take in and how much money it will spend. The budget determines which programs will grow, shrink, or be eliminated. Therefore, it is important for the state to manage its money wisely.

7. What does the state budget do?

____

____

____

____

____

The Budget Process *(page 647)*

A **budget** is a plan for how much one expects to earn and how one proposes to spend the money.

In Texas, the governor and legislative committee propose a budget. Two-year budgets are set during the regular session of the legislature. About 12 months before the legislature meets, agencies that spend state funds report to the Legislative Budget Board and the Governor's Office of Budget and Planning. The agencies list what they spent and estimate what they will need for the next two years.

8. Who is responsible for proposing the state budget?

____

____

____

____

____

(continued)

Chapter 29-3

How the State Spends Money *(pages 647–648)*

A House–Senate budget committee, in the state legislature, creates the budget. The budget for **fiscal** (financial) year 2002–2003 is $114 billion. It includes money for state workers' raises, improving Medicaid eligibility for children, and an insurance plan for some teachers.

Education accounted for 31 percent of the budget. Other major expenses included economic development and criminal justice programs.

9. How is most of the budget spent?

____

____

____

____

____

Where the State Gets Its Money *(page 648)*

Most of Texas's revenue comes from a general sales tax. Food and medicine are not taxed. The tax on motor fuels is the second largest source of revenue. Other sources include taxes on the sale of motor vehicles, manufactured houses, utility services, alcoholic beverages, and tobacco products.

The major tax on business in Texas is the **franchise tax.** This tax is based on the value of machinery and equipment that businesses use to produce income. Service businesses pay little or no franchise tax. Because Texas has changed from a product economy to a service economy, the franchise tax has become less important.

Texas also receives money from sources other than taxes. Like other states, Texas receives many grants from the federal government. Additional sources include land and mineral rights, investment of state funds, and fees for state services and permits. Sometimes the state receives a **windfall,** or money from an unexpected source. In 1998, for example, Texas received a settlement of millions of dollars in a tobacco lawsuit.

(continued)

10. What is the second largest source of revenue in Texas?

____

____

____

____

____

Influences on the Process *(page 649)*

Many people and factors influence the budget process. Federal decisions affect state budgets. Court decisions at the federal and state levels may direct what a state can and cannot do. The state courts might say that the legislature may not use money in certain ways. Individuals and groups work to promote their interests. They pressure budget officials on many important issues.

11. How do individuals and groups influence the budget process?

____

____

____

____

____

Name ____________________ Date ____________ Class ____________

Reading Essentials and Study Guide

Chapter 30-1

For use with textbook pages 656–660

Types of Local Government

Key Terms

general-law city A small city of less than 5,000 in population that functions under the general laws of Texas and provides basic services *(page 657)*

home-rule city A city that does whatever it wants as long as it does not break state or federal laws, and increases its tax base by annexing nearby land *(page 657)*

mayor-council A form of city government in which the mayor has full executive authority. There are strong mayor and weak mayor types of this form, however. *(page 657)*

ordinance A local law *(page 658)*

council-manager A form of city government in which the mayor has less power and the city council hires a professional city manager to manage the affairs of the city and prepare the city budget *(page 658)*

commission A form of city government in which voters elect commissioners, each of which is in charge of a particular city department *(page 658)*

appraise To determine the value *(page 658)*

commissioners court The governing body of a county, made up of one elected commissioner from each county district *(page 659)*

precinct One of four districts within a county *(page 659)*

real estate Property in buildings and land *(page 660)*

★ DRAWING FROM EXPERIENCE

Who runs your city? What county do you live in? What services does your city or county provide? What is the name of your school district?

In the last chapter you learned about state government. In this section, you will learn about the different types of local government and how they affect your life.

★ ORGANIZING YOUR THOUGHTS

Use the diagram below to help you take notes as you read the summaries that follow. Identify and describe the three forms of city government in Texas.

Forms of City Government

1.	3.	5.
2.	4.	6.

(continued)

Name ______________________ Date ______________ Class ______________

Reading Essentials and Study Guide

★ **READ TO LEARN** *Write in complete sentences to answer the following questions. Use correct spelling, punctuation, and grammar.*

Local Governments at Work *(pages 656–657)*

The work of local governments affects people every day. Some services that local governments provide are police and fire protection, garbage collection, water and sewer services, and education. Texas has three basic types of local government:

A. City
B. County
C. Special districts

7. What services do local governments provide?

____

____

____

Two Kinds of City Government *(page 657)*

Some cities and towns are called municipalities. If a city government incorporates by citizen request, it is a municipal government. There are two types of cities in Texas:

A. General-Law City Small cities of less than 5,000 in population may incorporate as a general-law city. These cities operate under the general laws of Texas. They often provide only basic services such as police and fire protection and water and sewer service.

B. Home-Rule City About one-fourth of Texas cities are home-rule cities. They can do what they want unless it is prohibited by state or federal laws. These cities try to increase their tax base by growing. To do this, they often annex nearby land into the city limits. They have to provide city services to the annexed area within four-and-one-half years.

8. How do general-law cities and home-rule cities differ?

____

____

____

____

(continued)

Organization of City Governments *(pages 657–658)*

There are three common forms of city governments in Texas:

A. **Mayor-council** This type of city government is used by some Texas cities. The mayor has full executive authority. In strong-mayor cities, the mayor is responsible for day-to-day operations of the city, hiring and firing department heads, and vetoing city council actions. Houston and El Paso are examples of strong-mayor cities. In weak-mayor cities, however, the mayor's powers are limited and he shares administrative duties with the city council. City councils pass **ordinances,** or local laws.

B. **Council-manager** The mayor has less power in council-manager cities. The mayor presides over council meetings and has only one vote, like other members of the city council. The city council hires a professional city manager. The city manager manages the affairs of the city and prepares the city budget. Dallas and San Antonio have this form of government.

C. **Commission** The voters elect commissioners to run the government in commission cities. Each commissioner is in charge of a department, such as public safety or human services. The mayor has little power, presiding over meetings and acting as a spokesperson for the council. This is the least common form of local government in Texas. Galveston and Sweetwater have this form of government.

9. How does a commission city differ from a council-manager city?

____

____

____

____

____

City Governments Need Funds *(pages 658–659)*

Local governments need money in order to operate and provide services. Cities have several sources of revenue. The most important source is property taxes. Owners of land, houses, and other buildings pay property tax. These taxes depend on the financial worth of the property. Tax assessors inspect the property, **appraise,** or determine

(continued)

the value, and make recommendations to the city. Other sources of revenue include sales tax, fees for services such as garbage collection, building permits, and fines for traffic violations.

Local governments in Texas spend their money on services such as public safety, police and fire protection, jail maintenance, parks, streets, bridges, animal shelters, airports, and libraries. Sometimes local governments need money for special, long-term projects, such as building a sports arena. Then the government may get the money by selling bonds. Bonds are certificates issued by a government that guarantee payment plus interest. Local governments may also ask for money from the state and federal governments to pay for certain programs.

10. How is property tax determined?

____

____

____

____

County Government *(page 659)*

The county level of government was originally created to govern rural areas. It is still the most important unit of local government. There are 254 counties in Texas. Each is an administrative area of the state and is staffed by locally elected officials.

One of the most important responsibilities of county governments is to help the state government. Counties collect state taxes, handle election matters, and issue licenses. County courthouses keep records of births, deaths, marriages, and property ownership. Texas counties work with state and federal agencies to provide services and programs for citizens.

11. What are some responsibilities of county governments?

____

____

____

____

(continued)

Name ______________________ Date ______________ Class ______________

Reading Essentials and Study Guide

Chapter 30-1

County Officials *(pages 659–660)*

County government is set up the same way in every county. Each Texas county has a **commissioners court.** The commissioners court determines the county's budget, sets the property-tax rate, and decides how county money will be spent.

Each county is divided into four districts called **precincts.** Each precinct elects a county commissioner. The commissioners serve four-year terms. A county judge is elected in a countywide election and also serves for four years. The county judge is responsible for the day-to-day administration of the county and heads the commissioners court.

The commissioners court does not conduct trials. It makes policies and directs county business. County business includes building and repairing roads and bridges, operating the courthouse and jail, and maintaining county hospitals, museums, libraries, parks, and airports.

12. What does the commissioners court do?

____

____

____

____

____

Financing County Government *(page 660)*

The most important sources of revenue for counties are property taxes and bonds. Counties collect taxes on most **real estate** property (buildings or land). Personal property such as automobiles and airplanes may also be taxed. The commissioners court sets the tax rate. Counties also raise money by issuing bonds after voter approval. Bonds pay for long-term construction projects. Other sources of income for counties include fees for permits, taxes on liquor and motor fuel, and fees for vehicle registration.

County budgets are approved by the commissioners court. Fast-growing counties may need more funds for road and bridge construction. Counties with high crime rates may spend more on law enforcement, courts, and jails.

(continued)

Name ______________ Date ______________ Class ______________

13. What are the two most important sources of revenue for counties?

____

____

____

____

Special Districts *(page 660)*

Another form of local government is the special district. These districts are created to meet a specific need. Special districts include school districts, rapid transit authorities, river authorities, and water control and improvement districts.

School districts are the most common kind of special district. Each school district is directed by an elected board of trustees known as a school board. The school board makes school policies, hires teachers, sets salaries, takes care of school buildings, and provides transportation. Money for school districts comes from federal, state, and local funds.

Community college districts support the development of junior or community colleges. A board of trustees is elected to administer the community college district.

14. What does a school board do?

____

____

____

____

____

Name ______________________ Date ______________ Class ______________

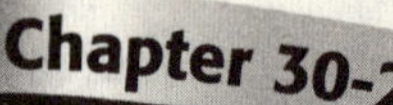

For use with textbook pages 662–665

Participation in Government

Key Terms

nonpartisan election Not connected with a particular political party *(page 663)*

watchdog role A political party's monitoring of the activities of other parties *(page 664)*

special interest group An organization of people who share a common interest and seek to exert influence over a particular aspect of government *(page 664)*

★ DRAWING FROM EXPERIENCE

What does the term democracy mean to you? Have you ever written to an elected official about an issue or concern? Have you ever volunteered in your community? What did you do? Why is it important for people to participate in government?

In this section, you will learn about ways citizens can be involved in government and politics. You will also discover why all citizens have a duty to participate in government.

★ ORGANIZING YOUR THOUGHTS

Use the diagram below to help you take notes as you read the summaries that follow. List ways people can participate in government through political parties and special interest groups.

Ways to Participate in Government

Through Political Parties	Through Special Interest Groups
1.	4.
2.	5.
3.	6.

(continued)

Name ______________________ Date ______________ Class ______________

Chapter 30-2

★ **READ TO LEARN** *Write in complete sentences to answer the following questions. Use correct spelling, punctuation, and grammar.*

Democratic Principles *(pages 662–663)*

Both the United States and Texas were founded on the principle that citizens should govern themselves. The founders set up democratic governments for the nation and the state. Texans have the right and duty to support their democratic government. A democratic government is founded on three important beliefs:

A. The needs and opinions of each citizen are important.
B. To serve the people, the government should consider the different needs, values, and experiences of its citizens.
C. Citizens should participate in government.

7. What three beliefs form the basis of democracy?

____

____

____

____

____

Individual Participation *(page 663)*

Government officials do their jobs more effectively when they know what the people want. People can express their views by talking to or writing to government officials. Voting is another important way to express concerns. Citizens help make many important decisions when they vote. They also elect individuals to carry out specific government tasks. To vote in Texas elections, a person must be a U.S. citizen and 18 years or older. He or she must also be a resident of the state and county and be registered to vote for at least 30 days before election day.

Many people are involved in government through volunteer work. Volunteers make a difference in their communities in many ways. They read to young children at public libraries, answer phones at crisis hot lines, and work in political campaigns.

(continued)

Reading Essentials and Study Guide

8. How can citizens express their views and concerns?

___

___

___

___

___

Running for Political Office *(page 663)*

Anyone can run for public office. In order to get elected, candidates must campaign to win support. Campaigns give candidates and voters a chance to express their opinions and concerns. Some officials in government are paid. Others donate their time to help meet the needs of citizens.

9. Why do candidates campaign?

___

___

___

___

___

Political Parties in Texas *(pages 663–664)*

Voting is one of the most important ways of taking part in a democracy. Texas has four types of elections:

A. Primary elections
B. General elections
C. Special elections
D. Local elections

In **nonpartisan elections** candidates are not identified with any political party.

One of the most important ways citizens can affect government decision making is by taking part in political parties. The ideas and actions of each individual citizen are important. There can also be great advantage to working together.

(continued)

Name ______________________ Date ______________ Class ______________

Reading Essentials and Study Guide

Chapter 30-2

Political parties serve several functions. They nominate people to run for office and campaign for their candidates. Once elections are held, political parties play an important part in organizing government. They recommend qualified candidates for government positions. Parties also work to unite government leaders so they can better carry out their duties. Political parties also keep track of the activities of other parties. This is called the **watchdog role.** Each party tries to keep informed about the activities of others. This process helps keep citizens informed.

Until recently, more voters in Texas belonged to the Democratic Party than to the Republican Party. Now both parties compete for voter support. Having active political parties is good for Texas. The parties work hard to recruit good candidates and to publicize the issues. They also encourage citizens to be active in campaigns and elections. Besides the Democratic and Republican Parties, the Reform Party, Libertarian Party, and the Green Party have appeared on Texas ballots.

10. Why are active political parties good for Texas?

____

____

____

____

____

Special Interest Groups *(pages 664–665)*

Special interest groups (SIGs) are organizations of people who have common interests and seek to exert influence over a particular aspect of government.

SIGs are somewhat like political parties. However, their focus is generally narrower and more specific. SIGs and political parties also differ in their activities. One of the main functions of political parties is to nominate and elect candidates. SIGs may support candidates, but winning elections is not their goal. Instead, they want to influence public officials.

Some SIGs make certain that the civil rights of minorities are protected. SIGs include labor groups, racial and ethnic groups, political interest groups, religious groups, and environmental groups.

(continued)

Name ______________________ Date ______________ Class ______________

Chapter 30-2

Political interest groups focus on many different issues. Women's groups, such as the Texas League of Women Voters, publish reliable voter information. The Sierra Club is involved with maintaining clean air and water. The League of United Latin American Citizens works hard to ensure social justice and equal opportunities for Latinos.

11. How do special interest groups differ from political parties?

____

____

____

____

____

Directly Influencing Government *(page 665)*

Special interest groups often try to get officials elected who agree with their views. They encourage people who support their goals to run for office. They publicly endorse them. They give money to these candidates.

SIGs also try to get the general public to support their goals. They buy advertisements. They hold public events to make their point and shape public opinion. Another method SIGs use to reach their goals is lobbying. Lobbying is trying to persuade government leaders to support a particular cause. Lobbyists may appear before legislative committees, testify in court hearings, and visit legislators and other officials. Some groups hire professional lobbyists. In other groups, members volunteer to lobby.

12. Why do special interest groups lobby?

____

____

____

____

____